A noble lady and her son

HOW THEY LIVED

VOLUME II

*An Anthology of original accounts written
between 1485 and 1700*

Compiled by

MOLLY HARRISON

and

O. M. ROYSTON

BASIL BLACKWELL
OXFORD
1965

Reprinted 1965

Printed in Great Britain for BASIL BLACKWELL & MOTT, LTD.
by A. R. MOWBRAY & CO. LIMITED in the City of Oxford
and bound at the KEMP HALL BINDERY

CONTENTS

LIST OF PLATES

iv

ACKNOWLEDGEMENTS

The authors and publishers wish to thank the following for permission to reproduce copyright material:

PLATES

H.M. the Queen, 2; H.G. the Duke of Rutland, 27; The Hon. Robin Nevill, frontispiece; The Trustees of the British Museum, 4(a), 4(b), 11, 19; Bibliothèque Nationale, Paris, 3; The Mayor and Corporation of Bristol, 1; The Victoria and Albert Museum, 5, 22; The Trustees of the National Gallery, 21; The Bodleian Library, Oxford, 15, 25, 28(a), 28(b), 32; The Guildhall Library, 20; The Trustees of the Tate Gallery, 13; Mme. A. Eccen van Setten, 12; Lady Richmond, 30; The Abbot of Ampleforth, 8; Dr. J. F. Stent, 16; Radio Times Hulton Picture Library, 6(b), 9, 10, 17, 18, 23, 24, 26, 28(a); B. T. Batsford Ltd., *Life in Elizabethan England* 6(a); The Vicar of Durnford, 14; The Vicar of Fairford, 7; The Hon. Judge Irwin Untermeyer and Thames and Hudson Ltd., *English Needlework, Tapestries and Textiles*, 29; Thomas Agnew Esq., 31

PHOTOGRAPHS

The Ministry of Works, frontispiece; O. H. Downing A.P.F.S. 7; The Yorkshire Evening Press, 8; Frans Popken, 12; R. B. Fleming, 20; John McCrindle M.P.A., 27; Sydney W. Newbery, 31; The City Museum and Art Gallery, Birmingham, 30; F. Futcher and Son, 14.

FOREWORD

This book is about the lives, thoughts and feelings, the behaviour and the intentions of people who lived in England between 1485 and 1700. It is an anthology of extracts from writings of varied kinds made by many different people, for all kinds of reasons: some are letters describing situations or protesting against injury or injustice; others are official documents laying down laws and practices. Some extracts are from imaginative works—plays, poems, stories—which inevitably give us, among the fiction, a good deal of contemporary fact; others are straightforward descriptions written appreciatively, critically or impartially by travellers, men of letters, or social commentators.

The illustrations, too, are all contemporary. These drawings, paintings, woodcuts, brasses, stained glass and carvings, recorded real people, and situations as they were at the time. Nothing has been redrawn for purposes of reproduction, for we believe that human eyes and manual skill change as times change and any redrawing is bound to have in it the flavour of the draughtsman's own period.

In selecting our material from the vast amount available we have tried to ensure that the principal aspects of English social life are shown. Preference has been given, when possible, to material less often quoted; well-known sources being drawn on only where it appeared essential. The material is divided into chapters corresponding to certain broad aspects of living, and within these chapters the extracts are grouped round common themes and arranged as far as possible in chronological order. At the beginning of each chapter, and elsewhere when it was thought necessary, there are authors' comments, which are intended to give background information, rather than to explain the extracts. The plates are arranged chronologically throughout the book; the line drawings are placed adjacent to the relevant extracts.

Our English language has, of course, changed considerably

since our ancestors wrote these statements about themselves, and the question of spelling gave us cause for thought. We have kept the original spelling in a few of the simpler extracts so that the reader may see how different it is from ours and get fun from making comparisons. But for the sake of clarity and understanding we have modernized most of the extracts slightly, and we have in many cases selected only the more interesting or important parts of a document. In order to put two hundred and fifteen years within the covers of one volume we have had to ration every speaker—at times harshly, but always with the purpose of giving as much of the flavour of the period as possible.

The 'they' of the title are English men, women and children, but we have decided to include some extracts and some illustrations from continental sources. Many foreign travellers came to England at this time and recorded their impressions when they reached home. The English gentleman also began to travel abroad extensively, and saw how cultured Frenchmen and Italians lived; he liked to furnish his home with Flemish wall hangings, Dutch paintings, Venetian glass and French cabinets, as these successive fashions spread. It does not seem too great an extension of our purpose to include, here and there, illustrations of scenes which English travellers could have seen and enjoyed and in time copied.

There is too little here about poor people, but that is surely one of the facts of history. In these 215 years in England, as in all periods in all parts of the world, most people were poor, ignorant, illiterate and insignificant. They did not write diaries or make speeches, and only by chance, and very occasionally, do they figure in illustrated records. But underneath the story of how the wealthy, the vocal, and the adventurous lived, we hope you may find brief echoes of families whose purpose it was to serve others, and who probably enjoyed a good deal of their service. They become more in evidence as time passes; men were learning, in these centuries, to think for themselves in religious and political matters and, inevitably, the 'common man' began to appear. Throughout the Tudor period there was a strong undercurrent of independent thought running in England.

The Tudor monarchs had to take account of this; the Stuarts struggled against it with disastrous results.

In later centuries our society has continued to learn, slowly and often painfully, how to give effect to the dangerous idea that the individual human being matters.

M. H.

SOME IMPORTANT ENGLISHMEN OF THE PERIOD

Architects	John Thorpe	1570–1610
	Inigo Jones	1573–1652
	Christopher Wren	1632–1723
Craftsmen	Christopher Saxton	1570–1596
	John Speed	1552–1629
	Grinling Gibbons	1648–1721
	Francis Bird	1667–1731
Explorers	Martin Frobisher	1535–1594
	Sir Francis Drake	1540–1596
	Sir Walter Raleigh	1552–1618
	Henry Hudson	? –1611
	Sir Thomas Roe	1580–1644
	Lord Baltimore	1580–1632
	William Penn	1644–1718
Inventors	William Gilbert	1540–1603
	Sir John Harington	1561–1612
	Robert Hooke	1635–1703
	Thomas Newcomen	1663–1729
Musicians	Thomas Tallis	1505–1585
	William Byrd	1542–1623
	John Bull	1562–1628
	Thomas Morley	1557–1603
	John Dowland	1563–1626
	Orlando Gibbons	1583–1625
	Henry Lawes	1595–1662
	Henry Purcell	1658–1695
Painters	Hans Holbein	1497–1543
	Nicholas Hilliard	1537–1619
	Isaac Oliver	1556–1617

Reformers	John Colet	1467–1519
	Sir Thomas More	1478–1535
	Thomas Cranmer	1489–1556
	William Tyndale	1492–1536
	John Hampden	1594–1643
	Oliver Cromwell	1599–1658
	George Fox	1624–1691
Scientists	Francis Bacon	1561–1626
	William Harvey	1578–1657
	Robert Boyle	1627–1691
	John Ray	1627–1705
	Isaac Newton	1642–1727
	Edmund Halley	1656–1742
Writers	Edmund Spenser	1532–1599
	Sir Philip Sidney	1554–1586
	Christopher Marlowe	1564–1593
	William Shakespeare	1564–1616
	Ben Jonson	1573–1637
	John Donne	1573–1631
	George Herbert	1593–1633
	John Milton	1608–1674
	John Bunyan	1628–1688
	John Dryden	1631–1700
	Samuel Pepys	1633–1703

CHAPTER I

GENERAL DESCRIPTION

AS TO THE COUNTRY

Source: Italian Relations, VII, 1551, by Daniele Barbaro, Venetian Ambassador to Edward VI, 1549–50.

Nature has endowed it with beauty and great bounty, and among its chief endowments is that of most fine and excellent wools. 'Tis also rich in metals, having tin and lead in greatest quantity, to such an extent that, in addition to what is used in the island, the worth of two millions in gold is exported to Antwerp as to a centre whence it is distributed to other places. And there are animals of all kinds, and such abundant grazing that for a single crown a thousand sheep can be fattened. In some places grains are plentiful, and they would be much more so if the people did not shirk toil; but they have what they need, and do not seek more . . . although neither vines nor olives are found there, yet, besides what they procure in sufficiency (from abroad) by their convenient position for sea trade, they can do with less, as they use beer in place of wine, and butter and oil from turnips in place of (olive) oil. They make salt in several places, and there is no tax on it; they make firewood in abundance, and can procure enough vegetables and saffron, and plenty of fish; moreover, lodgings are excellent and most commodious, a sure sign of the country's wealth.

'NOW A DAYES', c. 1520

Source: Ballads from Manuscripts, ed. F. J. Furnivall (Ballad Soc., Vol. I, 1868–72).

> We Englisshemen beholde
> Our auncient customs bolde,
> more preciouser than golde,
>   be clene cast away,

And other new be fownd
the which (ye may understand)
that causethe all your land
   So gretly to decay.

. . . .

Envy waxith wonders strong,
the Rich(e) doth the poore wrong:
God of his mercy sufferith long
   the devill his workes to worke.
The townes go down, the land decayes;
Off cornefeyldes, playne layes;
Gret men makithe now a dayes
   A shepecott in the churche.

The places that we Right holy call,
Ordeyned For christyan buriall,
Off them to make an ox stall
   thes men be wonders wyse.
Commons to close and kepe;
Poor folk for bred (to) cry and wepe;
Towns pulled downe to pastur shepe:
   this ys the new gyse!

Alyauntes here have ther way,
And Englysshmen cleane decay,
the one half must nedes play;
   this ys a comon welth!
Other landes avaunced bee,
And by and sell among us free;
And thus our own commodite
   Doth clene undo our selff.

Marchauntes use subtility,
the church livith viciously,
the commons are in poverty,
   this lond goth to wast:
Marchaunt men travell the contre,
plowmen Dwell in the cyte,

Which wyll Destroy the land shortly:
That will be sene in hast!

. . . .

Greate De(ar)th and much idelnes,
lytle mony and much sicknes,
gret pryd and smale Riches,
   How can these agree?
Gret auctorite and smale wisdom,
Symple officers and gret extorsion:
Lyght offence and sore correction,
   An end of this must bee.

. . . .

many gammers and few archers,
gay cortyars and yll warryers,
many craftesmen and halff beggers,
   both in townes and cyty.
Frenche ware hither ys browght,
and englishe hand craft gothe to nowght.
Halffe this Realme, it ys unwrowght!
   Alas, for pure pytty!

. . . .

The former of heven above all thing,
In the celestiall court sittyng,
thre in one withowt begynnyng,
   the father and sonne and holy goost!
Off thy infinyte mercy
send to us some Remedy!
Or els I fear shortly
   this Realm wyl be lost.

SEDITION, 1550

Source: J. M. Cowper, 'The Way to Wealth', in *Select Works of Robert Crowley* 1872.

The causes of Sedition muste be roted oute. If I shuld demaunde of the pore man of the contrey what thinge he thinketh to be the cause of Sedition, I know his answere. He woulde tel me that the great fermares, the grasiers, the riche buchares, the men of lawe, the marchauntes, the gentlemen, the knightes, the lordes, and I can not tel who; men that have no name because they are doares in al thinges that ani gaine hangeth upon. Men without conscience. Men utterly voide of Goddes feare. Yea, men that live as thoughe there were no God at all! Men that would have all in their owne handes; men that would leave nothyng for others; men that would be alone on the earth; men that bee never satisfied. Cormerauntes, gredye gulles; yea, men that would eate up menne, women and chyldren, are the causes of Sedition! They take our houses over our headdes, they bye our growndes out of our handes, they reyse our rentes, they leavie great (yea unreasonable) fines, they enclose oure commens! No custome, no lawe or statute can kepe them from oppressyng us in such sorte, that we knowe not whyche waye to turne us to lyve. Very nede therefore constrayneth us to stand up agaynst them! In the countrey we can not tarye, but we must be theyr slaves and laboure tyll our hertes brast, and then they must have al. And to go to the cities we have no hope, for there we heare that these unsaciable beastes have all in theyr handes. Some have purchased, and some taken by leases, whole allyes, whole rentes, whole rowes, yea whole streats and lanes, so that the rentes be reysed, some double, some triple, and some four fould to that they were wythin these xii yeres last past. Yea, ther is not so much as a garden grownd fre from them. No remedye therfore, we must nedes fight it out, or else be brought to the lyke slavery that the French men are in! These idle bealies wil devour al that we shal get by our sore laboure in our youth, and when we shal be old and impotent, then shal we be driven to begge and crave of them that wyl not geve us so muche as the crowmes that fall from their tables. Such is the pytie we se in them! Better it were therfore, for us to dye lyke men, then after so great misery in youth to dye more miserably in age!

. . . . . .

Nowe if I should demaund of the greedy cormerauntes what thei thinke shuld be the cause of Sedition, they would saie:— 'The paisant knaves be to welthy, provender pricketh them! They knowe not them selves, they knowe no obedience, they regard no lawes, thei would have no gentlemen, thei wold have al men like themselves, they would have al thinges commune! Thei would not have us maisters of that which is our owne! They wil appoint us what rent we shal take for our groundes! We must not make the beste of oure owne! These are joly felowes! Thei wil caste doune our parckes, and laie our pastures open! Thei wil have the law in their own handes! They wil play the kinges! They wyll compel the kinge to graunt theyr requestes! But as they like their fare at the breakefaste they had this laste somer, so let them do againe. They have ben metely well coled, and shalbe yet better coled if they quiet not them selves. We wyll tech them to know theyr betters. And because they wold have al commone, we wil leave them nothing. And if they once stirre againe, or do but once cluster togither, we wil hang them at their own dores! Shal we suffer the vilaines to disprove our doynges? No, we wil be lordes of our own and use it as we shal thinke good!'

ABUSES

Source: Sir Thomas More, *Utopia*, 1516.

. . . make a law that they which plucked down farms and towns of husbandry shall re-edify them, or else yield and uprender the possession thereof to such as will go to the cost of building them anew. Suffer not these rich men to buy up all to engross and forestall, and with their monopoly to keep the market alone as please them. Let not so many be brought up in idleness; let husbandry and tillage be restored; let clothworking be renewed, that there may be honest labours for this idle sort to pass their time in profitably, which hitherto either poverty hath caused to be thieves, or else now be either vagabonds or idle serving men, and shortly will be thieves.

THE COUNTRYSIDE

Source: Hentzner *Travels in England,* 1598.

The soil is fruitful, and abounds with cattle, which inclines the inhabitants rather to feeding than ploughing, so that near a

B

third part of the land is left uncultivated for grazing. The climate is most temperate at all times, and the air never heavy, consequently maladies are scarcer, and less physic is used there than any where else. There are but few rivers: though the soil is productive, it bears no wine; but that want is supplied from abroad by the best kinds, as of Orleans, Gascon, Rhenish, and Spanish. The general drink is beer, which is prepared from barley, and is excellently well tasted, but strong, and what soon fuddles. There are many hills without one tree, or any spring, which produce a very short and tender grass, and supply plenty of food to sheep; upon these wander numerous flocks, extremely white, and whether from the temperature of the air, or goodness of the earth, bearing softer and finer fleeces than those of any other country: this is the true Golden Fleece, in which consist the chief riches of the inhabitants, great sums of money being brought into the island by merchants, chiefly for that article of trade. The dogs here are particularly good. It has mines of gold, silver, and tin, (of which all manner of table utensils are made, in brightness equal to silver, and used all over Europe), of lead, and of iron, but not much of the latter. The horses are small but swift. Glasshouses are in plenty here.

Source: Thomas Platter, *Travels in England,* 1599.

Of field crops there is a splendid profusion in England, corn, rye, barley, oats, beans, hops, garden produce, apples, pears, many species of purple plums, cherries, which however ripen rather late.

Of game there are deer of every shade in plenty, both in the woods and in enclosed parks, likewise red deer, stags and other game, small in size and quantity however, and no black game or roebuck; sheep are abundant, and since there are no wolves in England they are easier to keep, the wool is extremely good, and the cloth is rated very high. There are plenty of foxes and hares and a great many rabbits all over England, and the rabbits are often found in enclosed gardens, or running about the open fields and woods. Tame fourfooters also abound, as for instance fine oxen and cows, which, like the sheep, are put out to graze in the summer without a herdsman.

Horses are plentiful too, but wretched and small, though very nimble, the riding horses are geldings, and mostly excellent. And it is forbidden to take these horses out of the country without the queen's passport.

A PLOUGHMAN'S DAY

Source: Gervase Markham, *Farewell to Husbandry.* 1653.

We will suppose it to be after Christmas, or about Plow Day. . . . At this time the Plowman shall rise before four o'clock in the morning, and after thanks given to God for his rest, and the success of his labours, he shall go into his stable or beast-house, and first he shall fodder his cattle, then clean the house and make the booths clean; rub down the cattle, and cleanse their skins from all filth. Then he shall curry his horses, rub them with cloths and wisps, and make both them and the stable as clean as may be. Then he shall water both his oxen and horses, and housing them again, give them more fodder and to his horse by all means provender, as chaff and dry pease or beans, or oat-hulls, or clean garbage (which is the hinder ends of any grain but rye), with the straw chopped small amongst it, according as the ability of the husbandman is.

And while they are eating their meat, he shall make ready his collars, hames, treats, halters, mullers and plow-gears seeing everything fit and in its due place, and to these labours I will allow two hours; that is, from four the clock till six. Then he shall come into breakfast, and to that I allow him half an hour, and then another half hour to the yoking and gearing of his cattle, so that at seven he may set forth to his labours; and then he shall plow from seven o'clock in the morning till betwixt two and three in the afternoon. Then he shall unyoke and bring home his cattle, and having rubbed them, dressed them and cleansed them from all dirt and filth, he shall fodder them and give them meat. Then shall the servants go in to their dinner, which allowed half an hour, it will then be towards four of the clock; at what time he shall go to his cattle again, and rubbing them down and cleansing their stalls, give them more fodder; which done, he shall go into the barns, and provide and make ready fodder of all kinds for the next day. . . .

This being done, and carried into the stalls, ox-house, or other convenient place, he shall then go water his cattle, and give them more meat, and to his horse provender; and by this time it will draw past six o'clock; at which time he shall come in to supper, and after supper he shall either sit by the fireside, mend shoes for himself and their family, or beat and knock hemp or flax, or pick and stamp apples or crabs for cider or vinegar, or else grind malt on the querns, pick candle-rushes, or do some husbandly office till it be fully eight o'clock. Then he shall take his lanthorn and candle, and go see his cattle, and having cleansed his stalls and planks, litter them down, look that they are safely tied, and then fodder and give them meat for all night. Then, giving God thanks for benefits received that day, let him and the whole household go to their rest till the next morning.

MANNERS

Source: Hentzner, *Travels in England*, 1598.

The English are serious, like the Germans; lovers of shew, liking to be followed wherever they go by whole troops of servants, who wear their masters' arms in silver, fastened to their left arms, a ridicule they deservedly lay under. They excel in dancing and music, for they are active and lively, though of a thicker make than the French; they cut their hair close on the middle of the head, letting it grow on either side; they are good sailors, and better pirates, cunning, treacherous, and thievish; above three hundred are said to be hanged annually at London; beheading with them is less infamous then hanging; they give the wall as the place of honour; hawking is the general sport of the gentry; they are more polite in eating than the French, devouring less bread, but more meat, which they roast in perfection; they put a great deal of sugar in their drink; their beds are covered with tapestry, even those of farmers; they are often molested with the scurvy, said to have first crept into England with the Norman conquest; their houses are commonly of two stories, except in London, where they are of three and four, though but seldom of four; they are built of wood, those of the richer sort with bricks; their roofs are low, and, where the owner has money, covered with lead.

They are powerful in the field, successful against their enemies, impatient of anything like slavery; vastly fond of great noises that fill the ear, such as the firing of cannon, drums, and the ringing of bells, so that it is common for a number of them, that have got a glass in their heads, to go up into some belfrey, and ring the bells for hours together for the sake of the exercise. If they see a foreigner very well made, or particularly handsome, they will say, It is a pity he is not an Englishman!

CHILDREN

Source: E. Chamberlayne, *Angliae Notitia, or The Present State of England*, 1687.

The Condition of Children in England is different from those in our Neighbour-Countries.

As Husbands have a more absolute Authority over their Wives, and their Estates, so Fathers have a more absolute Authority over their Children. Fathers may give all their Estates unintailed from their own Children, and all to any one Child, and none to the rest; the Consideration whereof, keeps the Children in great awe.

Children, by the Common Law of England, are, at certain Ages, enabled to perform certain acts.

A Son at the Age of 14, may chuse his Guardian, may claim his Land holden in Socage, may consent to Marriage, may, by Will dispose of Goods and Chattels.

At the Age of 15, he ought to be sworn to his Allegiance to the King.

At 21, he is said to be of full Age, may then make any Contracts, may pass, not only Goods, but Lands by Will, which in other Countries may not be done, till the Annus Consistentiae, the Age of 25, when the heat of Youth is somewhat abated, and they begin to be stayed in mind, as well as in growth.

A Daughter at 7 years is to have aid of her Father's Tenants to marry her, for at those years she may consent unto Marriage, though she may afterwards dissent.

At 9 she is Dowable, as if then, or soon after she could virum sustinere, and thereby Dotem promereri.

At 12, she is enabled to ratifie and confirm her former consent given to Matrimony; and if at that Age she dissent not, she is bound for ever; she may then make a Will of Goods and Chattels.

At 14, she might receive her Lands into her own hands, and was then out of Wardship, if she was 14 at the Death of her Ancestor.

At 16 (though at the Death of her Ancestor she was under 14) she was to be out of Wardship; because then she might take a Husband, who might be able to perform Knights Service.

At 21, she is enabled to Contract or Alienate her Lands by Will, or otherwise.

The eldest Son inherits all Lands, and to the younger Children are disposed Goods and Chattels, and commonly the eldest Son's Wife's Portion; and besides, they are carefully educated in some Profession or Trade.

If there be no Son, the Lands, as well as Goods, are equally divided amongst the Daughters.

LIFE DURING THE CIVIL WAR

Source: Lady Fanshawe's Memoirs.

We that had till that hour lived in great plenty and great order, found ourselves like fishes out of the water, and the scene so changed that we knew not at all how to act any part but obedience, for from as good a house as any gentleman in England had, we came to a baker's house in an obscure street, and from rooms well furnished, to lie in a very bad bed in a garret, to one dish of meat, and that not the best ordered, no money, for we were poor as Job, nor clothes more than a man or two brought in their cloak bags: we had the perpetual discourse of losing or gaining towns and men; at the windows the sad spectacle of war, sometimes plague, sometimes sickness of other kinds, by reason of so many people being packed together, as I believe, there never was before of that quality; always in want, yet I must needs say that most bore it with a martyr-like cheerfulness. For my own part, I began to think we should all, like Abraham, live in tents all the days of our lives.

CHAPTER II

TOWNS

In medieval England some regions were rich and others poor. With increasing trade and wealth, conditions were levelling out to a certain extent in the sixteenth and seventeenth centuries. No other town came anywhere near the metropolis in size or wealth or importance. By 1600 London's population had reached about 150,000, and in the next hundred years, in spite of the Plague of 1665 which killed twice as many people as lived in the largest provincial town, it reached nearly 450,000. This growth was viewed with alarm by government and people alike. In 1563 a royal proclamation prohibited new building in London or within three miles of its gates and the letting of any house to more than one family. But both prohibitions were frequently ignored.

Many provincial towns were becoming stronger and, with growing prosperity, were trying to free themselves from the remains of their earlier dependence upon Crown or Church. Scores of new charters were granted to towns and many former charters were re-granted with new privileges.

LONDON

EASTCHEAP IN 1589. (*Wilkinson's Londonia Illustrata*)

Source: Italian Relations of England, c. 1500, Camden Society.

It abounds with every article of luxury, but the most remarkable thing in London is the wonderful quantity of wrought silver.

BILLINGSGATE IN 1598. (*Wilkinson's Londonia Illustrata*)

In one single street, named the Strand, leading to St. Paul's, there are fifty-two goldsmith's shops, so rich and full of silver vessels. And these vessels are all either salt-cellars or drinking-cups, or basins to hold water for the hands, for they eat off that fine tin, which is little inferior to silver. (pewter)

A GENTLEMAN GOES SHOPPING.

Source: Thomas Dekker, *The Seven Deadly Sins of London*, 1606.

In every street carts and coaches make such a thundering as if the world ran upon wheels. At every corner men, women and children meet in such shoals, that posts are set up on purpose to strengthen the houses, lest with jostling one another they should shoulder them down. Besides hammers are beating in one place, tubs hooping in another, pots clinking in a third, water tankards running at tilt in a fourth. Here are porters sweating under burdens, there merchants' men bearing bags of money.

RIVER TRAFFIC IN LONDON

Source: Thomas Platter, *Travels in England,* 1599.

And while a very fine bridge is built across this stream, it is more customary to cross the water or travel up and down the town . . . by attractive pleasure craft, for a number of tiny streets lead to the Thames from both ends of the town; the boatmen wait there in great crowds, each one eager to be first to catch one, for all are free to choose the ship they find most attractive and pleasing, while every boatman has the privilege on arrival of placing his ship to best advantage for people to step into.

The wherries are charmingly upholstered and embroidered cushions laid across the seats, very comfortable to sit on or lean against, and generally speaking the benches only seat two people next to one another; many of them are covered in, particularly in rainy weather or fierce sunshine. They are extremely pleasant to travel in and carry one or a couple of boatmen.

DRINKING WATER IN LONDON

The Water Bearer

Source: Thomas Platter, *Travels in England,* 1599.

Spring or drinking-water is enclosed in great well-sealed stone cisterns in different parts of the town, is let off through cocks into special wooden iron-bound vessels with broad bottoms and narrow tops, which poor labourers carry to and fro to the houses on their shoulders and sell.

WATER SUPPLY

Source: John Taylor, *Carrier's Cosmography*, 1634.

Some ten years since, fresh water there was scant,
But with much cost they have supplied that want.
By a most exc'lent water-work that's made,
And to th' Town in Pipes it is conveyed,
Wrought with most artificial engines, and
Performed by th' Art of the Industrious hand
Of Mr. William Maltby Gentleman.
So that each man of note there always can
But turne a cock within his house, and still
They have fresh water always at their will.
This have they all, unto their great content,
For which they each do pay a yearly rent.

Source: The Journeys of Celia Fiennes, 1685–1698.

(*Plymouth*) . . . there are severall good Conduits to convey the water to the town, which conveyance the famous Sir Francis Drake (which did encompass the world in Queen Elizabeths days and landed safe at Plymouth) he gave this to the town; . . .

(*Norwich*) . . . in the middle was a great Well house with a wheele to wind up the water for the good of the publick; a little farther is a large pond walled up with brick a mans height with an entrance on one end, a little farther was a building on which they were at work design'd for a Water house to supply the town by pipes into their houses with water, . . .

(*Leicester*) . . . They have a water house and a water mill to turn the water into the pipes to serve the town, as it is in London, it comes but once a day so they save the water in deep leaden tubbs or cisterns for their use, there are wells in some streetes to draw water by a hand wheele for the common use of the town; . . .

(*Shrewsbury*) . . . there is a Water house which supplys the town through pipes with water, but its drawn up with horses and it seemes not to be a good and easye way, so they intend to make it with a water Engine in the town; . . .

COFFEE HOUSES

Source: M. Misson's *Memoirs*, translated by Mr. Ozell, 1719.

You have all Manner of News there: You have a good Fire, which you may sit by as long as you please: You have a Dish of Coffee; you meet your Friends for the Transaction of Business, and all for a Penny, if you don't care to spend more.

FIRE-FIGHTING

Source: W. S. Prideaux, *Memorials of the Goldsmiths' Company.*

24th February 1643.   A precept from the Lord Mayor requiring the Company to provide ladders, hooks, and buckets, for the quenching of fire.   It is agreed to provide 3 dozen leather buckets, and the rest at the Warden's discretion.

8th December 1644.   Order that the engine for the quenching of fire shall be used by two or three almsmen, who are all to be 'fit to take their turns', and are to be paid 6*d.* each.

FIGHTING A FIRE.

Source: The Life and Times of Anthony Wood, antiquary, of Oxford, 1632–1695, described by himself.

2 Sept., 1666, a lamentable fire broke out in London in the morning, being Sunday. The wind being eastward blew clouds of smoke over Oxon the next day, and cheifly Tuesday, and the sunshine was much darkned. The same night also the moone was darkened by clouds of smoak and looked reddish. The fire or flame made a noise like the waves of the sea. The city by this fire and the pest much impoverished, discontented, afflicted, cast downe. Therby chimney money taxed, contributions for some time lost. The country cries out because there is soe much plenty and no transportation. Many farmers broke; clapt up in prison because they cannot pay their rent, corne being soe cheap. Wheras on the other side, Holland is soe poore for want of transportation that corne is there 20s. a bushell.

The Fire. Soe suddenly did it come and therby caused such distraction and severall forgat their names when they with their money or goods under their armes were examined by the watch that then immediatly was appointed. Others that had occasion to write letters a day or 2 after it ended, forgat the day of the mounth and the mounth of the year. Others quite distracted for the generall loss they have received. Thousands utterly undone that had houses there. Those that had a house to-day were the next glad of the shelter of an hedge or a pigstie or stable. Those that were this day riding wantonly in coaches, were, the next, glad to ride in dung-carts to save their lives. Those that thought the ground too unworthy to be touched by their feet, did run up to the knees in dirt and water to save themselves from the fury of fire or the falling of houses. Those that faired deliciously this day and nothing curious enough to satiate their palatts, were within few days following glad of a browne crust. Those that delighted themselves in downe bedds and silken curteynes, are now glad of the shelter of a hedge.

Source: Schedule of Bye-laws attached to roll or manor of Bishops Hall in Chelmsford, 1564. (Essex Record Office, D/DM M7.)

First, it is ordained that every inhabitant of the town shall scour and make clean the common gutter coming through the town, once in every month. Under pain of forfeiture 12d.

Item, that neither the butcher nor any person at any time hereafter shall cast any horns, bones or any other filth in the street or in the river there, penalty 3s. 4d.

Item, that no inhabitant of any house shall kill any cattle or make any slaughter within his house, to the hurt and annoyance of his neighbours, penalty 20s.

Source: 'Civil and Uncivil Life, 1579', W. C. Hazlett: *Inedited Tracts.*

The manner of the most gentlemen and noblemen is to house themselves (if possibly they may) in the suburbs of the city, because the air there being somewhat at large, the place is healthy; and through the distance from the body of the town, the noise not much and so consequently quiet. Also for comfort, we find many lodgings, both spacious and roomy, with gardens and orchards very delectable.

PROVINCIAL TOWNS

Celia Fiennes, travelling throughout England during the closing years of the seventeenth century, noted many developments in the towns she visited.

Source: The Journeys of Celia Fiennes, 1685–1698.

. . . as I observe most of the great towns and cittys have about them little villages as attendants or appendix's to them which are a sort of suburbs, there being stragling houses for the most part all the way between that and the gates; . . .

. . . I went to this Newcastle in Staffordshire to see the makeing the fine tea-potts cups and saucers of the fine red earth, in imitation and as curious as that which comes from China, but was defeated in my design, they comeing to an end of their clay they made use of for that sort of ware and therefore was removed to some other place where they were not settled at their work, so could not see it;

Taunton is a large town haveing houses of all sorts of buildings both brick and stone but mostly timber and plaister; its a very neate place and looks substantial as a place of good trade; you meete all sorts of country women wrapp'd up in manteles called West Country rockets, a large mantle doubled together of a sort of serge, some are linsywolsey, and a deep fringe or fag at the lower end; these hang down some to their feete some only just below the wast, in the summer they are all in white garments of this sort, in the winter they are in red ones; I call them garments because they never go out without them and this is the universal fashion in Somerset and Devonshire and Cornwall; . . .

Gloucester . . . here they follow knitting, stockings gloves wastcoates and peticoates and sleeves all of cotten, and others spinn the cottens.

Leeds is a large town, severall large streetes cleane and well pitch'd and good houses all built of stone, some have good gardens and steps up to their houses and walls before them; this is esteemed the wealthyest town of its bigness in the Country, its manufacture is the woollen cloth the Yorkshire Cloth in which they are all employ'd and are esteemed very rich and very proud; . . .

Liverpool which is in Lancashire is built just on the river Mersey, mostly new built houses of brick and stone after the London fashion; the first original was a few fishermens houses and now is grown to a large fine town and but a parish and one Church, tho' there be 24 streetes in it; there is indeed a little Chappell and there are a great many Dessenters in the town; its a very rich trading town the houses of brick and stone built high and even, that a streete quite through lookes very handsome, the streetes well pitched; there are abundance of persons you see very well dress'd and of good fashion; the streetes are faire and long, its London in miniature as much as ever I saw any thing; . . .

Colchester . . . a long building like stalls on purpose to lay their baize when exposed to saile, great quantetyes are made here and sent in Bales to London that is 44 miles distant, the whole town is employ'd in spinning weaveing washing drying and dressing their baize, in which they seeme very industrious; there I saw the Card they use to comb and dress the baize, which they call them teazels which are a kind of rush tops or something like them which they put in frames or laths of wood; the town looks like a thriveing place by the substantiall houses, well pitched streetes which are broad enough for two Coaches to go a breast, besides a pitch'd walke on either side by the houses, secured by stumps of wood and is convenient for 3 to walke together; their buildings are of timber of loame and lathes and much tileing, the fashion of the Country runs much in long roofes and great cantilivers and peakes; out of these great streetes runs many little streetes but not very narrow, mostly old buildings except a few houses builded by some Quakers that are brick and of the London mode; . . .

Nottingham is the neatest town I have seen, built of stone and delicate large and long Streetes much like London and the houses lofty and well built, the Market place is very broad—out of which runns 2 very large streetes much like Holborn but the buildings finer and there is a Pyaza all along one side of one of the Streetes, with stone pillars for walking that runns the length of the Streete, which is a mile long; all the streetes are of a good size all about the town and well pitch'd, there are severall good houses in the town, there are 3 or 4 large houses of the Duke of Newcastles with the Castle, which is a fine thing stands very high on a hill and when you come to the Castle you ascend 40 steps to the Court and Hall, the roomes are very lofty and large, 6 or 7 state roomes, and a long gallery hung with fine pictures of the family, the wanscoate is most of Cedar; . . . the Chamber of State is hung with very rich tapistry so much silver and gold in it that the 3 pieces that hung the roome cost 1500£; . . .

They make brick and tile by the town; the manufacture of the town mostly consists in weaving of Stockings, which is a very ingenious art; there was a man that spunn Glass and made severall things in Glass birds and beasts, I spunn some of the glass and saw him make a Swan presently, with divers coulloured glass he makes Buttons which are very stong and will not breake; Nottingham is famous for good ale so for Cellars they are dugg out of the rocks and so are very coole.

Winchester is a large town was once the metropolis, there is a wall encompassing it with severall Gates, the streets are pretty good large and long, the buildings but low and old, only some

PLATE 1

Swearing-in the Mayor of Bristol. The retiring Mayor holds the bible, and the clerk reads the oath

PLATE 2

A painting on wood of the opening of Parliament

few in the Close which are new built of the Doctors houses by the Colledge and the Church; the Dean's house is a good old house, timber buildings, there are some of the roomes lofty and large, a dineing drawing room and bed chamber very good, a long Gallery runns through the house and opens into the Garden by a descent of severall stone stepps; the Garden is but small, there are green and gravel walkes higher and lower but its all in an old fashion'd form, . . .

Oxford opens to view 2 mile off; its scituation is fine on a round hill, environ'd round with hills adorn'd with Woods and Enclosures, yet not so neare as to annoy the town, which stands pleasant and compact; there is a fine Causy for neare two mile by the road for the Schollars to walke on; the Theater stands the highest of all and much in the middle encompass'd with the severall Colledges and Churches and other Buildings whose towers and spires appeares very well at a distance; the Streetes are very cleane and well pitched, and pretty broad, the High Streete is a very noble one, soe large and of a greate length; in this is the University Church, called St. Maryes, which is very large and lofty but nothing very Curious in it.

The Theater is a Noble Pile of building its paved with black and white marble exceeding large and lofty built round and supported by its own architecture all stone, noe pillars to support it; . . .

Newcastle . . . their shops are good and are of distinct trades, not selling many things in one shop as is the custom in most country towns and cittys; here is one market for Corne another for Hay besides all other things which takes up two or three streetes; . . .

ELECTION OF A MAYOR (in Norwich)

Source: The Journeys of Celia Fiennes, 1685–1698.

. . . they elect him the first of May and then prepare for his being sworne on Holy Thursday, they new washe and plaister their houses within and without . . . all the streete in which this major elects house is very exact in beautifying themselves

C

and hanging up flags the coullours of their Companyes and dress up pageants and there are playes and all sorts of shows that day, in little what is done at the Lord Major of London show; then they have a great feast with fine flaggs and scenes hung out, musick and danceing; I was in the hall they keep their feast in and saw some of their preparations for that day . . .

CHAPTER III

DRESS

During the sixteenth and seventeenth centuries a succession of
writers—English and foreign—commented upon the extravagance
and expensiveness of the clothes worn by wealthy Englishmen and

their wives. Of what was worn by the majority of people we know very little.

Fashion stemmed from the Court and it is therefore understandable that garments were exaggerated and ostentatious in Tudor times. Queen Elizabeth loved fine clothes and jewels, and it was said at her death that her wardrobe numbered dresses in thousands and wigs in hundreds.

Elizabeth issued several edicts against lavishness in dress, as previous monarchs had done, but since she ignored these rules herself it is not surprising that they were not generally obeyed. Hers was an age of change and opportunity and those with new money and new social ambitions wanted to 'put their money on their backs'. Discretion and modesty were not in vogue.

Phillip Stubbes, a rigid Calvinist and bitter enemy of Popery, wrote a number of books dealing with divinity and morality. The title page of *The Anatomie of Abuses* ran:

The Anatomie of Abuses, containing a Discoverie, or briefe Summarie of such Notable Vices and Corruptions, as nowe raigne in many Christian Countreyes of the Worlde: but especiall in the Countrey of Aligna: Together with most fearefull Examples of Gods Judgementes, executed upon the wicked for the same, as well in Aligna of late, as in other places, elsewhere.

Very godly, to be read of all true Christians, everywhere: but most chiefly, to be regarded in England.

SUMPTEOUS ATTYRE

Source: Phillip Stubbes, *Anatomie of Abuses,* 1585.

But now there is suche a confuse mingle mangle of apparell . . . and suche preposterous excesse thereof, as every one is permitted to flaunt it out in what apparell he lusteth himself, or can get by any kinde of meanes. So that it is very hard to know who is noble, who is worshipfull, who is a gentleman, who is not; for you shal have those which are neither of the nobilitie, gentilitie, nor yeomanrie, no, nor yet any magistrate or officer in the common wealthe, go daiely in silkes, velvettes, satens, damasles, taffaties, and suche like; notwithstanding that they be bothe base by birthe, meane by estate, and servile by callyng.

MEN'S DRESS

Source: Phillip Stubbes, *Anatomie of Abuses,* 1585.

Hats. Sometymes they use them sharpe on the croune, pearking up like the spere, or shaft of a steeple. . . . Othersome be flat and broad on the crowne, like the battlementes of a house. . . . And as the fashions bee rare and straunge, so is the stuffe whereof their hattes be made divers also; for some are of silke, some of velvet, some of taffatie, some of sarcenet, some of wooll,... And so common a thing it is, that every servyng man, countrieman, and other, even all indefferently, dooe weare of these hattes.

Ruffes. They have great and monsterous ruffes, made either of cambrike, holland, lawne, or els of some other the finest cloth that can be got for money, whereof some be a quarter of a yarde deepe, yea, some more, very fewe lesse, so that they stande a full quarter of a yearde (and more) from their necks, hanging over their shoulder points in steade of a vaile. . . . the devill, as he, in the fulnesse of his malice, first invented these great ruffes, so hath he now found out also two great pillers to beare up and maintaine this his kingdom of pride withal. . . . The one arch or piller . . . is a certaine kind of liquid matter, which they call starch, wherein the devill hath willed them to washe and dive their ruffes well, whiche, beeyng drie, will then stande stiffe and inflexible about their neckes. The other piller is a certaine device made of wiers crested for the purpose, whipped over either with gold thred, silver, or silke, and this he calleth a supportasse or underpropper; this is to bee applied round about their neckes under the ruffe, upon the out side of the bande, to beare up the whole frame and bodie of the ruffe, from fallying and hangyng doune.

Shirtes. Their shirtes . . . are either of camericke, holland, lawne, or els of the finest cloth that maie be got. And of these kinds of shirtes every one doethe weare alike; . . . And these shirtes . . . are wrought throughout with needle worke of silke, and such like, and curiously stitched with open seame, and many other knackes besides, more then I can describe; . . .

Dublets. Their dublets are no lesse monstrous then the rest;

for now the fashion is to have them hang downe to the middle of their theighes, . . . being so hard quilted, stuffed, bombasted, and sewed, as they can neither worke, nor yet well playe in them, through the excessive heate thereof; and therefore are forced to weare them lose about them for the most parte, otherwise they could very hardly eyther stoupe or decline to the grounde, so stiffe and sturdy they stand about them. . . . and stuffed with foure, five, or sixe pound of bombast at the least: I say nothing of what their dublets be made, some of saten, taffatie, silke, grograine, chamlet, gold, silver, and what not! slashed, jagged, cut, carved, pincked, and laced with all kinde of costly lace of divers and sondrey colours . . .

Shoes. . . . they have corked shoes, pinsnets, and fine pantoffles, whiche beare them uppe a finger or two from the ground, whereof some be of white leather, some of blacke, and some of red; some of black velvet, some of white, some of red, some of greene, razed, carved, cut, and stitched all over with silke, and layd on with golde, silver, and such like; . . .

Coats and Jerkins. Their coates and jerkins, as they be divers in colours, so be they divers in fashions; for some be made with collors, some without, some close to the body, some loose, which they cal mandilians, covering the whole body down to the thigh, like bags or sacks, that were drawne over them, hiding the dimensions and lineaments of the body; some are buttoned down the brest, some under the arme, and some down the backe, some with flaps over the brest, some without; some with great sleeves, some with small, and some with none at all; some pleated and crested behinde, and curiously gathered, some not; . . .

Clokes. They have clokes also in nothing discrepant from the rest, of divers and sundrye colours, white, red, tawnie, blacke, greene, yellow, russet, purple, violet and infinite other colours; some of clothe, silke, velvet, taffetie, and such like, whereof some be of the Spanishe, French, and Dutch fashions—some shorte, scarsly reaching to the girdlestead or waste, some to the knee, and othersome trailing uppon the grounde (almost), liker gownes then clokes; then are they garded with velvette gardes, or els laced with costly lace, either of golde, silver, or at the leaste of silke, three or foure fingers broade, down the balke, about the skirts, and every where els. And nowe of late they use to garde their clokes rounde about the skirtes with (bables), I should saie bugles, and other kinde of glasse, and all to shine to the eye. Besides al this, they are so faced, and withal so lined, as the inner side standeth almost in as muche as the outside; some have sleeves, other some have none; some have hoodes to pull over the head, some have none; some are hanged with poyntes and tassells of golde, silver, or silke, some without all this.

Bootehose. They have also bootehoose, whiche are to be wondred at, for they be of the finest clothe that may be got, yea, fine enought to make any band, ruffe, or shirte, needefull to be worne; yet this is bad enough to weare next their greasie bootes. And would to God this were all; but (oh phy for shame!) they must be wrought all over, from the gartering place upwarde, with needle woorke, clogged with silke of all colours, with byrdes, foules, beastes, and antiques purtraied all over in sumptuous sorte.

WOMEN'S DRESS

Source: Phillip Stubbes, *Anatomie of Abuses*, 1585.

Hair. . . . thei are not simplie content with their owne haire, but buye other haire, either of horses, mares, or any other straunge beastes, dying it of what colour they list themselves. And if there be any poore woman . . . that hath faire haire, these nice dames will not rest till they have bought it. Or if any children have faire haire, they will entice them into a secret place, and for a penie or two they will cut of their haire; as I heard that one did . . . of late, who, meeting a little childe with very faire haire, inveigled her into a house, promised her a penie, and so cutte off her haire.

Head-dresses. Then on toppes of these stately turrets (I meane their . . . heades . . .) stand their other capitall ornaments, as French-hood, hatte, cappe, kercher, and such like, whereof some be of velvet, some of taffatie, some (but few) of wooll, some of this fashion, some of that, and some of this colour, some of that, accordyng to the variable phantasies of their serpentine mindes. . . . They have also other ornaments . . . whiche they call . . . cawles, made netwise, to the ende, as I thinke, that the clothe of golde, clothe of silver, or els tinsell . . . may the better appeare, and shew it selfe in the bravest maner;

Ruffs, etc. The women . . . use great ruffes and neckerchers of holland, laune, camericke, and such clothe, as the greatest threed shall not be so big as the least haire that is; and lest they should fall downe, they are smeared and starched in the devil's liquor, I meane starche—after that dried with great diligence, streaked, patted, and rubbed very nicely, and so applied to their goodly necks, and, withal, underpropped, with supportasses . . . beyond all this, . . . three or foure degrees of minor ruffes, placed . . . one beneath an other, and al under the mayster devilruffe; . . . these great ruffes are . . . pleated, and crested full curiously, God wot. Then, last of all, they are either clogged with gold, silver, or silke lace of stately price, wrought all over with needle worke, speckeled and sparkeled here and there with the sunne, the mone, the starres, and many other antiques strange to beholde. Some are wrought with open worke downe to the midst of the ruffe and further; some with close worke, some wyth purled lace so cloied, and other gewgawes so pestered, as the ruffe is the least parte of it selfe. Sometimes they are pinned upp to their eares, sometimes they are suffered to hange over theyr shoulders, like windemill sailes fluttering in the winde, and thus every one pleaseth her selfe in her foolish devises;

Dublets and Jerkins. The women also have . . . dublettes and jerkins, as men have . . . buttoned up the breast, and made with winges, weltes, and pinions, on the shoulder poyntes, as mannes apparel is, for all the worlde;

Gowns, etc. Their gownes be no lesse famous then the rest, for some are of silke, some of velvet, some of grograine, some of taffatie, some of scarlet, and some of fine clothe, . . . If the whole gowne be not silke or velvet, then the same shall be layd with lace, two or three fingers broade, all over the gowne, or els the most parte; or . . . garded with great gardes of velvet, every gard fower or sixe fingers broad at the least, and edged with costly lace; ... some (have) sleeves hanging downe to their skirtes, trailing on the ground, and cast over their shoulders like cowe tailes. Some have sleeves much shorter, cut up the arme, and poincted with silk ribbons very gallantly, tied with true loves knottes. ... Then have they petticoates of the best clothe that can be bought, and of the fairest dye that can be made. ... they have kirtles ... either of silke, velvett, grograine, taffatie, satten, or scarlet, bordered with gardes, lace, fringe, and I can not tell what besides. So that, when they have all these goodly robes upon them, women seeme to be the smallest part of themselves, not ... women of flesh and bloude, but rather puppits ..., consisting of ragges and cloutes compacte together.

Trinkets. ... their fingers must be decked with golde, silver, and precious stones, their wreastes with bracelettes, and armelettes of golde, and other costly jewelles, their handes covered with their sweet washed gloves imbroidered with golde, silver, and what not; and to suche abhomination it is growen, as they must have their looking-glasses caried with them wheresoever they goe; and good reason, for els how could they see the devil in them?

FASHIONABLE ELIZABETHAN BARBERS

Source: Stubbes, *Anatomie of Abuses.* 1583.

There are no finer fellows under the sun, nor experter in their science of barbing than they be. They have invented such strange fashions and monstrous manners of cuttings, trimmings, shavings and washings, that you would wonder to see. When you come to be trimmed, they will ask you whether you will be cut to look terrible to your enemy or amiable to your friend. When they come to the cuttings of the hair, what snipping and snapping of scissors is there, what tricking and trimming. And when they come to washing, oh how gingerly they behave themselves therein, for they have their sweet balls of soap wherewithal they use to wash. Thus come warm cloths to wipe and dry him. The last action is the payment of money and in the end your cloak shall be brushed and 'God be with you gentleman!'

FASHIONS

The Reverend William Harrison wrote vivid descriptions of the clothes worn in Elizabethan England. He later became Canon of Windsor.

Source: William Harrison, *A Description of England*, 1587.

The fantastical folly of our nation (even from the courtier to the carter), is such that no form of apparel liketh us longer than the first garment is in the wearing, if it continue so long, and be not laid aside to receive some other trinket newly devised by the fickle-headed tailors, who covet to have several tricks in cutting, thereby to draw fond customers to more expense of money. . . . such is our mutability, that to-day there is none to the Spanish guise, to-morrow the French toys are most fine and delectable, ere long no such apparel as that which is after the high Almain fashion, by-and-bye the Turkish manner is generally best liked of, otherwise the Morisco gowns, the Barbarian fleeces, the mandilion worn to Colley-weston ward, and the short French breeches make a comely vesture that, except it were a dog in a doublet, you shall not see any so disguised as are my countrymen of England. And as these fashions are diverse, so likewise it is a world to see the costliness and the curiosity, the excess and the vanity, the pomp and the bravery, the change and the variety, and finally the fickleness and the folly, that is in all degrees, insomuch that nothing is more constant in England than inconstancy of attire. Oh, how much cost is bestowed nowadays upon our bodies, and how little upon our souls! How many suits of apparel hath the one, and how little furniture hath the other! How long time is asked in decking up of the first, and how little space left wherein to feed the latter! How curious, how nice also, are a number of men and women, and how hardly can the tailor please them in making it fit for their bodies! How many times must it be sent back again to him that made it! What chafing, what fretting, what reproachful language, doth the poor workman bear away! And many times when he doth nothing to it at all, yet when it is brought home again it is very fit and handsome. Then must we put it on, then must the long seams of our hose be set by a plumb-line, then we puff, then we blow, and finally sweat till we drop, that our clothes may stand well upon us. I will say nothing of our heads, which sometimes are polled, sometimes curled, or suffered to grow at length like woman's locks, many times cut off, above or under the ears, round as by a wooden dish. Neither will I meddle with our variety of beards, of which some are shaven from the chin like those of Turks, not a few cut short like to the beard of Marquess Otto, some made round like a rubbing-brush, others with a pique de vant (O! fine fashion), or now and then suffered to grow long, the barbers being grown to be so cunning in this behalf as the tailors. And therefore if a man have a lean and straight face, a Marquess Otto's cut will make it broad and large; if it be platter-like, a long, slender beard will make it seem the narrower; if he be weasel-beaked, then much hair left on the cheeks will make the owner look big like a bowdled hen, and so grim as a goose. . . . Many old men do wear no beards at all. Some lusty courtiers also and gentlemen of courage do wear either rings of gold, stones, or pearl in their ears, whereby they imagine the workmanship of God not to be a little amended.

Source: Thomas Platter, *Travels in England*, 1599.

Now the women-folk of England, who have mostly blue-grey eyes and are fair and pretty, have far more liberty than in other lands, and know just how to make good use of it, for they often stroll out or drive by coach in very gorgeous clothes, and the men must put up with such ways, and may not punish them for it, indeed the good wives often beat their men, and if this is discovered, the nearest neighbour is placed on a cart and paraded through the whole town as a laughing-stock for the victim, as a punishment—he is informed—for not having come to his neighbour's assistance when his wife was beating him. They lay great store by ruffs and starch them blue, so that their complexion shall appear the whiter, and some may well wear velvet for the street—quite common with them—who cannot afford a crust of dry bread at home I have been told. English burgher women usually wear high hats covered with velvet or silk for headgear, with cut-away kirtles when they go out, in old-fashioned style. Instead of whalebone they wear a broad circular piece of wood over the breast to keep the body straighter and more erect.

A LIGHT GARMENT, AND YET SUFFICIENT
AGAINST ALL RAINY WEATHER

Source: Sir Hugh Platt, *A Jewell House of Art and Nature*, 1594.

This garment will not be much dearer than our ordinary riding clokes. It may be made as light or lighter than our usual garments. A cloke may be prepared in such a manner, as that notwithstanding a continual rain, it shall not grow much more ponderous, then it was being dry.

This is done by putting a sufficient quantity of Linseed oyl, mixed with Rosin, and boiled to a vernish, with Verdigrease, Vermillion, or what else you will choose to colour the same, and when you find that it is not clammy, but casts a bright colour upon a rag of cloth dipt in it, then dip therein your cloth, whereof you would make your garment, and spread it abroad and let it dry leisurely.

17TH CENTURY FASHIONS

Seventeenth-century writers continued to mock at fashionable dress, but costume no longer reflected social status so much as political and religious views. Differences of outlook and practice between Puritans and Royalists showed in various degrees of soberness or frivolity in what they wore. The cropped hair, dark and very plain garments and tall black hats of the middle of the century were only worn by Puritans with extremely strict views. Times were serious and difficult for everybody and the majority of people wore a simplified version of Royalist dress, but active supporters of the exiled King often flaunted their lace and ribbons and curls as political banners.

At the Restoration, fashion was released from political or religious covention and styles again became lavish.

Source: Sir William Brereton, Bart., *Travels in Holland, the United Provinces, England, Scotland and Ireland*, 1634–1635.

Touching the fashion of the citizens, the women here wear and use upon festival days six or seven several habits and fashions; some for distinction of widows, wives and maids, others apparelled according to their own humour and phantasy. Many wear (especially of the meaner sort) plaids, which is a garment of the same woollen stuff whereof saddle-cloths in England are made, which is cast over their heads, and covers their faces on both sides, and would reach almost to the ground, but that they pluck them up, and wear them cast under their arms. Some ancient women and citizens wear satin straight-bodied gowns, short little cloaks with great capes, . . . young maids not married all are bare headed; some with broad thin ruffs, which lie flat to their shoulders, and others with half bands with wide necks, either much stiffened or set in wire, which comes only behind; and these ruffs some are more broad and thick than others.

Source: John Evelyn, *Tyrannus or The Mode*, 1661.

It was a fine silken fop which I spied walking th'other day through Westminster-Hall, that had as much Ribbon about him as would have plundered six shops, and set up twenty Country Pedlers: All his Body was dres't like a May-pole, or a Tom-a Bedlam's Cap. A Fregat newly rigg'd kept not half such a clatter in a storme, as this Puppets Streamers did when the Wind was in his Shroud's; the Motion was Wonderfull to behold, and the Colours were Red, Orange, and Blew, of well gum'd Sattin, which argu'd a happy fancy: but so was our Gallant over charg'd, . . . whether he did weare this Garment, or (as a Porter) bear it only, was not easily to be resolv'd.

Source: Life and Times of Anthony Wood, antiquary, of Oxford, 1632–1695, *described by Himself.*

Dec. 1663. A strange effeminate age when men strive to imitate women in their apparell, viz. long periwigs, patches in their faces, painting, short wide breeches like petticotes, muffs, and their clothes highly scented, bedecked with ribbons of all colours. And this apparell was not only used by gentlemen and others of inferior quality, but by souldiers especially those of the Life Gard to the King, who would have spanners hanging on one side and a muff on the other, and when dirty weather some of them would relieve their gards in pattens.

On the other side, women would strive to be like men, viz., when they rode on horsback or in coaches weare plush caps like monteros, wither full of ribbons or feathers, long periwigs which men use to weare, and riding coate of a red colour all bedaubed with lace which they call vests, and this habit was cheifly used by the ladies and maids of honor belonging to the Queen, brough in fashion about anno 1662.

FASHION SET BY KING AND COURT

Source: Pepys's Diary.

Nov. 28th, 1665. The King and Court, they say, have now finally resolved to spend nothing upon clothes but what is of the growth of England; which, if observed, will be very pleasing to the people, and very good for them.

Oct. 8th, 1666. The King hath yesterday in Council declared his resolution of setting a fashion for clothes, which he will never alter. It will be a vest, I know not well how; but it is to teach the nobility thrift, and will do good.

Oct. 15th, 1666. This day the King begins to put on his vest, and I did see several persons of the House of Lords and Commons too, great courtiers, who are in it; being a long cassocke close to the body, of black cloth, and pinked with white silke under it, and a coat over it, and the legs ruffled with black riband like a pigeon's leg; and upon the whole I wish the King may keep it, for it is a very fine and handsome garment. . . .

AN ABSURD FASHION

Source: Thomas Mace, *Musick's Monument,* 1676.

I remember there was a Fashion, not many Years since, for Women in their Apparel to be so Pent up by the Straitness, and Stiffness of the Gown-Shoulder-Sleeves, that they could not so much as Scratch Their Heads, for the Necessary Remove of a Biting Louse; nor Elevate their Arms scarcely to feed themselves Handsomly; nor Carve a Dish of Meat at a Table, but their whole Body must needs Bend towards the Dish.

UMBRELLAS

Source: Quotation from Gladys Scott Thomson, *Life in a Noble Household* (Cape, 1937).

A 'new-fangled notion' which came to England from the East, was introduced into the Duke of Bedford's family in 1689, when a workman submitted this bill to His Lordship:

	£	s.	d.
For wood and iron work to two umbrellas to rule (measure)	1	7	0
For 17¾ yards of ticking to make the umbrellas at 1s. 3d. per yard	1	5	0
For 16¾ ounces of worsted fringe to the umbrellas at 5d. per ounce		6	8
For making the umbrellas		6	0
For a piece of tape and tacks		2	0
For a sacking bottom and nails		12	0
For 2 long screws and nuts		2	6
For a plain mat to pack them in		1	0

CHAPTER IV

BUILDINGS

In the Middle Ages the best craftsmanship in wood and stonework had been devoted to ecclesiastical building, but the sixteenth century was a period of rising prosperity, when men of all classes except the poorest built themselves new houses.

Henry VIII, interested in the new Renaissance style of architecture in Italy, encouraged Italian artists and craftsmen to come to England. With the breakaway from the Church of Rome, however, the flow of Italian workmen ceased and Renaissance influence made no further headway in this country for many years, except indirectly through the Low Countries.

The new houses varied naturally with the wealth of the owner, the environment and the available building materials. But so general was the interest in house building that even Dr. Andrew Borde, the eminent physician, gave general advice to his readers.

Much of our information about later building comes from legal documents and ecclesiastical records. Celia Fiennes, travelling through England and Wales on horseback at the end of the century recorded many details of the buildings she saw.

ADVICE

Source: Borde, *A Compendyous Regyment*, 1567.

. . . he that wyll builde, let him make his foundacyon upon a gravaly grounde myxte with clay, or els let him buylde upon a roche or stone, . . . or els upon a hylles syde. And order and edyfye the house so that the pryncypall and chiefe prospectes may be east and weest, specyally north east, south east, and south west, . . . Make the hall under such a fashion, that the parler be anexed to the heade of the hall. And the butterye and pantry be at the lower ende of the hal, the seller under the pantry . . . the kychen set somwhat a base from the buttry and pantry, . . . the pastry house and the larder house anexed to the kychen, . . . let the pryve chambre be anexed to ye chambre of astate, with other chambers necessarie for the buyldynge, so that many of the

PLATE 3

Country revels

PLATE 4

(a) a Royal feast

(b) A wealthy man at home

chambers may have a prospecte into the Chapell. . . . the bake house and brewe house shulde be a distaunce from . . . other buyldynge, . . .

. . . it is a commodyous and a pleasaunt thynge to a mansion to have an orchard of soundry fruytes, but it is more commodiouse to have a fayre gardayn repleted with herbes of aromatyck and redolent savours, . . . Also a parke repleted with dere and conyes is a necessary and a pleasaunt thynge to be anexed to a mansyon. A dove house also is a necessary thynge aboute a mansyon place. And amenge other thynges a payre of buttes is a decent thynge . . . and other whyle for a greate man necessary it is for to passe his tyme with bowles in an aly . . .

MATERIALS

William Harrison noted many changes in England between 1577 and 1587.

Source: Harrison, *A Description of England,* 1587.

The ancient manours and houses of our gentlemen are yet, and for the most part, of strong timber, in framing whereof our carpenters have beene and are worthilie preferred before those of like science among all other nations. Howbeit such as he latelie builded are commonlie either of bricke or hard stone, or both; their roomes large and comelie, and houses of office further distant from their lodgings. Those of the nobilitie are likewise wrought with bricke and hard stone, as provison may best be made: but so magnificent and statelie, as the basest house of a baron dooth often match in our daies with some honours of princes in old time.

During the seventeenth century timber was becoming increasingly scarce, and in many areas regulations were made concerning its use in house-building.

Source: Proclamations (British Museum).

There hath been such consumption of timber in the Realm that in the very City of London they are now driven to build with beech and other timber of small continuance which in time

D

will be the notorious peril and decay of the city. It is now commanded that no part of a tree that may serve for any use of timber shall be converted to coal or firewood; and, for the better preservation of timber, from the feast of St. Michael no one shall erect any new house, or the forepart of any house within the city and suburbs, except all outer walls and windows be made wholly of brick, or brick and stone. Moreover, the forefront thereof shall be made of that uniform order and form as shall be prescribed, for that street where the building shall be, by the chief magistrates of the City.

PETITION FOR LICENCE TO BUILD A COTTAGE

Source: Letter to Sir Thomas Kitson, Kt., at London. (Bury St. Edmunds and West Suffolk Record Office, E 3/15.7/4.3.); 28 March, 1598.

Sir—Thomas Rodger the younger—an honest true labouring man in his trade of plowright & one that hitherto has had his dwelling in the town of Fornham all Saints—But now there being no house for him to bestowe himself in, neither can he provide himselfe elsewhere, but ready to lye in the street, hath made his humble suit that we would in his behalf be humble suitors to your worship that it might please you to give him licence to build himself up a cottage or poor dwelling-place upon a piece of the common next the east end of your pasture called the Mare Close, and that he might by your worship's good means have authority to enclose for the situation thereof $\frac{1}{2}$ rood of ground by your ditch of the said pasture, in such manner and form as your steward by viewing same thinks both convenient and meet.

But because many have interest of common in that plot of ground, as well as in the rest adjoining, and amongst those many, the poor man fears he shall not get all their consent before your worship's good liking thereof may be had. And to the end that your worship may be advertized whose consents are already given, And who they be that humbly sue in his behalf—the underwritten have severally subscribed name or mark.

(11 names follow)

Endorsement. My master was pleased to grant this request, & to give him a load of timber & two loads of bricks towards the same house—Condition—he to hold it for the lives of himself & his present wife, paying 2/- p.a. and keeping the pale in sufficient repair, . . . And that the longer liver of them both shall leave the said house now to be built sufficiently repaired fit and meet to serve for another of his quality or otherwise as best shall please Sir Thomas or his next successors to dispose or appoint there.

SMALL HOUSES

Source: Parsonage Terriers from Devonshire and Leicestershire.

Alphington, Devon (c. 1601). There are 4 houses: hall and parlour under one roof, kitchen and malthouse under another, the third a barn, the fourth a shippon with a new stable and a corn chamber, which I have built.

Lockington, Leicestershire (1638). The vicarage house stands southeast from the Church, on the left hand on the entry of it is a hall with plaistered walls, with a chimney in it, over it is a chamber wherein is a garner to lye in corne.
Item on the east side of the hall is a buttery & all this makes one bay of building.
Item Two little parlours one whereof has a study in it on the north side of the hall. With two chambers over them containing two bayes of building.
Item on the right hand of the entry is a kitchen with an oven in it almost a bay of building.
Item Southward from the house is a barn for corne . . .

GRANDER BUILDINGS

Source: E. Chamberlayne, *Angliae Notitia, or the Present State of England,* 1687.

Churches throughout all England, and all publick Edifices, are generally of Solid Stone, covered with Lead; Cathedral and Collegiate-Churches every where ample and magnificent; and the Churches in Market-Towns and Opulent Villages spacious and solid enough, beautified either with very high Pyramids, or Steeples, or at least with stately high Towers. Houses in Cities, that were heretofore usually of Wood, are now built of good Stone or Brick, and cover'd with Slate or Tyle; the Rooms within, formerly Wainscotted, are now hung with Tapistry, or other convenient Stuff, and are ceiled with Plaister, excellent against the rage of fire, against the cold, and to hinder the passage of all dust and noise.

The Modern Buildings have been far more slight, and of less continuance than the Ancient.

The Houses of the Nobles and Rich are abundantly furnished with Pewter, Brass, fine Linnen, and Plate: The mean Mechanicks and ordinary Husbandmen want not Silver Spoons, or some Silver Cups in their Houses.

The Windows every where glazed, not made of Paper or Wood, as is usually in Italy or Spain. Chimneys in most places, no Stoves, although the far more Southern parts of Germany can hardly subsist in the Winter without them.

A PALACE

Source: The Journal of Frederick, Duke of Wirtemberg, 1592.

(in Herts.) . . . went to see the magnificent palace Theobalds, belonging to the Lord High Treasurer of England, which is reckoned one of the most beautiful houses in England, as in truth it is.

First of all his Highness inspected the handsome and delightful hall, which is so ornamental and artistic that its equal is not easily to be met with; for, besides other imbellishments in it, there is a very high rock, of all colours, made of real stones, out of which gushes a splendid fountain that falls into a large circular bowl or basin, supported by two savages. This hall has no pillars: it is about sixty feet in length and upwards of thirty wide.

The ceiling or upper floor is very artistically constructed: it contains the twelve signs of the zodiac, so that at night you can see distinctly the stars proper to each; on the same stage the sun performs its course, which is without doubt contrived by some concealed ingenious mechanism. On each side of the hall are six trees, having the natural bark so artfully joined, with birds' nests and leaves as well as fruit upon them, all managed in such a manner that you could not distinguish between the natural and these artificial trees; and, as far as I could see, there was no difference at all, for when the steward of the house opened the windows, which looked upon the beautiful pleasure-garden, birds flew into the hall, perched themselves upon the trees, and began to sing. In a word, this hall is so elegantly adorned with paintings and otherwise that it is right royal, and well worth the seeing.

There are also many other spacious halls and fine galleries in this splendid palace, with very artistic paintings and correct landscapes of all the most important and remarkable towns in Christendom, as well as tables of inlaid-work and marble of various colours, all of the riches and most magnificent description.

In another hall is depicted the kingdom of England, with all its cities, towns and villages, mountains and rivers; as also the armorial bearings and domains of every esquire, lord, knight, and noble who possess lands and retainers to whatever extent. In short, all the apartments and rooms are adorned with beautiful tapestries and the like to such a degree that no king need be ashamed to dwell there.

Some rooms in particular have very beautiful and costly ceilings, which are skilfully wrought in joiner's work and elegantly coloured, . . .

HOUSES IN VARIOUS DISTRICTS

Source: The Journeys of Celia Fiennes, 1685–1698.

(In Cornwall) . . . His house stands on a high hill in the middle of a parke with severall rows of trees with woods beyond it; the house is built all of white stone like the rough coarse marble and cover'd with slate; they use much lime in their cement which makes both walls and cover look very white; there is a Court walled round with open iron gates and barrs; the entrance is up a few stone steps into a large high hall and so to a passage that leads foreright up a good stair-case; on the right side is a large common parlour for constant eating in, from whence goes a little roome for smoaking that has a back way into the kitchin, and on the left hand is a great parlour and drawing roome wanscoated all very well, but plaine, the great parlour is Cedar, out of that is the drawing-roome, which is hung with pictures of the family; that goes into the garden which has gravel walks round and across, but the squares are full of goosebery and shrub-trees and looks more like a kitchen garden . . . out of which is another garden and orchard which is something like a grove, green walks with rows of fruit trees; . . .

(In Wilts.) . . . the house stands finely to the river, a brick building, you enter into a walled Court low up 12 stepps at least into a noble hall, on the left hand was a parlour and on the right a large drawing roome a little parlour and large Staires up to severall very handsom Chambers furnish'd with good tapestry and damaske and some velvets which was new, because the fire had spoiled most of the goods but the house was built just in the same figure; the kitchins and offices are all under the Roomes of State and they go down steps to it under the arch of stepps that ascend to the hall; out of the drawing roome by Glass doors you enter the Garden on a terrass and that by stepps so to severall Walks of Gravel and Grass and to the Gardens one below another with low walls to give the view all at once; here was fine flowers and greens dwarfe trees and oring and lemon trees in rows with fruite and flowers at once, and some ripe, they are the first oring trees I ever saw; here are stately woods and walks.

(In Wilts.) . . . the Earle of Pembroke . . . has a very fine house (Wilton) with large courts one within another: at the Entrance there is a lofty Hall with good pictures, 3 or 4 dineing roomes and drawing roomes of State with very good bed chambers and well furnished velvet damaske and tissue; one gallery and the dineing roome was all wanscoated with pictures of the family; there is a drawing roome and anti-roome the wanscoate is painted with the whole History of the Arcadia romance made by Sir Philip Sidney brother to the then Countess of Pembrooke and composed by him in the fine woods above the house.

Another room is painted with all sorts of sports Hunting Hawking etc., they are all finely painted on the ceileing and very lofty: . . .

The Gardens are very fine, with many gravel walks with grass squaires set with fine brass and stone statues, with fish ponds and basons with figures in the middle spouting out water, dwarfe trees of all sorts and a fine flower garden, much wall fruite: . . .

(In Norwich)... their building timber and they playster on laths which they strike out into squares like broad free stone on the outside, which makes their fronts look pretty well, and some they build high and contract the roofes resembling the London houses but none of brick except some few beyond the river which are built of some of the rich factors like the London buildings; . . ,

(In Bury St. Edmunds) . . . this high house is an apothecarys at least 60 steppes up from the ground and gives a pleaseing prospect of the whole town, . . . except this the rest are great old houses of timber and mostly in the old forme of the country which are long peaked roofes of tileing; this house is the new mode of building, 4 roomes of a floore pretty sizeable and high, well furnish'd, a drawing roome and chamber full of China and a Damaske bed embroyder'd, 2 other roomes, Camlet and Mohaire beds, a pretty deale of plaite in his wives chamber, parlours below and a large shop; he is esteem'd a very rich man; he shewed me a Curiosity of an Herball all written out with every sort of tree and herb dryed and cut out and pasted on the leaves— it was a Doctor of Physicks work that left it him as Legacy at his death, it was a fine thing and would have delighted me severall dayes . . .

(In Bristol) . . . the buildings of the town are pretty high most of timber work, the streetes are narrow and something darkish, because the roomes on the upper storys are more jutting out, soe contracts the streete and the light; the suburbs are better buildings and more spacious streetes; . . .

GARDENS

Harrison commented on the general interest in gardening among all classes of the population. Italian influence showed itself in the gardens at Hampton Court and Nonesuch and Lord Burleigh's gardens at Theobalds with their elaborate labyrinths and fountains were show places.

Source: Harrison, *A Description of England,* 1577.

If you looke into our gardens annexed to our houses, how woonderfullie is their beauty increased, not onelie with floures, . . . and varietie of curious and costlie workmanship, but also with rare and medicinable hearbes sought up in the land within these fortie yeares: so that in comparison of this present, the ancient gardens were but dunghills and laistowes to such as did possesse them. How art also helpeth nature, in the dailie colouring, dubling and inlarging the proportion of our floures, it is incredible to report: for so curious and cunning are our gardeners now in these daies, that they presume to doo in maner what they list with nature, and moderate hir course in things as if they were hir superiours. It is a world also to see how manie strange hearbs, plants, and annuall fruits, are dailie brought unto us from the Indies, Americans, Taprobane, Canarie Iles, and all parts of the world. . . .

There is not almost one noble man, gentleman, or merchant, that hath not great store of these floures, which now also doo begin to wax so well acquainted with our soiles, that we may almost accompt of them as parcell of our owne commodities. They have no lesse regard in like sort to cherish medicinable hearbs fetched out of other regions neerer hand: insomuch that I have seene in some one garden to the number of three hundred or foure hundred of them, if not more; of the halfe of whose names, within fortie yeeres passed we had no maner knowledge. . . .

And even as it fareth with our gardens, so doth it with our orchards, which were never furnished with so good fruit nor with such variety as at this present. For, beside that we have most delicate apples, plums, pears, walnuts, filberts, etc., and those

A Formal Garden.

of sundry sorts, planted within forty years past, . . . so have we
no less store of strange fruit, as apricots, almonds, peaches, figs,
corn-trees in noblemen's orchards. I have seen capers, oranges
and lemons, and heard of wild olives growing here. . . .

THE GARDENS AT HAMPTON COURT

Source: Thomas Platter, *Travels in England*, 1599.

. . . the gardener conducted us into the royal pleasaunce.

By the entrance I noticed numerous patches where square
cavities had been scooped, as for paving stones; some of these
were filled with red brick-dust, some with white sand, and some
with green lawn, very much resembling a chess-board. The
hedges and surrounds were of hawthorn, bush firs, ivy, roses,
juniper, holly, English or common elm, box and other shrubs,
very gay and attractive.

There were all manner of shapes, men and women, half men
and half horse, sirens, serving-maids with baskets, French lilies
and delicate crenellations all round made from the dry twigs
bound together and the aforesaid evergreen quick-set shrubs,
or entirely of rosemary, all true to the life, and so cleverly and
amusingly interwoven, mingled and grown together, trimmed
and arranged picture-wise that their equal would be difficult to
find.

And just as there is a park on the one hand, so opposite this
in the middle of the other side there is a maze, similarly decorated
with plants and flowering trees, and two marble fountains, so
that time shall not drag in such a place; for should one miss one's
way, not only are taste, vision and smell delighted, but the glad-
some birdsongs and plashing fountains please the ear, indeed
it is like an earthly paradise.

THE GARDEN OF THEOBALDS

Source: Hentzner, *Travels in England*, 1598.

. . . the garden, encompassed with a ditch full of water, large
enough for one to have the pleasure of going in a boat, and rowing
between the shrubs; here are great variety of trees and plants;

labyrinths made with a great deal of labour; a jet d'eau, with its bason of white marble; and columns and pyramids of wood and other materials up and down the garden. After seeing these, we were led by the gardener into the summer-house, in the lower part of which, built semicircularly, are the twelve Roman emperors in white marble, and a table of touchstone; the upper part of it is set round with cisterns of lead, into which the water is conveyed through pipes, so that fish may be kept in them, and in summertime they are very convenient for bathing; in another room for entertainment very near this, and joined to it by a little bridge, was an oval table of red marble.

A Playing Card, showing a formal garden.

CHAPTER V

FURNISHINGS

The closing years of the fifteenth century brought an end to a long period of strife, and with a new feeling of comparative security men began to find time to turn their attention to their houses. English homes began, very gradually, to be something other than fortified dwellings.

Early in the sixteenth century the chief room was still the hall, as it had been in the Middle Ages. Later in the century large houses were built with a 'long gallery' on the first floor. This was the chief room for the family and was like a long corridor, with windows along one side. Farmhouses and cottages were usually only one room thick and this accounts for the high-pitched roofs, particularly in the Cotswolds. Bedrooms, or 'chambers' above were partitioned with wood and one led out of another, without a passage.

By the time of Elizabeth all but the poorest lived well, and writers commented frequently on the recent increase in comfort. Walls were panelled, or covered with hangings, ceiling beams were carved and windows frequently glazed instead of being covered with horn. Chests and cupboards stood against the walls to display the family plate of pewter, silver or silver gilt. Chairs were still rare and most people sat on benches or settles.

In seventeenth-century homes, the walls were panelled in oak or pine, and in fashionable houses the panels often served as settings for portraits by English and foreign painters. Stucco ceilings were elaborately decorated, chimney pieces richly carved, and woven rush matting provided a more hygienic floor covering than strewn rushes. Carpets on floors were still rare; people who had them laid them across tables or hung them on the walls.

Furniture became more comfortable during the seventeenth century and upholstery gradually came into use in fashionable homes. Inventories suggest that many middle class homes were lavishly furnished, but even the wealthy lacked much that we, to-day, consider essential.

ENGLISH WAYS

Source: Dr. Levinus Lemmius, M.A. (1560) quoted in an appendix to Harrison, *A Description of England.*

. . . the neate cleanlines, the exquisite finenesse, the pleasaunte and delightfull furniture in every poynt for household, wonderfully rejoysed mee; their chambers and parlours strawed over with sweete herbes refreshed me; their nosegayes finely entermingled wyth sundry sortes of fragrante floures in their bedchambers and privy roomes, with comfortable smell cheered mee up and entirelye delyghted all my sences. And this do I thinck to be the cause that Englishmen, lyving by such holesome and exquisite meate, and in so holesome and healthfull ayre, be so fresche and cleane coloured; their faces, eyes and countenaunce carying with it and representing a portly grace and comelynes, geveth out evident tokens of an honest mind; in language very smoth and allective, but yet seasoned and tempered within the limits and bonds of moderation, not bombasted with any unseemly termes, or infarced with any clawing flatteries or allurementes.

CHANGES IN ENGLAND, 1577–1587

Source: Harrison, *A Description of England,* 1587.

. . . in noble mens houses it is not rare to see abundance of Arras, rich hangings of tapistrie, silver vessell, and so much other plate, as may furnish sundrie cupbords, to the summe oftentimes of a thousand or two thousand pounds at the least: whereby the value of this and the rest of their stuffe dooth grow to be almost inestimable. Likewise in the houses of knights, gentlemen, merchantmen, and some other wealthie citizens, it is not geson to behold generallie their great provision of tapistrie, Turkis worke, pewter, brasse, fine linen, and thereto costlie cupbords of plate, . . .

. . . inferiour artificers and manie farmers, who by vertue of their old and not of their new leases have for the most part learned also to garnish their cupbords with plate, their joined beds with tapistrie and silke hangings, and their tables with carpets and fine naperie, whereby the wealth of our countrie . . . doth infinitelie appeare.

. . . the exchange of vessell, as of treene platters into pewter, and woodden spoones into silver or tin. For so common were all sorts of treene stuffe in old time, that a man should hardlie find foure peeces of pewter (of which one was peradventure a salt) in a good farmers house, and yet for all this frugalitie, (if it so be justly called) they were scarse able to live and paie their rents at their daies without selling of a cow, or an horse, or more, although they paid but foure pounds at the utter most by the yeare.

The wals of our houses on the inner sides . . . be either hanged with tapisterie, arras worke, or painted cloths, wherin either diverse histories, or hearbes, beasts, knots, and such like are stained, or else they are seeled with oke of our owne, or wainescot brought hither out of the east countries, whereby the roomes are not a little commended, made warme, and much more close than otherwise they would be.

INTERIOR DECORATION

There were no architects in the modern sense of the word. For a grand house the plans were often drawn up by a master mason. He and his workmen built the shell of the house, the master carpenter was responsible for internal details such as walls, ceilings and fireplaces. In his diary the Earl of Cork records his negotiations with he craftsmen engaged upon the interior decoration of his new house.

Source: Diary of the Earl of Cork.

I have agreed with Christopher Watts, freemason and carver, who dwells in Horse Street, Bristol, to make me a very fair chimney, also for my parlour, which is to reach up close to the ceiling, with my coat of arms complete, with crest, helmet, coronet, supporters, mantling and foot-pace, which he is to set up and finish all at his own charges, fair and graceful in all respects, and for that chimney I am to pay £10, and I am to find carriage also. He is also to make twelve figures each three foot high, to set upon my staircase for which he demands 20s. apiece, and I offer him 13s. 4d. And he is presently to cut one of them with the figure of Pallas with a shield. One with a coat with a coronet is to be cut for a trial.

INVENTORIES

Sir Ralph Verney, writing to his brother in 1645, describes the preparations for taking an inventory at the family home, Claydon, in Buckinghamshire. 'Fripperies' were hanging closets for gowns.

Source: Verney Papers.

... the odd things in the roome my Mother keept herself, the iron closet, the little roome betweene her bed's head and the backstairs, the little and great fripperies, your owne greene wrought velvet furniture, the looking-glasses (there should be at least four), leather carpets for the drawinge and dininge roomes, the stooles with nailes guilt, the great cabanet like yours, the tapestry, the great branch candle-stick, all such wrought work as my Mother had from London and was not finished, the booke of martirs and other bookes in the withdrawinge-roome, the preserving-room, the spicery with furnaces and brewing vessels, plat left for the children's use, all the lockes that are loose in the closet.

Most inventories refer to well-to-do households. Ordinary families did not usually possess enough to warrant any careful assessment. The following, however, is the probate inventory of a rural labourer:

Source: Maidstone Record Office, PRC 11/21 Jan. 23 1662.

An Invintory of the goods and Chattalls and Cattall of Bartholmawe Burch latt of Shaddoxhurst in the County of Kent Labarer deceseed Taken and aprised by us whose names are hereunto subscribed the day and yere above written:
Item in the hall one tabel one cubord one Kneeding trofe tene chayer a payer of pothanggeres: a payer of tongs: a grid ierne a salt Box
Item in the Milke house five tonges six bowles three plattares a payer of scalls
Item in the hall chamber one beed and beedsteedell three Bolsters fower blankets one Coverlett one truckell beedstall one linin trendell, one wollin trindell fowr Chestes
Item in the drinke hows three tubes two Barralls and other old lomber and a Chayrne

Item one hay Cutter one hand saw and other old (   ) and a mattock
Item Bords and Shelfes and old Lomber
Item without dores wood and heye and Botts (?)
Item three Cowes
Item one hoge
Item one Birding peece
Item things un seene and forgott
        Nathanell Manering   Thomas Yates.

LIGHTING BY CANDLES

Source: Pepys's Diary.

Dec. 15th, 1664. This night I begun to burn wax candles in my closett at the office, to try the charge, and to see whether the smoke offends like that of tallow candles.

THINGS NECESSARY FOR AND BELONGING TO A DINEING ROME

Randle Holme, of Chester, was, in 1664, appointed Server of the Chamber in Extraordinary to King Charles II, which office exempted him from arrest and from serving on juries. He later described the equipment considered necessary for various rooms of the house:

Source: Randle Holme, *An Academie of Armory*, 1682.

The Rome well wanscotted about, either with Moontan and panells or carved as the old fashion was; or else in larg square panell.

The Rome hung with pictures of all sorts, as History, Land-skips, Fancyes, &c.

Larg Table in the midle, either square to draw out in Leaves, or Long, or Round or oval with falling leaves.

Side tables, or court cubberts, for cups and Glasses to drink in, Spoons, Sugar Box, Viall and Cruces for Viniger, Oyle and Mustard pot.

Cistern of Brass, Pewter, or Lead to set flagons of Beer, and Bottles of win in.

PLATE 5

A glass roundel showing a middle-class home

PLATE 6

(*a*) Interior of a glassworks, showing furnace, glass blowing and pack carriers setting out

(*b*) **A sugar factory.** Notice the cane being cut, the syrup being extracted and moulds being filled

A Turky table cover, or carpett of cloth or Leather printed. Chaires and stooles of Turky work, Russia or calves Leather, cloth or stuffe, or of needlework. Or els made all of Joynt work or cane chaires.

Fire grate, fire shovell, Tongs, and Land Irons all adorned with Brass Bobbs and Buttons.

Flower potts, or Allabaster figures to adorn the windows, and glass well painted and a Larg seeing Glass at the higher end of the Rome.

A Faire with-drawing Rome at the other end of the dineing Rome well furnished with a Table, Chaires and stooles &c.

THINGS USEFULL ABOUT A BED, AND BED-CHAMBER

Source: Randle Holme, *An Academie of Armory*, 1682.

Bed stocks, as Bed posts, sides, ends, Head and Tester.
Mat, or sack-cloth Bottom.
Cord, Bed staves, and stay for the feet.
Curtain Rods and hookes, and rings, either Brass or Horn.
Beds, of chaffe, Wool or flocks, Feathers, and down in Ticks or Bed Tick.
Bolsters, pillows.
Blankets, Ruggs, Quilts, Counterpan, caddows.
Curtaines, Valens, Tester Head cloth, all either fringed, Laced or plaine alike.
Inner curtaines and Valens, which are generally White silk or Linen.
Tester Bobbs or Wood gilt, or covered sutable to the curtaines Tester top either flatt, or Raised, or canopy like, or half Testered
Basis, or the lower Valens at the seat of the Bed, which reacheth to the ground, and fringed for state as the uper Valens, either with Inch fring, caul fring, Tufted fring, snailing fring, Gimpe fring with Tufts and Buttons, Vellem fring, &c.

E

A Bedroom.

THE CHAMBER

Hangings about the Rome, of all sorts, as Arras, Tapestry, damask, silk, cloth or stuffe: in paines or with Rods, or gilt Leather, or plaine, else Pictures of Friends and Relations to Adorne the Rome.

Table, stands, dressing Box with drawers, a larg Myrour, or Looking glass. Couch, chaire, stoles, and chaires, a closs-stole.

Window curtaines, Flower potts, Fire grate, and a good Fire in the winter, Fire shovel, Tongs, Fork and Bellowes.

NEW EQUIPMENT

Mrs. Elizabeth Freake was a well-to-do housewife who, like many others, kept careful recipe and account books and a diary of household matters. Her sisters were evidently in comfortable circumstances also and helped her equip a new house:

Source: Mrs. Elizabeth Freake, Her Diary, 1671–1714. (Edited by Mary Carbery.)

1698. *Jully* 16. . . . My Deer sister Norton sentt me Towards Furnishing my bare walls A Large Fine Tortershell Cabynett, which now stands in my best Chamber, vallued att neer A hundred pounds. With some Fine China for the Topp of Itt. My deer sister Austin sentt me Towards my house furniture Five Greatt China Jarrs for my best Chamber (now In my Closet carefully laid up by Eliz. Frek) And a New Long Cane squab—now stands In the greatt Parlor.

Abutt the same Time I bought for my self A new Green Damask bed, & all my Tapstry hangings for the Parlor And two Chambers & the Dining Roome; with two greatt Glasses And A New damask Coach lined with A Damask & scarlett silk coosey for my selfe, with severall other Nessesarys to aboutt the value of Thre hundrid and fiffty pounds, . . .

LOOKING GLASSES

Celia Fiennes noted that some of the wealthy houses she visited were lavishly equipped with looking-glass. At Chippenham Park she wrote:

. . . there was no looking-glass but on the chimney-piece and just opposite in the place a looking glass used to be was 4 pannells of glass in length and 3 in breadth set together in the wanscoate; the same was in another drawing roome which was for my Lord; the dineing roome had this looking glass on the two peers between the three windows it was from the top to the bottom 2 pannells in breadth and 7 in length, so it shews one from top to toe; . . . the common roomes are all new convenient and neate with double doores lined to prevent noises; . . .

CHAPTER VI

FOOD

The increasing luxury of the Elizabethan home was reflected in the meals eaten. All but the poorest people ate lavishly, each 'course' of a family dinner consisting of a full dinner as we understand it to-day. The townsman's diet differed little from that of the countryman, for he often kept his own animals or, at any rate, farms and fields were near at hand.

Dr. Andrew Boord, in his *Breviary of Helthe*, wrote much sound advice on life in general and sees good food as helping 'To comforte the herte':

A DOCTOR'S ADVICE

Source: Andrewe Boord, *Breviary of Helthe*, 1547.

There is nothynge that doth comfort the hert so muche beside god as honest myrth and good company. And wyne moderatly taken doth letyficate and dothe comfort the hert, and good breed dothe confyrme and doth stablyshe a mannes herte. And al good and temperate drynkes the which doth ingender good blode doth comfort the herte. Al maner of cordyalles and restoratives and al swete or dulcet thynges doth comfort the hert, and so doth maces and gynger, rere egges and poched egges nat harde, theyr yolkes be a cordiall.

MEAL-TIMES

Harrison disliked extravagances but approved of good solid eating, though not in excess. Although most classes ate well, the times of meals varied between nobility, merchants and countrymen. These varying customs, which began as conveniences, tended to become social dividers. With improved supplies, foodstuffs which had once been rare came to be considered as fit 'onlie to the inferior sort'.

Source: Harrison, *A Description of England*, 1577.

Heretofore there hath beene much more time spent in eating and drinking then commonlie is in these daies, for whereas of old we had breakefasts in the forenoone, beverages, or nuntions after dinner, and thereto reare suppers generallie when it was time to go to rest. . . . Now these od repasts—thanked be God—are verie well left, and ech one in maner . . . contenteth himselfe with dinner & supper onelie.

With us the nobilitie, gentrie, and students, doo ordinarilie go to dinner at eleven before noone, and to supper at five, or between five and six at afternoone. The merchants dine and sup seldome before twelve at noone, and six at night especiallie in London. The husbandmen dine also at high noone as they call it, and sup at seven or eight: but out of the tearme in our universities the scholars dine at ten. As for the poorest sort they generallie dine and sup when they may, so that to talke of their order of repast, it were but a needlesse matter.

FOOD HABITS

Source: Harrison, *A Description of England*, 1577.

. . . in this season wherein we live, there is no restreint of anie meat, either for religions sake or publike order, but it is lawfull for everie man to feed upon what soever he is able to purchase, except it be upon those daies whereon eating of flesh is especiallie forbidden by the lawes of the realme, which order is taken onelie to the end our numbers of cattell may be the better increased, & that aboundance of fish which the sea yeeldeth, more generallie received. Beside this, there is great consideration had in making of this law for the preservation of the navie, and maintenance of convenient numbers of sea faring men, both which would otherwise greatlie decaie, if some meanes were not found whereby they might be increased. But how soever this case standeth, white meats, milke, butter & cheese, which were woont to be accounted of as one of the chief staies throughout the Iland, are now reputed as food appertinent onelie to the inferiour sort, whilest such as are more wealthie, doo feed upon the flesh of all kinds of cattell accustomed to be eaten, all sorts of fish taken upon our coasts and in our fresh rivers, and such diversitie of wild and tame foules as are either bred in our Iland or brought over unto us from other countries of the maine.

GLUTTONY

Stubbes' account of the changes in eating habits is less praising. He does not approve of the new wealth as Harrison does. Fynes Moryson, who had travelled through the chief countries of Europe, compares English eating habits not unfavourably with Italian.

Source: Stubbes, *Anatomie of Abuses*, 1585.

And nowe a dayes, if the table be not covered from the one ende to the other, as thicke as one dish can stand by an other, with delicate meate of sundrie sorts, one cleane different from an other, and to everie dishe a severall sawce, appropriate to hys kinde, it is thought . . . unworthy the name of a dinner! Yea, so many dishes shal you have pestering the table at once, as the . . . devouringst glutton, or the greediest cormorant that ever was, can scarce eate of every one a little. And these many shal you have at the first course, as many at the second, and, peradventure, moe at the third; besides other swete condiments, and delicate confections of spiceries, and I can not tell what! And to these dainties, all kinde of wines are not wanting, you may bee sure. . . . I have heard my father say, that in his dayes one dishe or two of good wholesome meate was thought sufficient for a man of great worshippe to dine withall, and if they had three or foure kinds, it was reputed a sumptuous feast. A good peece of beefe was thought then good meate, and able for the best, but nowe, it is thought too grosse for their tender stomackes to disgest;

. . . every countrey, cittie, towne, village, and other places, hath abundance of ale-houses, tavernes, and innes, whiche are so fraught with maultwormes, night and day, that you woulde wonder to see them. You shall have them there sitting at the wine and good-ale all the day long, yea, all the night too, peradventure a whole weeke together, so long as any money is left, swilling, gulling, and carousing, from one to an other, till never a one can speak a ready word.

RESTRAINT IN EATING

Source: Fynes Moryson, *Itinerary*, 1617.

The Italian Sansovino is much deceived, writing, that in general the English eat and cover the table at least four times in the day; for howsoever those that journey and some sickly men staying at home may perhaps take a small breakfast, yet in general the English eat but two meals (of dinner and supper) each day, and I could never see him that useth to eat four times in the day. And I will profess for myself and other Englishmen, passing through Italy so famous for temperance, that we often observed, that howsoever we might have a pullet and some flesh prepared for us, eating it with a moderate proportion of bread, the Italians at the same time, with a charger full of herbs for a sallad, and with roots, and like meats of small price, would each of them eat two or three penny-worth of bread. And since all fulness is ill, and that of bread worst, I think we were more temperate in our diet, though eating more flesh, than they eating so much more bread than we did. It is true that the English prepare largely for ordinary diet for themselves and their friends coming by chance, and at feasts for invited friends are so excessive in the number of dishes, as the table is not thought well-furnished, except they stand one upon another. Neither use they to set drink on the table, for which no room is left, but the cups and glasses are served in upon a side table, drink being offered to none, till they call for it.

TABLE MANNERS

Source: Thomas Coryat, *Crudities.* 1611.

The Italians do always at their meals use a little fork when they cut their meat. This form of feeding I understand is generally used in all places in Italy, their forks being for the most part made of iron or steel and some of silver, but those are used only by gentlemen. The reason of this their curious custom is because the Italian cannot by any means endure to have his dish touched with fingers, seeing all men's fingers are not alike clean. Hereupon I myself thought good to imitate the Italian fashion by this forked cutting of meat.

STORES REQUIRED FOR A CREW OF 15 MEN AND A BOY

The extension of trade and a demand for new luxuries sent fishermen further and further afield and the East Anglian fishing boats began to work beyond the accustomed coastal waters and developed Yarmouth into a sizeable port. An anonymous writer put forward an interesting project in 1615 for catching and marketing Yarmouth herring. He set forth his plans in a tract which provides a detailed account of the expense of fitting out a boat for a 16-week fishing season. The herring was to be sold in continental ports and the boat was to return loaded with pitch, hemp, flax and corn.

Source: Britaine's Busses or a Computation as well of the Charge of a Busse or Herring-Fishing Ship. 1615.

Beere. A gallon of beer a day 'which is the allowance made in the king's ships', which at 40/- a tun would cost £16.0.0. for the voyage.

Bisket. 1 lb. a day 'as in his Majesty's ships'; total cost, £10.13.4.

Oatmeale or Peaze. 1 gallon a day; cost at 4/- a bushel, £2.16.0.

Bacon. '2 pounds of bacon for 4 meales in a weeke.' Total cost at 2/2d. a stone, £6.18.8.

Fresh Fish. 'They may take, daily, out of the sea, as much fresh fish as they can eate.'

Butter. 'To allow every man and boy (to butter their fish, or otherwise to eate as they like,) a quarter of a pound of butter a day, that is for each person 28 pounds of butter, that is halfe a firkin of Suffolk butter'; total cost at 20/- a firkin, £8.0.0.

Cheese. ½ lb. of Holland cheese a day at 23/4d. the 'hundred waight'; total cost, £9.6.8.

Vinegar. 3 pints a day among 16 people; total cost £1.0.0.

The following stores were also taken:—*Aquivita*, 4 gallons; *Zantoyle*, 2 gallons; *Honny*, 2 gallons; *Sugar*, 4 lb.; *Nutmegge*, ¼ lb.; *Ginger*, ½ lb.; *Pepper*, 1 lb.

A NEW DIET TABLE APPROVED BY THE GOVERNING BODY OF ST. BARTHOLOMEW'S HOSPITAL IN APRIL, 1687

Source: Sir Norman Moore, *The History of St. Bartholomew's Hospital*, 1918.

Sunday
    10 ounces of Wheaten Bread
    6 ounces of Beefe boyled without bones
    1 pint and a halfe of Beef Broth
    1 pint of Ale Cawdell
    3 pints of 6 shilling Beere

Monday
    10 ounces of Wheaten Bread
    1 pint of Milk Pottage
    6 ounces of Beefe
    $1\frac{1}{2}$ pints of Beefe Broth
    3 pints of Beere

Tuesday
    10 ounces of Bread
    halfe a pound of Boyled Mutton
    3 pints of Mutton Broth
    3 pints of Beere

Wednesday
    10 ounces of Bread
    4 ounces of Cheese
    2 ounces of Butter
    1 pint of Milk Pottage
    3 pints of Beere

Thursday
    The same allowance as Sunday
    1 pint of Rice Milke

Friday
    10 ounces of Bread
    1 pint of Sugar Soppes
    2 ounces of Cheese
    1 ounce of Butter
    1 pint of Water Gruell
    3 pints of Beere

Satturday
    The same allowance as Wednesday.

A BILL OF FARE FOR GENTLEMEN'S HOUSES
OF LESSER QUALITY

Many housewives made collections of their recipes and ways of housekeeping. Again, it is the quantity of materials and the time spent which strike us as remarkable:

Source: Hannah Woolley, *The Queen-like Closet*, 1684.

THE FIRST COURSE IN SUMMER-SEASON

1. A Boiled Pike or Carp stewed.
2. A very fine Pudding boiled.
3. A Chine of Veal, and another of Mutton.
4. A Calves Head Pie.
5. A Leg of Mutton rosted whole.
6. A couple of Capons, or a Pig, or a Piece of roste Beef, or boiled Beef.
7. A Sallad, the best in season.

FOR THE SECOND COURSE TO THE SAME

1. A Dish of fat Chickens roasted.
2. A cold Venison Pasty.
3. A Dish of fryed Pasties.
4. A Jole of fresh Salmon.
5. A couple of Lobsters.
6. A Dish of Tarts.
7. A Gammon of Bacon or dry'd Tongues.

After these are taken away, then serve in your Cheese and Fruit. Note, that this Bill of Fare is for Familiar Times.

RECIPES

Source: Hannah Woolley, *The Queen-like Closet*, 1684.

1. *To make Ale to drink within a week.* Turn it into a Vessel which will hold Eight Gallons, and when it hath done working,

ready to bottle, put in some Ginger sliced, and an Orange stuck
with cloves, and cut here and there with a Knife, and a pound and
a half of Sugar, and with a stick stir it well together, and it will
work afresh; when it hath done working, stop it close, and let it
stand till it be clear, then bottle it up, and put a Lump of Sugar
into every Bottle, and then stop it close, and knock down the
Corks, and turn the Boles the Bottom upwards, and it will be
fit to drink in a Weeks time.

2. *To make the best Orange Marmalade.* Take the rinds of the
deepest coloured Oranges, boil them in several Waters till they
are tender, then mince them small, and to one pound of Oranges,
take a pound of Pippins cut small, one pound of the finest Sugar,
and one Pint of Spring-water, melt your Sugar in the Water over
the fire, and scum it, then put in your Pippins, and boil them till
they are very clear, then put in the Orange Rind, and boil them
together, till you find by cooling a little of it, that it will jelly
very well, then put in the juice of two Oranges, and one Limon,
and boil it a little longer; and then put it up in Galley-pots.

3. *To make Misers for Children to eat in Afternoons in Summer.*
Take half a pint of good small beer, two spoonfuls of Sack, the
Crum of half a penny Manchet two handfuls of Currans washed
clean and dried, and a little of grated-Nutmeg, and a little Sugar,
so give it to them cold.

4. *To make very good Cake.* Take a peck of Flower, four pound of
Currans well washed, dryed and picked, four pounds of Butter,
one pound of Sugar, one Ounce of Cinamon, one Ounce of
Nutmegs, beat the Spices, and lay it all night in Rosewater,
the next day strain it out, then take one pint and a half of good
Ale-yest, the Yolks of four Eggs, a pint of Cream, put a pound of
the butter into the warmed Cream, put the rest into the Flower
in pieces, then wet your Flower with your Cream, and put in
your Currans, and a little Salt, and four or five spoonfuls of
Caraway-comfits and your Spice, mix them all and the Yest well
together, and let it lie one hour to rise, then make it up and Bake
it in a Pan buttered: It may stand two hours.

5. *To Candy Flowers.* Boil some Rosewater and Sugar together,
then put in your Flowers, being very dry, and boil them a little,

then strew in some fine Sugar over them, and turn them, and boil them a little more, then take them from the fire, and strew some more Sugar over them, then take them out and lay them to dry, and open them, and strew Sugar over them; they will dry in a few hours in a hot day.

HOUSEHOLD HINTS

Source: Hannah Woolley, *The Queen-like Closet*, 1684.

1. *To keep Flowers all the year.* Take any sort of pretty Flowers you can get, and have in readiness some Rosewater made very slippery by laying Gum-Arabick therein. Dip your Flowers very well, and swing it out again, and stick them in a sieve to dry in the Sun, some other of them you may dust over with fine Flower, and some with searced Sugar, after you have wetted them, and so dry them. Either of them will be very fine, but those with Sugar will not keep so well as the other; they are good to set forth Banquets and to garnish dishes, and will look very fresh, and have their right smell.

2. *To perfume Gloves.* Take four Grains of Musk and grind it with Rosewater, and also eight grains of Civet, then take two spoonfuls of Gum-dragon steeped all night in Rosewater, beat these to a thin jelly, putting in half a spoonful of Oil of Cloves, Cinamon and Jessamine mixed together, then take a Spunge and dip it therein, and rub the Gloves all over thin, lay them in a dry clean place eight and fourty hours, then rub them with your hand till they become limber.

3. *Plague Water.* Take Rosemary, Red Balm, Burrage, Angelica, Carduus, Celandine, Dragon, Featherfew, Wormwood, Peny-royal, Elecampane roots, Mugwort, Bural, Tormentil, Egrimony, Sage, Sorrel, of each of these one handful, weighed weight for weight, put all these in an earthen Pot, with four quarts of white Wine, cover them close, and let them stand eight or nine days in a cool Cellar, then distil it in a Glass still.

NEW BEVERAGES

As exploration increased new commodities were brought to Europe and changes in social customs followed. A description of several new drinks introduced gives details of various ways of making them. There is no reference to the use of tea in England—this was largely an eighteenth-century development.

Source: John Chamberlayne, *The Manner of Making Coffee, Tea and Chocolate . . . with their Vertues,* 1685.

. . . a Drink termed Coffee, which was heretofore in use amongst Arabians, and Egyptians, and which is now a dayes in very great request amongst the English . . .

. . . it shall be well rosted; after which having beaten it unto very fine Powder, you may make use thereof, in an equal proportion according to the number of the people that will drink it: Viz. the third part of a spoonful for each person, and putting a little Sugar thereto: and after having let it boyl a small time, you must pour it into little dishes of porcelain or any other sort, and so let it be drunk by little and little, as hot as it can possible be indur'd, but especially fasting. . . .

So great is the number of those persons, who at present do drink of Chocolate, that not only in the West Indies, whence this Drink has its Original and beginning, but also in Spain, Italy, Flanders, etc. . . . and lately much used in England, as Diet and Phisick with the Gentry. . . . We in England usually boyl the Chocolate with the water, and some to make it more dainty, though less wholesome, use therein Eggs and Milk.

CHAPTER VII

HEALTH AND MEDICINE

Men and women of all classes lived in insanitary conditions such as we in our day cannot even imagine. There were very few qualified doctors and only rich people had any kind of medical attention. The death-rate was very high and parents took it for granted that only very few of their numerous children were likely to grow up.

Bishop Latimer complained 'At our tyme physic is a remedy only for rich folks . . . for the poor is not able to wage the physician'.

All classes made great use of home-made recipes and, in a crisis, submitted themselves to the mercies of a barber-surgeon or a local 'wise woman'.

The foremost school of medicine in the late sixteenth century was at Padua, where Vesalius had, in 1543, published a very important book on the structure of the human body. William Harvey studied at Padua, before he announced, in 1616, his discovery of the systematic circulation of the blood.

VISITING A SICK FRIEND.
A glass panel from a merchant's house in Leicester, 1500

Dr. Andrew Boorde, a witty, wise and much-travelled physician, wrote a great deal and gave much sound and human advice on all manner of subjects. His introduction to *The Breviary of Helthe* gives an idea of how all-embracing was his point of view, and how tinged with religious emphasis.

A WOODCUT OF ANDREW BOORDE.

The Breviary of Helthe . . . for all manner of syckenesses and diseases the whiche may be in man, or woman dothe folowe. Expressinge the obscure termes of Greke, Araby, Latyn and Barbary in to englysh concerning Phisicke and Chierurgye compyled by Andrewe Boord of physicke Doctour and englysh man.

I do advertyse every sycke man, and al other men the whiche hathe any infyrmite sicknes or impedimet, above all thynges to pacify him selfe, or to arme him selfe with pactence, and to fixe his harte and mynd in christes death and passion and to call to his remembraunce, what paines, what adversyte, and what penury, and povertye Christ dyd suffer for us.

Lordes Ladies and Gentylmen, lerned and unlearned of what estate or degre so ever you be of, thynke not that no man can be holpen by no maner of medicines, yf so be god do sende the sicknes for he hath put a tyme to every man, over the which tyme no man by no arte nor science can not prolong that tyme for the nomber of the monthes and daies of mannes lyfe god knoweth.

JOY OR MYRTHE

Source: Andrewe Boord, *Breviary of Helthe,* 1547.

Myrthe comethe many wayes, the principall myrth is whan a man dothe lyve out of deedly synne, and nat in grudge of conscience in this worlde, and that every man doth rejoice in god, and in charite to his neyghbour, than be many other myrthes and consolacions, some beynge good and laudable and some vituperable, laudable myrthe is one man or one neyghbour to be mery with an other, with honesty and vertue, without swearynge and sclaunderynge, and rybaldry spekynge. Myrthe is in musicall instrumentes, and gostly and godly syngynge. Myrthe is whan a man lyveth out of det, and may have meat and drynke and cloth, although he have never a peny in his purse, but now a dayes he is mery that hath gold and sylver and ryches with lechery, and all is nat worthe a blewe poynt.

I do advertyse every man to remember that he must dye, howe, when and what tyme he can nat tell, wherfore let every man amende his lyfe and commyt him self to the mercy of god.

WATCHYNG OR THEY THAT CAN NAT SLEPE

Source: Andrewe Boord, *Breviary of Helthe,* 1547.

The cause. This impediment doth come thorowe ydelnesse or wekenesse of ye brayne, or els thorowe sicknesse, anger or

PLATE 7

Church memorials like this give authentic information about costume

PLATE 8

A mural. Notice the musical instruments on the wall, and the plaster ceiling

fastynge, or els thorowe solicitudnesse or replecion, or extreme heate, or extreme colde in the fete or suche lyke.

A remedy. Take of the oyle of violettes an ounce, of opium halfe an ounce, incorporate this togither with woman's milke and with a fyne lynnen cloth lay it to the temples, or els use to eat of letuce sedes, of white popy sedes, or mandragor sedes . . . of eche iii drams, but above all thynges myrthe is best to bedwarde.

DEEFNESS OR A MAN THAT CAN NAT HEARE

Source: Andrewe Boord, *Breviary of Helthe,* 1547.

The cause. This impediment may come to a man iii maner of wayes, either it doth come by nature, or els accydental by some stroke, or stripe, or bruise or fal or els it doth come by an humour the which dothe opylate or stoppe the organs of herynge.

A remedy. Yf it do come by nature, that is to say that one is borne deef, there is no maner of remedye but only god to do a miracle. Yf it do come accidentally, as by a stroke, a stripe, a bruise or a fall or such lyke and that by it the organs of herynge be closed up, there is no remedy but only god. Yf it do come of an humour there is remedy as thus. Fyrst put nothynge into ye eare except it be warme as blode. Than take the gall of an hare and myxe it with the grece of a foxe and with blacke wul instyll it into the eare. Or els take of the juce of wormewode and temper it with the gall of a bull and intynct black wull in it put it into the eare.

PRISON SICKNESS

Source: Andrewe Boord, *Breviary of Helthe,* 1547.

The cause. This infyrmyte doth come of corrupcion of the ayer and of the breth and fylth ye which doth come from men, as many men be to togyther in a lytle rome havynge but lytle open ayer.

F

The remedy. The chefe remedy is for man so to lyve and so to do that he deserve nat to be broughte into no preson. And yf he be in preson, eyther to get frendes to helpe him out or else to use some perfumes or to smell to some odiferous savours and to kepe the person clene.

REMEDIES FOR BALDNESS

Source: Andrewe Boord, *Breviary of Helthe,* 1547.

Shave the head and berde and anoynt the head with the grece of a foxe. Or els wasshe the head with the juce of beetes v or vi tymes or els stampe garlyke and rub the heed with it and after that washe it with veneger, do this v or vi tymes. Or els make ashes of garlyke and temper it with hony and anoynt the heed. . . . Anoynt the heed with the oyles of bitter almons, or with the oyle of wormwode, or with the oyle of spycarnad and such lyke oyles. . . . The oyle of myrtylles is good, or the oyle of galles or the oyle of walnuttes or the oyle of maydenhere.

CARE OF THE EYES

Source: Andrewe Boord, *Breviary of Helthe,* 1547.

These thynges be good for the eyes: Every thynge that is grene or blacke is good for a man to loke upon it. Also to loke upon golde is good for the syght and so is glasse, cold water and every colde thynge, excepte the wynde is good for the eyes, and no hote thinge, nor warme thinge is good for the eyes excepte womans mylke and the blode of a dove.

These thynges be evyll for the eyes: Every thynge that is hote is naught for ye eyes, the sonne, the fyre, the snowe and every thyng that is white is nat good for the syght and smoke, wepynge, the wynde, sycknes, reume, redynge in smal printed bokes, specially greke bokes, and onyons, garlyke, chibols and such lyke be nat good for ye eyes.

To klaryfy the eyes and the syght: Take of the sedes of oculi christi and put into the eyes ii, iii or iv sedes, or els take colde water and with a fyne lynnen cloth wasshe ye eyes divers tymes in a day, the ofter the better, and chaunge ye water oft that it may be fresshe and colde.

MADNESSE

Source: Andrewe Boord, *the Breviary of Helthe,* 1547.

There be four kindes of madnesse, whiche be to saye in latyn Mania, Melancholia, Frenisis, and Demoniacus. They the which be manyake, in their madnesse be full of divinacion, as thynkynge them selfe to conjure, or to create, or to make things (that) no man can do but god, and doth presume upon supernaturall thinges, thynkynge they can thinke or do the things the which is impossible for man to do.

Melancholia is an other kinde of madnesse and they the which be infested with this madnesse be ever in feare and drede, and dothe thynke they shall never do well, but ever be in peril either of soule or body or both, wherfore they do fle from one place to another, and can nat tel where to be except they be kept in safegarde.

Frenisis is another kinde of madnesse, and it doth come ever in a fever. They do rave and speke, and can nat tell what they say. Demoniacus is an other kinde of madnesse. And they the which be in this madnes be ever possessed of the devyl, and be develyshe persons and wyl do much harme and evyl, worser than they ye which be maniake, for maniake persons cometh of infirmites of the body, but demoniake persons be possessed of some evyl spirite.

ON SLEEP

Source: Borde, *A Compendyous Regyment,* 1567.

Whole men of what age or complexion soever they be of, shulde take theyr naturall rest and slepe in the nyght: and to eschewe merydall sleep. But and need shall compell a man to slepe after his meate: let hym make a pause, and than let hym stande & lene and slepe agaynst a cupborde, or els let hym sytte upryght in a chayre and slepe. Slepynge after a full stomacke doth ingendre dyvers infyrmyties, it doth hurte the splene, it relaxeth the synewes, it doth ingendre the dropses and the gowte, and doth make a man looke evyll colored. . . . To bedwarde be you mery, or have mery company aboute you, so that to bedwarde no angre, nor hevynes, sorowe, nor pensyfulnes, do trouble or disquyet you. To bedwarde, and also in the mornynge, use to have a fyre in your chambre, to wast and consume the evyl vapowres within the chambre, for the breath of man may putryfye the ayre within the chambre: I do advertyse you not to stande nor to sytte by the fyre, but stande or syt a good way of from the fyre, takynge the flavour of it, for fyre doth aryfie and doth drye up a mannes blode, and doth make sterke the synewes and joyntes of man. In the nyght let the wyndowes of your howse, specyallye of your chambre, be closed. When you be in your bedde, lye a lytle whyle on your lefte syde, and slepe on your ryght syde. . . . To slepe grovellynge upon the stomacke and bely is not good, oneles the stomacke be slowe and tarde of dygestion; but better it is to laye your hande, or your bedfelowes hande, over your stomacke, than to lye grovellynge. To slepe on the backe upryght is utterly to be abhorred: whan that you do slepe, let not your necke, nother your sholders, nother your hands, nor feete, nor no other place of your bodye, lye bare undiscovered. Slepe not with an emptye stomacke, nor slepe not after that you have eaten meate one howre or two after. In your bed lye with your head somwhat hyghe, leaste that the meate whiche is in your stomacke, thorowe eructuacions to some other cause, ascende to the oryfe of the stomacke. Let your nyght cap be of scarlet: and this I do advertyse you, to cause to be made a good thycke quylte of cotton, or els of pure flockes or of cleane wolle, and let the coverynge of it be of whyte fustyan, and laye it on the fetherbed that you do lye on; and in your bed lye not to hote nor to colde, but in a temporaunce. Olde auncyent Doctors of physicke sayth viii howres of slepe in sommer, and ix in wynter, is suffycent for any man: but I do thynke that slepe oughte to be taken as the complexion of man is.

TREATMENT OF LUNATICS

Source: Borde, *A Compendyous Regyment,* 1567.

. . . it apperyd of late dayes of a lunatycke man named Michel, the which went many yeres at lybertye, and at last he dyd kyll his wyfe and his wyfes suster, and his own selfe, wherefore I do advertyse every man the whiche is madde . . . to be kepte in savegarde, in some close house or chamber, where there is lytle lyght. And that he have a keper the whiche the madde man do feare . . . Also the chamber . . . that the madde man is in, let there be no paynted clothes, nor paynted walles, nor pyctures . . ., for suche thynges makethe them full of fantasyes, . . . And use fewe wordes to them, excepte it be for reprehensyon, or gentyll reformacyon yf they have any wytte . . . to understande . . .

THE PLAGUE

Epidemics of bubonic plague were frequent in London for centuries. The overcrowded and insanitary conditions, the ill-balanced diet and the neglect of personal hygiene of our forefathers produced surroundings ideal for infection. In spite of this and other diseases, every effort was made to keep life going as normally as possible. It was, however, difficult for a man to decide when to be cautious and leave the town and thus risk losing his business, as this dialogue shows:

Source: William Bullein, *A Dialogue against the Pestilence,* 1564.

Citizen. Good wife, the daily jangling and ringing of the bells, the coming in of the Minister to every house in ministring the communion, in reading the homily of death, the digging up of graves, the sparring in of windows, and the blazing forth of the blue cross, do make my heart tremble and quake. Alas, what shall I do to save my life?

Wife: Sir, we are but young, and have but a time in this world, what doth it profit us to gather riches together, and can not enjoy them? Why tarry we here so long? I do think every hour a year until we be gone . . . seeing that we have sent our children forth three weeks past into a good air and a sweet country, let us follow them. . . . Let us take leave of our neighbours, and return merely home again when the plague is past, and the dog days ended.

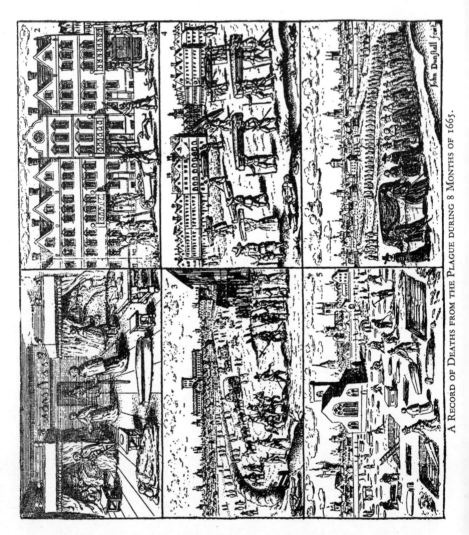

A RECORD OF DEATHS FROM THE PLAGUE DURING 8 MONTHS OF 1665.

John Dunstall fecit

1665.

	total.	Pl.
April 25	358.	2
May 2	388.	0
May 9	347	9
May 16	353	3
May 23	385	14
May 30	399	17
June 6	405	43
June 13	558	112
June 20	611	168
June 27	684	267
July 4	1006	470
July 11	1268	725
July 18	1761	1089
July 25	2785	1843
Auguſt 1	3014	2010
Auguſt 8	4030	2817
Aug. 15	5319	3880
Aug. 22	5568	4237
Aug. 29	7496	6102
Sept. 5	8252	6978
Sept. 12	7690	6544
Sept. 19	8297	7165
Sept. 26	6460	5532
Oct. 3	5720	4929
Oct. 10	5068	4327
Oct. 17	3219	2665
Oct. 24	1806	1421
Oct. 31	1388	1031
Nov. 7	1787	1414
Nov. 14	1359	1050
Nov. 21	0905	652
Nov. 28	0544	333
Dec. 5	0423	210
Dec. 12	0442	243
Dec. 19	0525	281

Source: Borde, *A Compendyous Regyment,* 1567.

Whan the Plages . . . is in a . . . countre, . . . houses the which be infected in towne or citte, be closed up both dores and wyndowes; and ye inhabytours shall nat come a brode, nother to churche: nor to markett, nor to any house or company, for infectyng other the which be clene without infection. . . .

I have known yt whan ye strawe and russhes hath ben cast out of a house infected, the hogges the which dyd lye in it, dyed of ye pestylence: . . .

. . . in such infeccyous tyme it is good for every man . . . to use dayly, specyally in ye mornyng and evenyng to burne Juneper, or Rosemary, or Baye leves, or Majerome or frankensence, . . .

Source: John Taylor, *The Wonderfull Yeare,* 1603.

. . . away they trudge thick and threefold, some riding, some on foote, some without bootes, some in their slippers, by water, by land, in shoales swom they west-ward: . . . Hacknies, water-men and wagons were not so terribly imployed many a yeare; so that within a short time, there was not a good horse in Smithfield, nor a coach to be set eye on: . . . the sight of a (Londoner's) flat-cap was more dreadful to a Lob[1] then the discharging of a caliver: a treble-ruffe . . . had power to cast a whole household into a cold sweat . . . to Bristowe (went) . . . an honest knowne citizen . . . with other company, travelling thither . . . and setting up his rest not to heare the sound of Bow-bell till next Christmas, was not withstanding in the hye way singled out from his company, and set upon by the Plague . . . The rest, at that word, shifted for themselves, and went on, hee (amazed to see his friends flye . . .) yeelded; and being but about fortie miles from London, . . . he called for help at the . . . inne . . . presently[2] the doores had their wooden ribs crusht in pieces, by being beaten together: the casements were shut more close than an usurers greasie velvet powch: the drawing windowes were hangd, drawne and quartred: not a crevis but was stopt, not a mouse-hole left open; . . . mine hoste and hostesse ranne over one another into the back-side, the maydes into the orchard, quivering

---

[1] Lob = country bumpkin.   [2] presently = at once.

and quaking, and ready to hang themselves on the innocent plumb-trees. . . . As for the tapster, he fled into the cellar, rapping out five or six plaine countrey oathes, that hee would drowne him-selfe in a most villainous stand of ale, if the sick Londoner stoode at the doore any longer.

A LETTER

Source: A letter to Sir Martin Stuteville (Time of Charles I).

Sir

Mr. Howlett I hope, delivered our Intelligence on Wednesday both what was written and what I told him upon newer relation. Henceforth you must not look to be supplied as you were wont. The plague is in the Doctor's parish, and the rest of our Intelli-gence is fled; and it grows very dangerous on both sides to continue an intercourse of Letters; not knowing what hands they pass through before they come to those to whom they are sent. Our Hobson[1] and the rest should have been forbidden this week, but that the message came too late. Howsoever it is his last.

The Bills are this Week for London, all Burials, one thousand two hundred and twenty two: whereof of the Plague five hundred and ninety three, of which within the walls a hundred and nine; walls and liberties together two hundred and twenty one. Parishes infected fifty seven.

'Tis true that the Plague was broken out in the Pantry: the King's baker's son dying thereof on Sunday, and another (a woman) then sick and sent away, died next day. The bread was all given away. Mr. Boswell told me yesterday that he was informed that one of the King's scholars of Westminster School was dead thereof, but carried thence sick some two or three days before he died. That my Lord Keeper hereupon had broke up house, using always to dine and sup in the same room the schollars did.

Yours most ready

to be commanded

Christ Coll.

July 9.

JOSEPH MEAD.

[1] The Cambridge carrier.

PLAGUE IN LONDON IN 1665

Source: Pepys's Diary.

June 7th. This day, much against my will, I did in Drury Lane see two or three houses marked with a red cross upon the doors, and 'Lord have mercy upon us' writ there; which was a sad sight to me, being the first of the kind that, to my remembrance, I ever saw. It put me into an ill conception of myself and my smell, so that I was forced to buy some roll-tobacco to smell and to chaw, . . .

June 11th. . . . I saw poor Dr. Burnett's door shut; but he hath, I hear, gained great goodwill among his neighbours, for he discovered it himself first and caused himself to be shut up of his own accord, which was very handsome.

July 12th. The people die so that now it seems they are fain to carry the dead to be buried by day-light, the nights not sufficing to do it in. And my Lord Mayor commands people to be within at nine at night, all as they say that the sick may have liberty to go abroad for ayre.

Sept. 3rd. Up; and put on my coloured silk suit very fine, and my new periwigg, bought a good while since but durst not wear because the plague was in Westminster when I bought it; and it is a wonder what will be the fashion after the plague is done as to periwiggs, for nobody will dare to buy any haire for fear of the infection, that it had been cut off of the heads of people dead of the plague.

Sept. 15th. . . . But, Lord! what a sad time it is to see no boats upon the River; and grass grows all up and down White Hall court, and nobody but poor wretches in the streets!

Oct. 16th. . . . how empty the streets are and melancholy, so many poor sick people in the streets full of sores; and so many sad stories overheard as I walk, every body talking of this dead, and that man sick, and so many in this place, and so many in that. And they tell me that in Westminster there is never a physician and but one apothecary left, all being dead; but that there are great hopes of a great decrease this week; God send it!

Oct. 26th. . . . The 'Change pretty full, and the town begins to be lively again, though the streets very empty, and most shops shut.

Dec. 24th. . . . at my old oyster shop in Gracious Streete, bought two barrels of my fine woman of the shop, who is alive after all the plague, which now is the first observation or enquiry we make at London concerning everybody we knew before it.

PHYSICIANS

Source: Nicholas Breton, *The Good and the Badde*, 1616.

A worthy physician is the enemy of sickness, in purging nature from corruption. His action is most in feeling of pulses, and his discourses chiefly of the nature of diseases. He is a great searcher out of simples, and accordingly makes his composition. He persuades abstinence and patience, for the benefit of health, while purging and bleeding are the chief courses of his counsel.

CONSULTING A DOCTOR. A GARDENER IS
BUSY BEYOND.

The apothecary and the chirurgeon are his two chief attendants, with whom conferring upon time, (he) grows temperate in his

cures. Surfeits and wantonness are great agents for his employment, when by the secret of his skill out of others' weakness he
gathers his own strength. In sum, he is a necessary member for
an unnecessary malady, to find a disease and to cure the diseased.

An unlearned and so unworthy physician is a kind of horse-
leech, whose cure is most in drawing of blood, and a desperate
purge, either to cure or kill, as it hits. His discourse is most of the
cures that he hath done, and them afar off; and not a receipt under
a hundred pounds, though it be not worth three halfpence. . . .
He is never without old merry tales and stale jests to make old
folks laugh, and comfits or plums in his pocket to please little
children; yea, and he will be talking of complexions, though he
know nothing of their dispositions; and if his medicine do a feat,
he is a made man among fools; but being wholly unlearned, and
ofttimes unhonest, let me thus briefly describe him: he is a plain
kind of mountebank and a true quacksalver, a danger for the
sick to deal withal, and a dizard in the world to talk withal.

SCURVY AMONG SAILORS

Source: John Woodall, *The Surgions Mate,* 1612.

The cheefe cause . . . is the continuance of salt diet, either fish
or flesh, as porke and the like, which is not to be avoyded at
sea, . . . another cause, is want of sufficient nourishing food, and
of sweete water, and also for want of Aqua vitae, wine, beere,
or other good water to comfort and warm their stomackes, which
by contrary windes men are too much incident unto in long
voiages howsover the Marchants are carefull, provident, and
bountifull in that point. . . .

. . . there is a good quantity of Juice of Lemmons sent in each
ship out of England by the great care of the Marchants, and intended onely for the releefe of every poore man in his neede. . . .

A REMEDY FOR COLIC

Source: Pepys's Diary.

Jan. 20th, 1665. . . . buying a hare and taking it home; which
arose upon my discourse today with Mr. Batten in Westminster

Hall, who showed me my mistake that my hare's foot hath not the joynt to it: and assures me he never had his cholique since he carried it about him: and it is a strange thing how fancy works, for I no sooner almost handled his foote but whereas I was in some pain yesterday and tother day and in fear of more today, I became very well, and so continue.

March 26th, 1665. . . . Now I am at a losse to know whether it be my hare's foot which is my preservative, for I never had a fit of the collique since I wore it, or whether it be my taking of a pill of turpentine every morning, or all together: but this I know, with thanks to God Almighty, that I am now as well as ever I can wish or desire to be; . . .

CLEANLINESS

Source: Pepys's Diary.

May 25th, 1662. To trimming myself, which I have this week done every morning, with a pumice stone, which I learnt when I was last at Portsmouth; and I find it very easy, speedy, and cleanly, and shall continue the practice of it. . . .

May 31st, 1662. Had Sarah to comb my head clean, which I found so foul with powdering and other troubles, that I am resolved to try how I can keep my head dry without powder; and I did also in a suddaine fit cut off all my beard, which I had been a great while bringing up, only that I may with my pumice-stone do my whole face, as I now do my chin, and to save time, which I find a very easy way and gentile. So she also washed my feet in a bath of herbs, and so to bed.

HOSPITAL CONDITIONS IN THE WINTER OF 1672

Source: F. N. L. Poynter (Ed.), *Journal of James Yonge* (1647–1721), *Plymouth Surgeon.*

The following winter I had the hospital full of men, at times above 200, for the most part sick, and that of malignant diseases, so that between Christmas and the end of March I fell sick 3 times of malignant spotted fevers, the last of which had well nigh killed me. My wife and both servants lay sick of the same disease by me, and during my lying-in this last time, my wife's sister, Elizabeth Cramporn (a good-natured ingenious girl, 22 years old) by watching and attendance among us got the disease and died, as did also Dr. Jennins (who was . . . infected by but one visit). Mr. Avent, my mate at the same time, lay down 8 weeks, and the chief nurse after 5 weeks died. Such a sad contagion was there among us; blessed be God all my family escaped.

A SURGEON'S FEES IN 1674

Source: F. N. L. Poynter (Ed.), *Journal of James Yonge* (1647–1721), *Plymouth Surgeon.*

My pay was 5s. per diem constant and 3d. per each man for medicines. I had also half-a-crown a day for each mate, and a mate for every 30 men, so as sometimes I had 4 mates' pay, and but one mate in being. The 3d. per diem seemed worst, but considering that many ran away as soon as they came, that most others were scurvy, which cost little, the 3d. per man did well enough, though it were a small reward.

CHAPTER VIII

LEISURE

Men and women of all classes loved sensation and many of the popular leisure pursuits seem to us to be barbarous. Pepys referred to them as 'rude and nasty' pleasures. Cromwell forbade cock-fighting because it disturbed the public peace and was accompanied by 'gaming, drinking, swearing, quarrelling and other dissolute practices'. Stubbes, of course, had critical views.

EVEN PLAYING CARDS WERE USED TO MAKE SATIRICAL REFERENCE TO CURRENT PROBLEMS.

One of Goldsmith's 'Cavalier' set of Playing Cards.

A Covenanting Scot & an English Independent differ about y things of this world

ACCOMPLISHMENTS OF EDWARD VI AND MARY

Source: Giralamo Cardano, an Italian physician, visiting the King in 1552. (Quoted in Burnet, *History of the Reformation*, 1829).

He had many tongues when he was yet but a child; together with the English, his natural tongue, he had both Latin and French; nor was he ignorant, as I hear, of the Greek, Italian and Spanish, and perhaps some more. But for the English, French and Latin, he was exact in them and apt to learn everything. Nor was he ignorant of logic, of the principles of natural philosophy, nor of music.

Source: Giacomo Soranzo, the Venetian Ambassador, 18th August, 1554 (*Cal. S.P. Venetian,* v).

Her Majesty takes great pleasure in playing on the lute and spinet, and is a very good performer on both instruments; and indeed before her accession she taught many of her maids of honour.

BEAR-BAITING

Source: Stubbes, *Anatomie of Abuses,* 1585.

. . . the bayting of a beare, besides that it is a filthie, stinking, and lothsome game, is it not a daungerous and a perilous exercise, wherein a man is in danger of his life everye minute of an houre? . . . What Christian hearte can take pleasure to see one poore beast to rent, teare, and kill an other, and all for his foolish pleasure? And although they be bloudie beasts to mankynd, and seeke his destruction, yet wee are not to abuse them, for his sake who made them, and whose creatures they are. For notwithstandyng that they be evill to us, and thirst after our bloud, yet are they good creatures in their own nature and kind, and made to set forthe the glorie, power, and magnificence of our God, and for our use, and therefore . . . wee ought not to abuse them.

COCK-FIGHTING

Source: Thomas Platter, *Travels in England,* 1599.

. . . in the city of London . . . cock-fights are held annually throughout three quarters of the year (for in the remaining quarter they told me it was impossible since the feathers are full of blood) and I saw the place which is built like a theatre. In the centre on the floor stands a circular table covered with straw and with ledges round it, where the cocks are teased and incited to fly at one another, while those with wagers as to which cock will win, sit closest around the circular disk, but the spectators who are merely present on their entrance penny sit around higher up, watching with eager pleasure the fierce and angry fight between the cocks, as these wound each other to death with spurs and beaks. And the party whose cock surrenders or dies loses the wager; I am told that stakes on a cock often amount to many thousands of crowns, . . .

BEAR- AND BULL-BAITING

Source: Thomas Platter, *Travels in England,* 1599.

Every Sunday and Wednesday in London there are bear-baitings . . . The theatre is circular, with galleries round the top for the spectators, the ground space down below, beneath the clear sky, is unoccupied. In the middle of this place a large bear on a long rope was bound to a stake, then a number of great English mastiffs were brought in and shown first to the bear, which they afterwards baited one after another: now the excellence and fine temper of such mastiffs was evinced, for although they were much struck and mauled by the bear, they did not give in, but had to be pulled off by sheer force, and their muzzles forced open with long sticks to which a broad ironpiece was attached at the top. The bears' teeth were not sharp so they could not injure the dogs; they have them broken short. When the first mastiffs tired, fresh ones were brought in to bait the bear.

When the first bear was weary, another one was supplied and fresh dogs to bait him, first one at a time, then more and more as it lasted, till they had overpowered the bear, then only did they come to its aid. This second bear was very big and old, and kept the dogs at bay so artfully with his paws that they could not score a point off him until there were more of them. When this bear was tired, a large white powerful bull was brought in, and likewise bound in the centre of the theatre, and one dog only was set on him at a time, which he speared with his horns and tossed in such masterly fashion, that they could not get the better of him, and as the dogs fell to the floor again, several men held the sticks under them to break their fall, so that they would not be killed. Afterwards more dogs were set on him, but

PLATE 9

The fyrſt Booke

of the perpendiculare intercepted with the Scale in the cliffes altitude befoꝛe meaſured, and diuide by the partes of the ſcale cutte, the quotient will ſhew the lyne Hypochenuſal, oꝛ diſtance of that parte of the ſhippe which your lyne viſuall touched from your eye, oꝛ adioyning the ſquare of the longitude firſte founde to the ſquare of the altitude, the rote quadꝛat of the pꝛoduct is alſo the true length of the line viſuall.

Example.

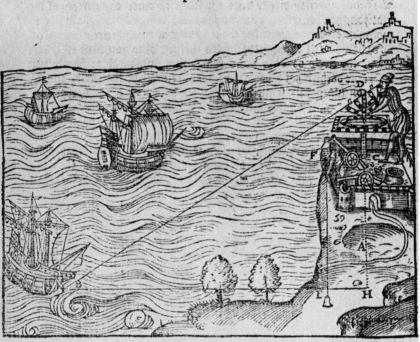

*A*Dmit I ſtande on the cliffe *A*, and ſee the ſhippe *B* lying at rode in the ſea, I deſire to know how farre off ſhe is from me, mine inſtrument conueniently placed at *C* (as is tofore declared) I turne my dimetient of my ſemicircle towarde the ſhippe, mouing it vp and downe till I eſpye through the ſightes the

A simple method of calculating distances

PLATE 10

A riverside scene. Notice the covered bridge

could not down him. Then another powerful bear was fetched and baited by six or seven dogs at a time, which attacked him bravely on all sides, but could not get the better of him because of his thick pelt.

Lastly they brought in an old blind bear which the boys hit with canes and sticks; but he knew how to untie his leash and he ran back to his stall.

FOOTBALL

Source: Stubbes, *Anatomie of Abuses*, 1585.

. . . for, as concernyng footeball playing, I protest unto you, it maie rather bee called a freendly kynde of fight then a plaie or recreation, a bloudie and murthering practise, then a fellowlie sporte or pastyme. For, dooeth not every one lye in waite for

his adversarie, seekyng to overthrowe hym, and to picke hym on his nose, though it bee upon harde stones, in ditche or dale, in valley or hill, or what place so ever it be, he careth not, so he maie have him downe? And he that can serve the moste of this fashion, he is counted the onely fellowe, and who but he? So that by this meanes, sometymes their necks are broken, some-tymes their backes, sometymes their legges, sometime their

G

armes, sometyme one parte thrust out of joynte, sometyme an other, sometyme their noses gush out with bloud, sometyme their eyes starte out; and sometymes hurt in one place, some-tymes in an other.

MAY DAY REVELS

Source: Stubbes, *Anatomie of Abuses,* 1585.

Against Maie, Whitsondaie, or some other tyme of the yeare, every parishe, towne, and village, assemble themselves together, bothe men, women, and children, olde and yong, even all indif-ferently; and either goyng all together, or devidyng themselves into companies, they goe some to the woodes and groves, some to the hilles and mountaines, some to one place, some to an other, where they spende all the night in pleasant pastymes, and in the mornyng they returne, bringing with them birch, bowes, and braunches of trees, to deck their assemblies withall. . . . But their cheefest jewell they bring from thence is their Maie poole, whiche they bring home with greate veneration, as thus: They have twentie or fourtie yoke of oxen, every oxe havyng a sweete nose-gaie of flowers tyed on the tippe of his hornes, and these oxen drawe home this Maie poole (this stinckyng idoll rather), which is covered all over with flowers and hearbes, bounde rounde aboute with stringes, from the top to the bottome, and sometyme painted with variable colours, with twoo or three hundred men, women, and children followyng it with greate devotion. And thus beyng reared up, with handkercheifes and flagges streamyng on the toppe, they strawe the grounde aboute, binde greene boughes about it, sett up sommer haules, bowers, and arbours hard by it; and then fall they to banquet and feast, to leape and daunce about it, . . .

CHURCH ALES

Source, Stubbes, *Anatomie of Abuses,* 1585.

. . . the Churche Wardens . . . of every parishe, with the consent of the whole parishe, provide halfe a score or twentie quarters of mault, wherof some they bye of the churche stocke, and some is given them of the parishioners themselves, . . . whiche mault beeyng made into very strong ale or beere, is sette to sale, either in the church or some other place assigned to that purpose. Then, when this . . . is sette abroche, well is he that can gette the soonest to it, and spend most at it; for he . . . is counted the godliest man, . . . because it is spent uppon his church forsoth! . . . In this kinde of practise they continue sixe weekes, a quarter of a yere, yea, halfe a yere together, swillyng and gullyng night and day, til they be as dronke as rattes, and as blockishe as beastes.

THE MONEY FROM CHURCH ALES

Source: Stubbes, *Anatomie of Abuses,* 1585.

. . . they repaire their churches and chappelles with it; they buie bookes for service, cuppes for the celebration of the sacramente, surplesses . . ., and . . . maintaine other extraordinary charges in their parishes besides.

BOWLING

Source: John Earle, *Micro-cosmographie,* 1628.

A bowl-alley is the place where there are three things thrown away besides bowls, to wit, time, money and curses, and the last ten for one. The best sport in it is the gamester's, and he enjoys it that looks on and bets not. It is the school of wrangling, and worse than the schools, for men will cavil here for an hair's breadth, and make a stir where a straw would end the controversy. No antic screws men's bodies into such strange flexures, and you would think them here senseless, to speak sense to their bowl, and put their trust in entreaties for a good cast. The bettors are the factious noise of the alley, or the gamesters' beadsmen that pray for them. They are somewhat like those that are cheated by great men, for they lose their money and must say nothing. It is the best discovery of humours; especially in the losers, where you have fine variety of impatience, whilst some fret, some rail, some swear, and others more ridiculously comfort themselves with philosophy. To give you the moral of it: it is the emblem of the world, or the world's ambition; where most are short, or over, or wide, or wrong-biased, and some few jostle in to the 'mistress' fortune. And it is here as in the court, where the nearest are most spited, and all blows aimed at the 'toucher'.

LEISURE UNDER THE COMMONWEALTH

Source: Parliamentary Ordinance, 1647.

To the end that there may be a convenient time allotted to scholars, apprentices, and other servants for their recreation: be it ordained That all scholars, apprentices, and other servants shall, with the leave and approbation of their masters respectively first had and obtained, have such convenient reasonable recreation and relaxation from their constant and ordinary labours on every second Tuesday in the month throughout the year, as formerly they used to have on . . . Holy Days. And that masters of all scholars, apprentices, and servants, shall grant unto them respectively such time for their recreations on the aforesaid second Tuesdays in every month, as they may conveniently spare from their extraordinary and necessary services and occasions. And it is further ordained by the said Lords and Commons, That if any difference shall arise between any master and servant concerning the liberty hereby granted, the next Justice of the Peace shall have power to hear and determine the same.

SPORTS AND RECREATIONS IN CHARLES II'S TIME

Source: Edward Chamberlayne, *Angliae Notitia, or The Present State of England,* 1676.

For variety of divertisements, sports and recreations no nation doth excel the English. (After mentioning the hunting, hawking, horse-racing, bowls, tennis and many other recreations of the nobility) . . . The citizens and peasants have hard-ball, football, skittles or nine-pins, shovel-board, stow-ball, goffe, trol-madam, cudgels, bear-baiting, bull-baiting, bow and arrow, throwing at

cocks, shuttle-cock, bowling, quoits, leaping, wrestling, pitching
the bar, and ringing of bells, a recreation used in no other country
of the world.

FINSBURY ARCHER'S TICKET FOR THE SHOOTING OF 1676.

A DAY IN THE COUNTRY

Source: Pepys's Diary.

29th May, 1662. With my wife and two maids and the boy took
boat and to Foxhall, where I had not been a great while. To the
Old Spring Garden, and there walked long, and the wenches
gathered pinks. Here we staid, and seeing that we could not
have anything to eat, but very dear, and with long stay, we went
forth again without any notice taken of us, and so we might have
done if we had had anything. Thence to the New one, where I

never was before, which much exceeds the other; and here we also walked, and the boy crept through the hedge and gathered abundance of roses; and, after a long walk, passed out of doors as we did in the other place, and here we had cakes and powdered beef and ale; and so home again by water with much pleasure.

HAVING ONE'S PORTRAIT PAINTED

Source: Pepys's Diary.

17th March, 1666. At noon home to dinner and presently with my wife out to Hales's, where I am still infinitely pleased with my wife's picture. I paid him £14 for it, and 25*s*. for the frame, and I think it is not a whit too deare for so good a picture. This day I begun to sit, and he will make me, I think, a very fine picture. He promises it shall be as good as my wife's, and I sit to have it full of shadows, and do almost break my neck looking over my shoulder to make the posture for him to work by.

A PRIZE FIGHT

Source: Pepys's Diary.

27th May, 1667. . . . Abroad, and stopped at the Bear-garden stairs, there to see a prize fought. But the house so full there was no getting in there, so forced to go through an alehouse into the pit, where the bears are baited; and upon a stool did see them fight, which they did very furiously, a butcher and a waterman. The former had the better all along, till by and by the latter dropped his sword out of his hand, and the butcher, whether not seeing his sword dropped I know not, but did give him a cut over the wrist, so as he was disabled to fight any longer. But, Lord! to see how in a minute the whole stage was full of watermen to revenge the foul play, and the butchers to defend their fellow, though most blamed him; and there they all fell to it to knocking down and cutting many on each side. It was pleasant to see, but that I stood in the pit, and feared that in the tumult I might get some hurt.

A FROST FAIR, 1684

Source: John Evelyn's Diary. Jan. 24th, 1684.

The frost continuing, more and more severe, the Thames, before London, was still planted with booths in formal streets, all sorts of trades and shops, furnished and full of commodities even to a printing press, where the people and ladies took a fancy to have their names printed, and the day and year set down when produced on the Thames; this humour took so universally, that it was estimated the printer gained five pounds a day, for printing a line only, at sixpence a name, besides what he got by ballads, etc. Coaches plied from Westminster to the Temple and from other stairs, to and fro, as in the streets; sleds, sliding with skates, or bull-baiting, horse and coach races, puppet-shows and interludes, cooks, tippling and other lewd places; so that it seemed to be a carnival on the water: . . . Many parks of deer were destroyed; and all sorts of fuel so dear, that there were great contributions to keep the poor alive.

SMOKING

The use of tobacco spread fast in England to the disgust of King James I and one, Barnaby Rich, who, in *The Honestie of this Age*, published in 1614, complained of the money wasted on it. He also contested the fact, admitted by Harrison below, of tobacco doing good. He stated that '7,000 houses live by the trade of tobacco-selling and if each of these takes but 2s 6d a day—and probably it takes 5s—the sum total amounts to £399,375 a year, "all spent in smoake".'

Source: Harrison's Chrononlogie.

1573. In these daies, the taking-in of the smoke of the Indian herbe called 'Tabaco', by an instrument formed like a little ladell, wherby it passeth from the mouth into the hed & stomach, is gretlie taken-up & used in England, against Rewmes & some other diseases ingendred in the longes & inward partes, & not without effect. This herbe as yet is not so comon, but that for want thereof divers do practize for the like purposes with the Nicetian, otherwise called in latine, 'Hyosciamus Luteus', or the yellow henbane, albeit, not without gret error; for, althoughe

The Illustration on the Title-page of *The Dancing Master*; or, plain and easie *Rules* for the Dancing of *Country-Dances,* with the *Tunes* to each *Dance.* To which is added the *Tunes* of the most usual *French Dances.* And also other New and Pleasant *English Tunes* for the *Treble-Violin.*
(*London,* Printed by *W.G.* and Sold by *J. Playford* and *Z. Watkins* at their Shop in the Temple. 1665.)

Gathering Peascods *Round for as many as will*

Goe all two Dubles round, turne S. That back a-gaine.

Men hands, and goe round in the inside, and come to your places. We. as much.

Men meet and clap hands, We. as much, while the men goe back, men meet againe and turne S. We. meet, men meet, while the We. go back, We. meet againe and turne S.

Sides, turne S. That a-gaine.

As before, the We. going first.

As before the We. meeting first.

Armes all, turn S. That againe.

Men hands as at the first.

Men meet as the first time.

Music and Instructions for Dancing *Gathering Peascods*; one of the Dances Published in the Above Book.

that herbe be a soverene healer of old ulcers & sores reputed incurable outwardly, yet is not the smoke or vapour thereof so profitable to be receaved inwardly. The herbe (Tobacco) is comonly of the height of a man, garnished with great long leaves like the paciens, (dock) bering seede, colloured, & of quantity like unto, or rather lesse then, the fine margeronie; the herbe it self yerely coming up also of the shaking of the seede. the collour of the floure is carnation, resembling that of the lemmon in forme: the roote yellow, with many fillettes, & therto very small in comparison, if you respect the substauns of the herbe.

READING

Despite far longer hours of work people had far more time to themselves than we do nowadays. There were fewer distractions and long periods when there was nothing more than local news and gossip to distract their thoughts. Few people could read, but the following list gives an idea of what an intelligent, though not literary, gentleman had read in his youth, in the very early years of the seventeenth century. After the Bible, he recommends to his grandson's attention:

Hooker's *Ecclesiastical Polity*, Sir W. Raleigh's *History of the World*, Plutarch's *Lives*, Camden's *Britannia*, my friend Sir Richard Baker's *Chronicles*, Xenophon's *Cyrus*, Tully's *Offices*, James I's *Basilicon Doron*. He adds:

'When I was young it was a defect not to be versed in Sir Philip Sidney. To refresh yourself with poetical stories you may take Sir Philip Sidney instead of all.'

A CULTURED GENTLEMAN'S PURSUITS

Here a lady describes the leisure interests of her husband, a wealthy Parliamentarian.

Source: The Life of Mrs. Lucy Hutchinson, written by herself—a fragment.

. . . he had a great love of music, and often diverted himself with a viol, on which he played masterly; and he had an exact ear and judgment in other music; he shot excellently in bows and guns, and much used them for his exercise; he had great judgment in paintings, graving, sculpture, and all liberal arts, and had many curiosities of value in all kinds; he took great delight in perspective glasses, and for his other rarities was not so much affected with the antiquity as the merit of the work; he took much pleasure in improvement of grounds, in planting groves, and walks, and fruit-trees, in opening springs and making fish-ponds.

(*Annalia Dubrensia*, 1636)

COTSWOLD GAMES. THESE WERE HELD NEAR CHIPPING CAMDEN ON THURSDAY AND FRIDAY
OF WHITWEEK FOR TWO AND A HALF CENTURIES.

CHAPTER IX

DRAMA

Strolling players had been a familiar feature of the English country-side throughout medieval times. Rich and poor were accustomed to seeing skilled dramatic performances and were familiar with poetry as a vehicle for story-telling, for entertainment and for the spread of news.

Skilled playwrights, well-trained and serious actors encouraged by the construction of new theatres gravitated naturally to London. The London crowds were critical and appreciative, and men of rank and fashion came by boat from Whitehall to see each play many times. Actors and playwrights alike could achieve fame and wealth on Bank-side.

FLOURISHING LONDON THEATRES

Source: Thomas Platter, *Travels in England,* 1599.

Daily at two in the afternoon, London has two, sometimes three plays running in different places, competing with each other, and those which play best obtain most spectators. The playhouses are so constructed that they play on a raised platform, so that everyone has a good view. There are different galleries and places, however, where the seating is better and more comfortable and therefore more expensive. For whoever cares to stand below only pays one English penny, but if he wishes to sit he enters by another door, and pays another penny, while if he desires to sit in the most comfortable seats which are cushioned, where he not only sees everything well, but can also be seen, then he pays yet another English penny at another door. And during the performance food and drink are carried round the audience, so that for what one cares to pay one may also have refreshment. The actors are most expensively and elaborately costumed; for it is the English usage for eminent lords or Knights at their decease to bequeath and leave almost the best of their clothes to their serving men, which it is unseemly for the latter to wear, so that they offer them for sale for a small sum to the actors.

How much time then they may merrily spend daily at the play everyone knows who has ever seen them play or act.

STRUCTURE OF A PLAYHOUSE

Source: Contract for building the Fortune Theatre at the cost of £440—dated Jan. 8, 1600.

. . . The frame of the said house to be set square and to contain four score foot of lawful assize every way square without, and fifty-five foot of like assize square every way within, with a good, sure and strong foundation of piles, brick, lime and sand both without and within to be wrought one foot of assize at the least above the ground. And the said frame to contain three storeys in height, the first or lower storey to contain twelve foot of lawful assize in height, the second storey eleven foot of lawful assize in height, and the third or upper storey to contain nine foot of lawful assize in height. All which storeys shall contain twelve foot and a half of lawful assize in breadth throughout, besides a jutty forwards in either of the said two upper storeys of ten inches of lawful assize, with four convenient divisions for gentlemen's rooms and other sufficient and convenient divisions for two-penny rooms, with necessary seats to be placed and set as well in those rooms as throughout all the rest of the galleries of the said house and with such-like stairs, conveyances and divisions without and within as are made and contrived in and to the late erected playhouse on the Bank, in the said parish of St. Saviour's, called the Globe; with a stage and tiring-house to be made, erected and set up within the said frame with a shadow or cover on the said stage. . . .

And which stage shall contain in length forty and three foot of lawful assize and in breadth to extend to the middle of the yard of the said house. The same stage to be paled in below with good, strong and sufficient new oaken boards, and likewise the lower storey of the said frame withinside; and the same lower storey to be also laid over and fenced with strong iron pikes. And the said stage to be in all other proportions contrived and fashioned like unto the stage of the said play-house called the Globe, with convenient windows and lights glazed to the said tiring-house, and the said frame, stage and staircases to be covered with tile and to have a sufficient gutter of lead to carry and convey the water from the covering of the said stage to fall backwards. And also all the said frame and the staircases thereof to be sufficiently enclosed without with lath, lime and hair, and the gentlemen's rooms and twopenny rooms to be sealed with lath, lime and hair, and all the floors of the said galleries, storeys and stage to be boarded with good and sufficient new deal boards of whole thickness where need shall be. And the said house, and other things before-mentioned, to be made and done, to be in all other contrivitions, conveyances, fashions, thing and things effected, finished and done, according to the manner and fashion of the said house called the Globe, saving only that all the principal and main posts of the said frame and stage forward shall be square and wrought pilaster-wise with carved proportions called satyrs to be placed and set on the top of every of the same posts. . . .

A PLEA FOR A PLAYHOUSE IN FINSBURY,
c. 1600

Source: Henslowe Papers, ed. W. W. Greg (1907); also in E. K. Chambers, *The Elizabethan Stage* (1923), vol. IV.

To the righte honorable the Lordes and others of her maiesties most honorable privie Councell:

In all humblenese, wee the Inhabitants of the Lordshipp of Fynisburye, within the parrishe of St. Gyles without Creplegate, London, doe certifie unto your honnours, That wheare the Servantes of the right honorable Earle of Nottingham have latelie gone aboute to erect and sett upp a newe Playehowse within the said Lordshipp, Wee could be contented that the same might proceede and be Tollerated (Soe it stande with your honnours pleasuers) For the reasons and Causes followeinge.

First, because the Place appoynted oute for that purpose Standeth very tollerable, neere unto the Feildes, and soe farr distant and remote frome any person or Place of accompt, as that none cann be Annoyed thearbie:

Secondlie, because the Erectours of the saied howse are contented to give a very liberall porcion of money weekelie, towardes the releef of our Poore, The nomber and necessity whereof is soe greate that the same will redounde to the contynuall comfort of the saied Poore:

Thirdlie and lastlie, wee are the rather Contented to accept this meanes of releif to our Poore, because our Parrishe is not able to releeve them, neither hath the Justices of the Sheire taken any order for any Supplie oute of the Countrye, as is enjoyned by the late Acte of Parliamente:

UNSEEMLY BEHAVIOUR AT THE PLAY

Performances were given in the daytime and there were no foot-lights and no curtain. Privileged members of the audience sat on stools among the actors, others stood below, exposed to the weather, or in covered galleries built round the stage.

Source: Stephen Gosson, *The Schoole of Abuse,* 1579.

In our assemblies at plays in London, you shall see such heaving, and shoving, such itching and shouldering to sit by women: such care for their garments, that they be not trod on: such eyes to their laps, that no chips light in them: such pillows to their backs, that they take no hurt: such masking in their ears, I know not what: such giving them pippins to pass the time: such playing at foot-saunt without cards: such tickling, such toying, such smiling, such winking, and such manning them home, when the sports are ended, that it is a right comedy to mark their behaviour, to watch their conceits, as the cat for the mouse, and as good as a course at the game itself, to dog them a little, or follow aloof by the print of their feet, and so discover by slot where the deer taketh soil. If this were as well noted as ill seen, or as openly punished as secretly practised, I have no doubt but the cause would be seared to dry up the effect, and these pretty rabbits very cunningly ferreted from their burrows.

For they that lack customers all the week, either because their haunt is unknown or the constables and officers of their parish watch them so narrowly that they dare not quetch, to celebrate the sabbath flock to theatres, and there keep a general market of bawdry. Not that any filthiness in deed is committed within the compass of that ground, as was done in Rome, but that every wanton and his paramour, every man and his mistress, every John and his Joan, every knave and his quean, are there first acquainted and cheapen the merchandise in that place, which they pay for elsewhere as they can agree.

COMMENTS BY A PLAYWRIGHT

Source: Ben Jonson, *The Devil is an Ass*, 1616. Act I, scene iii.

> Here is a cloke cost fifty pound, wife,
> Which I can sell for thirty, when I have seen
> All London in't, and London has seen me.
> Today I go to the Blackfriars playhouse,
> Sit in the view, salute all my acquaintance,
> Rise up between the acts, let fall my cloak,
> Publish a handsome man and a rich suit;
> And that's a special end why we go thither,
> All that pretend to stand for't on the stage;
> The ladies ask, 'Who's that?' For they do come
> To see us, as we do to see them.

Source: Ben Jonson, *Ode to Himself*, 1629.

> Come, leave the loathed stage,
>   And the more loathsome age;
> Where pride and impudence, in faction knit,
>   Usurp the chair of wit!
> Indicting and arraigning every day
>   Something they call a play.
>   Let their fastidious, vain,
>   Commission of the brain
> Run on and rage, sweat, censure, and condemn;
> They were not made for thee, less thou for them.

PLATE 11

Washday. Note beating, drying methods and the dress of the washerwomen

PLATE 12

Work on an estate

Say that thou pour'st them wheat,
  And they will acorns eat;
'Twere simple fury still thyself to waste
  On such as have no taste!
To offer them a surfeit of pure bread
  Whose appetites are dead!
No, give them grains their fill,
  Husks, draff, to drink or swill:
If they love lies, and leave the lusty wine,
Envy them not, their palate's with the swine.

A LOCAL PLAY

Provincial plays were still very much like medieval morality plays.

Source: R. Willis, *Mount Tabor,* 1639.

In the city of Gloucester, the manner is (as I think it is in other
like corporations) that when players of interludes come to the
town, they first attend the mayor, to inform him what noble-
man's servants they are, and so to get license for their public
playing; and if the mayor like the actors, or would shew respect
to their lord and master, he appoints them to play their first play
before himself and the aldermen and common council of the city;
and that is called the mayor's play, where everyone that will,
comes in without money, the mayor giving the players a reward
as he thinks fit to shew respect unto them. At such a play my
father took me with him, and made me stand between his legs,
as he sat upon one of the benches, where we saw and heard very
well. The play was called 'The Cradle of Security', wherein
was personated a king or some great prince, with his courtiers
of several kinds, amongst which three ladies were in special grace
with him; and they keeping him in delights and pleasures, drew
him from his graver counsellors, hearing of sermons, and listening
to good counsel and admonitions, that in the end they got him
to lie down in a cradle upon the stage, where these three ladies
joining in a sweet song rocked him asleep, that he snorted again,
and in the meantime closely conveyed under the cloths wherewithal he was covered, a vizard like a swine's snout upon his
face, with three wire chains fastened thereunto, the other end

H

whereof being holden severally by those three ladies, who fall
to singing again, and then discovered his face, that the spectators
might see how they had transformed him, going on with their
singing. Whilst all this was acting, there came forth of another
door at the farthest end of the stage, two old men, the one in blue,
like a sergeant at arms, with his mace on his shoulder, the other
in red, with a drawn sword in his hand, and leaning with the
other hand upon the other's shoulder; and so they two went
along in a soft pace round about by the skirt of the stage, till
at last they came to the cradle, when all the court was in greatest
jollity; and then the foremost old man with his mace stroke a
fearful blow upon the cradle; whereat all the courtiers, with the
three ladies and the vizard, all vanished; and the desolate prince
starting up bare-faced, and finding himself thus sent for to judgment, made a lamentable complaint of his miserable case, and
so was carried away by wicked spirits. This prince did personate
in the moral, the wicked of the world; the three ladies, Pride,
Covetousness, and Luxury; the two old men, the end of the world,
and the last judgment.

OBJECTIONS TO STAGE PLAYS IN LONDON

Many people objected on religious and moral grounds to the
behaviour of audiences at the London theatres. Puritan clergy preached
against stage performances and municipal authorities would have
banned them had not the courtiers intervened. The subject was hotly
debated in all quarters. At the outbreak of the Civil War theatres
were closed, and actors, among many others, remonstrated against
this ruling.

Source: A Letter from the Lord Mayor and Aldermen of London
to the Privy Council, July 28, 1597.

1. They are a special cause of corrupting their youth, containing nothing but unchaste matters, lascivious devices, shifts of
cozenage, and other lewd and ungodly practices, being so as
that they impress the very quality and corruption of manners
which they represent, contrary to the rules and art prescribed
for the making of comedies even among the heathen, who used
them seldom and at certain set times, and not all the year long
as our manner is. Whereby such as frequent them, being of the

base and refuse sort of people or such young gentlemen as have small regard of credit or conscience, draw the same into imitation and not to the avoiding the like vices which they represent.

2. They are the ordinary places for vagrant persons, masterless men, thieves, horse-stealers, whoremongers, cozeners, coney-catchers, contrivers of treason and other idle and dangerous persons to meet together and to make their matches to the great displeasure of Almighty God and the hurt and annoyance of her Majesty's people; which cannot be prevented nor discovered by the governors of the city for that they are out of the city's jurisdiction.

3. They maintain idleness in such persons as have no vocation, and draw apprentices and other servants from their ordinary works and all sorts of people from the resort unto sermons and other Christian exercises to the great hindrance of trades and profanation of religion established by her Highness within this realm.

4. In the time of sickness it is found by experience that many, having sores and yet not heart-sick, take occasion hereby to walk abroad and to recreate themselves by hearing a play. Whereby others are infected, and themselves also many things miscarry.

A DRAMATIST'S RETORT TO PURITAN OBJECTIONS TO PLAYS

Source: Thomas Nashe, *Pierce Penilesse,* 1592.

... the policy of plays is very necessary, howsoever some shallow-brained censurers ... mightily oppugn them. For whereas the afternoon, being the idlest time of the day, wherein men that are their own masters ... do wholly bestow themselves upon pleasure, and that pleasure they divide into gaming, following of harlots, drinking, or seeing a play: is it not then better ... that they should betake them to ... plays? Nay, what if I prove plays to be ... a rare exercise of virtue? First, for the subject of them (for the most part) it is borrowed out of our English chronicles, wherein our forefathers' valiant acts (that have lain long buried in rusty brass and worm-eaten books) are revived, and they themselves raised from the grave of oblivion, and brought to plead their aged honours in open presence; than which, what can be a sharper reproof to these degenerate effeminate days of ours?

How would it have joyed brave Talbot (the terror of the French) to think that after he had lain two hundred years in his tomb, he should triumph again on the stage, and have his bones new embalmed with the tears of ten thousand spectators at least, . . . who in the tragedian that represents his person imagine they behold him fresh bleeding. . . .

In plays, all cozenages, all cunning drifts over-gilded with outward holiness, all stratagems of war, all the cankerworms that breed on the rust of peace are most lively anatomized. They shew the ill-success of treason, the fall of hasty climbers, the wretched end of usurpers, the misery of civil dissension, and how just God is evermore in punishing of murder. . . .

. . . as for corrupting, . . . that's false; . . . for no play they have encourageth any man to tumults or rebellion, but lays before such the halter and the gallows; or praiseth or approveth pride, lust, prodigality or drunkenness, but beats them down utterly. As for the hindrance of trades and traders of the city by them, that is an article foisted in by the vintners, alewives, and victuallers who surmise, if there were no plays, they should have all the company that resort to them lie boozing and beer-bathing in their houses every afternoon. . . . What shall he do that hath spent himself? Where shall he haunt? Faith, when dice, lust, and drunkenness and all have dealt upon him, if there be never a play for him to go to for his penny, he sits melancholy in his chamber, devising upon felony or treason, and how he may best exalt himself by mischief.

A REMONSTRATION AGAINST THE CLOSING OF THE LONDON THEATRES, 1642

Source: The Actors Remonstrance, 1643.

Oppressed with many calamities and languishing to death under the burden of a long and (for aught we know) an everlasting restraint, we the comedians, tragedians and actors of all sorts and sizes belonging to the famous private and public houses within the city of London and the suburbs thereof, to you great Phoebus and your sacred Sisters, the sole patronesses of our distressed calling, do we in all humility present this our humble and lamentable complaint, by whose intercession to those powers who confined us to silence we hope to be restored to our pristine honour and employment.

First, it is not unknown to all the audience that have frequented the private houses of Black-friars, the Cock-pit and Salisbury-court, without austerity we have purged our stages from all obscene and scurrilous jests, such as might either be guilty of corrupting the manners, or defaming the persons of any men of note in the city or kingdom; that we have endeavoured, as much as in us lies, to instruct one another in the true and genuine art of acting, to repress bawling and railing, formerly in great request, and for to suit our language and action to the more gentle and natural garb of the times; that we have left off for our own parts, and so have commanded our servants, to forget that ancient custom which formerly rendered men of our quality infamous, namely the inveigling in young gentlemen, merchants' factors and prentices to spend their patrimonies and masters' estates upon us and our harlots in taverns; we have clean and quite given over the borrowing money at first sight of puny gallants or praising their swords, belts and beavers, so to invite them to bestow them upon us; and to our praise be it spoken, we were for the most part very well reformed, few of us keeping, or being rather kept by, our mistresses, betook ourselves wholly to our wives, observing the matrimonial vow of chastity. Yet for all these conformities and reformations we were by authority (to which we in all humility submit) restrained from the practice of our profession; that profession which had before maintained us in comely and convenient equipage, some of us by it merely being enabled to keep horses (though not whores) is now condemned to a perpetual, at least a very long temporary, silence, and we left to live upon our shifts or the expense of our former gettings, to the great impoverishment and utter undoing of ourselves, wives, children and dependants, besides which it is of all other our

extremest grievance, that plays being put down under the name
of public recreations, other public recreations of far more harm-
ful consequences (are) permitted still to stand in statu quo prius,
namely that nurse of barbarism and beastliness, the Bear-Garden,
where upon their usual days those demi-monsters are baited by
bandogs; the gentlemen of stave and tail, namely boisterous
butchers, cutting cobblers, hard-handed masons and the like
rioting companions, resorting thither with as much freedom as
formerly, making with their sweat and crowding a far worse
stink than the ill-formed beasts they persecute with their dogs
and whips; pick-pockets, which in an age are not heard of in
any of our houses, repairing thither, and other disturbers of the
public peace which dare not be seen in our civil and well-governed
theatres, where none use to come but the best of the nobility
and gentry; . . .

For ourselves, such as were sharers are so impoverished that,
were it not for some slender helps afforded us in this time of
calamity by our former providence, we might be enforced to act
our tragedies. Our hired-men are dispersed, some turned soldiers
and trumpeters, others destin'd to meaner courses, or depending
upon us, whom in courtesy we cannot see want for old acquaintance sakes. Their friends, young gentlemen that used to feast
and frolic with them at taverns, having either quitted the kin
in these times of distraction, or their money having quitted them,
they are ashamed to look upon their old expensive friends. . . .
Our fools who had wont to allure and excite laughter with their
very countenances, at their first appearance on the stage (hard
shifts are better than none) are enforced, some of them at least,
to maintain themselves by virtue of their baubles. Our boys, ere
we shall have liberty to act again, will be grown out of use, like
cracked organ-pipes, and have faces as old as our flags.

POST-RESTORATION DEVELOPMENTS

At the Restoration the theatres were reopened and Charles II
and his courtiers patronized them. The buildings were much improved:
there was a roof covering both actors and audience, artificial lighting
with candles, 'footlights', a drop curtain and painted scenery.
Women's parts were no longer played by boys, as before the Civil

War, but by women actresses. The plays written were frivolous and cynical and many well-brought-up young people were never allowed to visit the theatre. Here a writer sums up some of the differences between drama past and present:

Source: Richard Flecknoe, *A Short Discourse of the English Stage*, 1664.

(Up) to the last Age, they Acted nothing here but Playes of the holy Scripture or Saints Lives, and that without any certain Theaters or set Companies, till about the beginning of Queen Elizabeths Reign they began here to assemble into Companies, and set up Theaters, first in the City (as in the Inn-yards of the Cross-Keyes and Bull in Grace and Bishops-Gate Street at this day to be seen), till that Fanatick Spirit which then began with the Stage, and after ended with the Throne, banisht them thence into the Suburbs, as after they did the Kingdom, in the beginning of our Civil Wars. . . .

For Playes, Shakespear was one of the first who inverted the Dramatick Stile from dull History to quick Comedy, upon whom Johnson refin'd; . . . one saying wittily . . . of Shakespear's writings, that 'twas a fine Garden, but it wanted weeding. . . .

The chief faults of our (plays) are our huddling too much matter together, and making them too long and intricate; we imagining we never have intrigue enough till we lose our selves and Auditors, who should be led in a Maze, but not a Mist; and through turning and winding wayes, but so still as they may find their way at last. . . .

Beaumont and Fletcher were excellent in their kinde, but they often err'd against Decorum, seldom representing a valiant man without somewhat of the Braggadoccio, nor an honourable woman without somewhat of Dol Common in her; to say nothing of their irreverent representing Kings persons on the Stage, who shu'd never be represented but with Reverence. Besides, Fletcher was the first who introduc't that witty obscenity in his Playes, which like poison infused in pleasant liquor is alwayes the more dangerous the more delightful. . . .

It was the happiness of the Actors of those Times to have such Poets as these to instruct them and write for them; and no less of those Poets, to have such docile and excellent Actors to Act their Playes, as a Field and Burbidge, of whom we may say that he was a delightful Proteus, so wholly transforming himself into his Part, and putting off himself with his Cloathes, as he never (not so much as in the Tyring-house) assum'd himself again until the Play was done; . . .

Now, for the difference betwixt our Theaters and those of former times, they were plain and simple, with no other Scenes nor Decorations of the Stage, but onely old Tapestry, and the Stage strew'd with Rushes, with their Habits accordingly, whereas ours now for cost and ornament are arriv'd to the heighth of Magnificence; but that which makes our Stage the better makes our Playes the worse perhaps, they striving now to make them more for sight then hearing, whence that solid joy of the interior is lost, and that benefit which men formerly receiv'd from Playes, from which they seldom or never went away but far better and wiser then they came.

MASQUES

During the reign of James I operas and masques in the French and Italian style became fashionable. A masque involved singing, acting, dancing and playing and often the scenery and costumes were designed by a noted artist or architect.

In honour of the marriage of Princess Elizabeth, daughter of James I, a masque was held at Whitehall from 11th–16th February, 1613:

Source: Edmond Howes, *Annales,* 1615.

And that night, in honour of this joyful nuptial, there was a very stately masque of lords and ladies, with many ingenious speeches, delicate devices, melodious music, pleasant dances, with other princely entertainments of time, all which were singularly well performed in the Banqueting-house. The four honourable Inns of Court, as well the elders and grave benchers of each house as the towardly young active gallant gentlemen of the same houses, being of infinite desire to express their singular love and duteous affection to his Majesty, and to perform some memorable and acceptable service worthy their own reputation, in honour of this nuptial, and thereupon with great expedition they jointly and severally consulted and agreed amongst themselves to set out two several rich and stately masques, and to perform them bravely, without respect of charge or expenses, and from amongst themselves they selected the most pregnant and active gentlemen to be their masquers, who, to the lasting honour of themselves and their societies, performed all things as worthily. They employed the best wits and skilfullest artisans in devising, composing and erecting their several strange properties, excellent speeches, pleasant devices and delicate music, brave in habit, rich in ornaments, in demeanour courtly, in their going by land and water very stately and orderly; all which, with their rare inventions and variable entertainments of time, were such as the like was never performed in England by any society, and was now as graciously accepted of by his Majesty, the Queen, the Prince, the bride and bridegroom, from whom they received all princely thanks and encouragement. . . .

Upon Shrove Monday at night, the gentlemen of the Middle Temple and Lincoln's Inn, with their train for this business, assembled in Chancery Lane, at the house of Sir Edward Philips, Master of the Rolls, and about eight of the clock they marched thence through the Strand, to the court at Whitehall, in this manner. First rode fifty choice gentlemen richly attired, and as gallantly mounted, with every one his footman to attend him; these rode very stately like a vanguard. Next after, with fit distance, marched an antic or mock-masque of baboons, attired like fantastic travellers in very strange and confused manner, riding upon asses or dwarf jades, using all apish and mocking tricks to the people, moving much laughter as they passed with torches on either side to shew their state to be as ridiculous as the rest was noble. After them came two chariots triumphal, very pleasant and full of state, wherein rode the choice musicians of this kingdom in robes like to the Virginian priests, with sundry devices, all pleasant and significant, with two ranks of torches. Then came the chief masquers with great state in white Indian habit or like the great princes of Barbary, richly embroidered with the golden sun, with suitable ornaments in all points; about their necks were ruffs of feathers, spangled and beset with pearl and silver, and upon their heads lofty coronets suitable to the rest. They wore long silk stockings, curiously embroidered with gold to the mid-leg. Their buskins were likewise embroidered, and in their hands, as they rode, they brandished cane darts of the finest gold: their vizards were of olive colour, their hair long and black, down to their shoulders. The horses for rich shew equalled the masquers: their caparisons were enchased with suns of gold and ornamental jewels, with silver, scarfing over the whole caparison and about their heads, which made such a strange and glorious show, that it dazzled the eyes of the beholders with great admiration. . . .

The next day being Shrove Tuesday, the gentlemen of the Inner Temple and Gray's Inn, with their train and many other gallant young gentlemen of both those houses as their convoy, assembled themselves at Winchester House, being the appointed place for their rendezvous. This night's entertainment consisted of three several masques, viz. an antimasque of a strange and different fashion from others, both in habit and manners and very delectable; a rural or country masque consisting of many persons, men and women, being all in sundry habits, being likewise as strange, variable and delightful; the third, which they called the main masque, was a masque of knights, attired in arming doublets of carnation satin, richly embroidered with stars of silver plate beset with smaller stars, spangles and silver lace, between gorgets of silver mail, with long Venetian hose embroidered suitable to the rest, silk carnation stockings embroidered all over, their garters and roses answerable. Their hats were of the same stuff and embroidered, cut before like a helmet and the hinder part like a scallop, answering the skirts of their doublets; their hat-bands were wreaths of silver, in form of garlands of wild olives; their feathers white and carnation; their belts embroidered, silver swords, little Italian falling-bands and cuffs embroidered; their hair fair and long; their vizards fair and young; and concerning their sundry ingenious properties and devices already erected in the court hall, they were all excellent, fraught with art, state and delights, having all their actors correspondent.

CHAPTER X

MUSIC

During the sixteenth century secular music was becoming a rival to church music and virtually everybody sang and played an instrument. Drake, on his voyage round the world, found room in his tiny ship for musicians and wrote that he 'always dined and supped to the music of viols' and his crew were great singers. King Henry VIII and Queen Elizabeth were both good amateur composers and musicians, and there was much music-making at court. This fashion for creative music-making naturally spread throughout the country.

Large houses had a music room in which a large number of instruments were part of the furniture: a chest of viols (2 treble, 2 tenor

III

and 2 bass), a clavicord, lutes, recorders, virginals, organs, guitars, pipes and flutes were as much used as a chest and a stool. Shakespeare reflected the common attitude to music in his day:

> 'The man that hath no music in his soul,
> Nor is not moved with concord of sweet sounds,
> Is fit for treasons, stratagems, and spoils.'

THE DECAY OF SERIOUS MUSIC

Source: The Autobiography of Thomas Whythorne, c. 1576. Ed. J. M. Osborn, 1961.

In times past, music was chiefly maintained by cathedral churches, abbeys, colleges, parish churches, chantries, guilds, fraternities, etc., but when the abbeys, . . . etc. were suppressed, then went music into decay. To speak of music in houses, . . . divers noblemen and women, in time past, imitating the prince, would have organists and singingmen to serve God after the manner of that time with music in their private chapels, but that imitation is also left. Then for such as served for private recreation in houses, these were no less esteemed than the others. . . . Now I will speak of the use of music in this time present. First for the church, ye do and shall see it so slenderly maintained in the cathedral churches and colleges and parish churches that when the old store of the musicians be worn out . . . ye shall have few or none remaining except it be a few singingmen and players on musical instruments. . . . There be another sort of musicians that be named speculators, that is to say, they that do become musicians by study without any practice thereof. There have been of such who have made songs and have pricked them out, and yet could not sing a part of them themselves. . . .

I being desirous to have and enrich myself with some more such exercises and qualities as young folk for the most part do delight in, went to the dancing school and fencing school and also learned to play on the gittern and cittern, which two instruments were then strange in England, and therefore the more desired and esteemed—

THE TOWN WAITS OF NORWICH

Source: Records of the City of Norwich, ed. Hudson and Tingey, vol. II.

Norwich, Court on 4 Feb., 1576. The hole company of the waytes of this cittie did come here into this courte and craved that they myght have leve to playe commodies and upon interlutes and souch other places (plays) and tragedes which shall seme to them mete; which peticion by the whole concent of this courte is graunted to them so farre as they do not playe in the tyme of devine service and sermonnes.

Norwich, Court on 25 *Jan.,* 1589. This daye was redd in court a letter sent to Mr Maiour and his brethren from Sir Frauncys Drake wherby he desyreth that the waytes of this citie may bee sent to hym to go the new intendid voyage, wherunto the waytes beeyng here called doo all assent. Wherupon it is agreed that they shall have vj cloakes of stamell cloath made them redy before they go. And that a wagon shalbe provided to carry them and their instrumentes, and that they shall have iiij li. to buye them three new howboyes and one treble recordour and x li. to beare their chardgys. And that the citie shall hyer the wagon and paye for it. Also that the Chamberleyn shall paye Peter Spratt x s. for a saquebutt case, and the waytes to delyver to the Chamberleyn before they go the cities cheanes.

'THE FATHER OF ENGLISH MUSIC'

William Byrd (1543–1623) excelled in writing Church music, to both English and Latin words, madrigals, and music for strings and for the new keyboard instruments of the time. Here he suggests many reasons why everyone should learn to sing.

Source: Psalms, Sonnets and songs of sadness and pietie, 1588.

First, it is a knowledge easely taught, and quickly learned, where there is a good Master, and an apt Scoler.

2. The exercise of singing is delightfule to Nature, & good to preserue the health of Man.

3. It doth strengthen all parts of the brest, & doth open the pipes.

4. It is a singuler good remedie for a stutting & stamaring in the speech.

5. It is the best meanes to procure a perfect pronunciation, & to make a good Orator.

6. It is the onely way to know where Nature hath bestowed the benefit of a good voyce: which guift is so rare, as there is not one among a thousand, that hath it: and in many, that excellent guift is lost, because they want Art to expresse Nature.

7. There is not any Musicke of Instruments whatsoeuer, comparable to that which is made of the voyces of Men, where the voyces are good, and the same well sorted and ordered.

8. The better the voyce is, the meeter it is to honour and serue God therewith: and the voyce of man is chiefley to be imployed to that ende.

Omnis spiritus laudet Dominum.

> Since singing is so good a thing,
> I wish all men would learne to sing.

AN IMAGINARY DIALOGUE ABOUT MUSIC

Guests were expected to take their music with them, and music-making was the normal way of passing an evening with friends. In this imaginary dialogue about music, Philomathes (a lover of learning) admits with shame to his prother Polymathes (who is widely learned) that an ignorance of music is a serious social handicap.

Source: Thomas Morley, *A Plaine and Easie Introduction to Practicall Musicke,* 1597.

Poly. I praie you repeat some of the discourses which you had yester night at master Sophobulus his banket: For commonly he is not without both wise and learned guestes.

Phil. It is true in deede. And yester night, there were a number of excellent schollers, (both gentlemen and others:) but all the propose which then was discoursed upon, was Musicke.

Poly. I trust you were contented to suffer others to speake of that matter.

Phil. I would that had been the worst: for I was compelled to discover mine own ignorance, and confesse that I knewe nothing at all in it.

Poly. How so?

Phil. Among the rest of the guests, by chance, master Aphron came thether also, who falling to discourse of Musicke, was in an argument so quickely taken up & hotly pursued by Eudoxus and Calergus, two kinsmen of Sophobulus, as in his owne art he was overthrowne. But he still sticking in his opinion, the two gentlemen requested mee to examine his reasons, and confute them. But I refusing & pretending ignorance, the whole companie condemned mee of discurtesie, being fully perswaded, that I had beene as skilfull in that art, as they tooke mee to be learned in others. But supper being ended, and Musicke bookes, according to the custome being brought to the table: the mistresse of the house presented mee with a part, earnestly requesting mee to sing. But when after manie excuses, I protested unfainedly that I could not: everie one began to wonder. Yea, some whispered to others, demaunding how I was brought up: so that upon shame of mine ignorance I go nowe to seeke out mine old frinde master Gnorimus, to make my selfe his scholler.

The Elizabethan love of madrigal singing gradually gave place to a taste for instrumental music, and in musical gatherings concerts of viols came to replace those of voices only. The lute, which became the fashionable instrument for playing an accompaniment, was an expensive instrument. One writer of the time said it cost as much as a horse to keep because the wood was always breaking under the strain of the strings. Strings were so expensive that they were often given as presents, so the proper care of one's lute was important.

CARE OF A LUTE

Source: Thomas Mace, *Musick's Monument,* 1676.

. . . how to shelter your Lute in the worst weathers, (which is moist) you shall do well, ever when you Lay it by in the day-time, to put It into a Bed, that is constantly used, between the Rug and the Blanket; but never between the sheets, because they may be moist with Sweat, etc. . . . only to be excepted, That no Person be so inconsiderate, as to Tumble down upon the Bed whilst the Lute is There; For I have known several Good Lutes spoil'd with such a Trick.

A DIALOGUE BETWEEN THE AUTHOR AND HIS LUTE

Author. What makes thee sit so sad, my Noble Friend,
　　　　　As if thou wert (with sorrows) near Thy End?
　　　　　What is the Cause, my Dear-Renowned-Lute,
　　　　　Thou art of late so silent, and so mute?
　　　　　Thou seldom dost in Publick now appear;
　　　　　Thou art too Melancholly grown I fear.

Lute. What need you ask These Questions why 'tis so?
　　　　　Since 'tis too obvious for All men to know.
　　　　　The World is grown so Slight; full of New Fangles,
　　　　　And takes their Chief Delight in Jingle-Jangles:
　　　　　With fiddle-noises: Pipes of Bartholomew,
　　　　　Like those which Country-Wives buy, Gay and New,
　　　　　To please their Little Children when they Cry:
　　　　　This makes me sit and Sigh thus Mournfully.

PLATE 13

Two sisters and their babies

PLATE 14

Monumental brass of Edward Younge and family. Notice the large number of children

A MUSIC-PARTY.

THE IMPORTANCE OF MUSIC IN EDUCATION

Source: Thomas Mace, *Musick's Monument*, 1676.

Wheresoever you send your children to School, (I mean to the Grammar-School) indent so with the Master, that your children shall be taught one hour every day to sing, or one half day in every week at least, either by himself, or by some Musick-Master whom he should procure.

HOW TO GET AN ORGAN
FOR YOUR CHURCH

Source: Thomas Mace, *Musick's Monument*, 1676.

I would have you propose to yourselves some very great and urgent occasion, or necessity for a speedy raising of a sum of Money, supposing such an one as this: viz. the Parliament has made a great Tax to run quite through the Nation, such an one as . . . the Chimney-money; and it must be paid in presently, without any contradiction or delay.

This I know you would most certainly prepare to do, without accounting it impossible.

Now I say, do but suppose this, or some such like thing, and presently go about getting up the money, every man his share, and lay it by for that use, till your Organ be ready, and you will soon see it set up in your Parish Church.

VIOLS OR VIOLINS?

Music of all types continued to hold a large place in the life of the community during the Commonwealth. Puritans varied widely one from another in their religious beliefs, but all believed that God must be the centre of life and thought. It was for this reason that organs were removed from churches and that theatres were closed, but there was no fundamental opposition to the arts, including music.

Music was one of Cromwell's favourite recreations, and at the wedding of his daughter at Whitehall in 1657 there was music played by forty-eight violins, and mixed dancing.

John Evelyn, the diarist, did not like it when, in 1662, violins were used in church 'after ye French fantastical light way' to assist the organ, instead of 'ye ancient, grave and solemn wind music'. Such a custom, he wrote, was 'better suiting a tavern or a playhouse than a church'. Another writer comments on this development:

Source: Life and Times of Anthony Wood, antiquary, of Oxford, 1632–1695, described by Himself.

Jan. 1657. The gentlemen in privat meetings which A.W frequented, play'd three, four and five parts all with viols, as treble-viol, tenor, counter-tenor and bass, with either an organ or virginal or harpsicon joyn'd with them: and they esteemed a violin to be an instrument only belonging to a common fidler, and could not indure that it should come among them for feare of making their meetings seem to be vaine and fiddling. But before the restoration of K. Charles 2 and especially after, viols began to be out of fashion, and only violins used, as treble-violin, tenor and bass-violin; and the king according to the French mode would have 24 violins playing before him, while he was at meales, as being more airie and brisk than viols.

PLAYING THE VIOL.

MUSIC IN PEPYS' TIME

Source: Pepys's Diary.

Jan. 16th, 1660. . . . we went to the Green Dragon, . . . and there we sang of all sorts of things, and I ventured with good success upon things at first sight; and after that I played on my flageolet, and staid there till nine o'clock, very merry and drawn on with one song after another till it came to be so late. . . .

Nov. 21st, 1660. . . . at night to my viallin (the first time that I have played on it since I came to this house) in my dining room, and afterwards to my lute there, and I took much pleasure to have the neighbours come forth into the yard to hear me. . . .

April 24th, 1663. . . . all the afternoon fiddling upon my viallin (which I have not done many a day) while Ashwell danced, above in my upper best chamber, which is a rare room for musique.

May 5th, 1666. . . . About 11 I home, it being a fine moonshine and so my wife and Mercer come into the garden, and, my business being done, we sang till about twelve at night, with mighty pleasure to ourselves and neighbours, by their casements opening, and so home to supper and to bed.

July 22nd, 1663. To my brother Tom's barber and had my hair cut, while his boy played on the viallin, a plain boy, but has a very good genius. . . .

Jan. 13th, 1662. . . . Mr. Berkenshaw . . . staid with me a great while talking of musique, and I am resolved to begin to learn of him to compose, and to begin tomorrow, he giving of me so great hopes that I shall soon do it. . . .

March 24th, 1662. Long with Mr. Berkenshaw in the morning at my musique practice, finishing my song of 'Gaze not on Swans', in two parts, which pleases me well, and I did give him £5 for this month or five weeks that he hath taught me, which is a great deal of money and troubleth me to part with it.

Sept. 2nd, 1666. . . . I observed that hardly one lighter or boat in three that had the goods of a house in, but there was a pair of Virginalls in it.

PUBLICK CONSORTS

Towards the end of the seventeenth century communal domestic music-making was beginning to give place to more formal performance —public concerts and operas were becoming fashionable. The few specialized performers with a large audience replaced the traditional spontaneous creation of music.

Source: Roger North, *Memoirs of Musick.*

The first of those was in a lane behind Pauls, where there was a chamber organ that one Phillips played upon, and some shopkeepers, and foremen came weekly to sing in consort, and to hear and enjoy ale and tobacco; . . . and their musick was chiefly out of Playford's Catch book. (Catch that catch can, or a choice Collection of Catches, Rounds, and Canons, for 3 or 4 Voyces.)

The next essay was of the elder Banister, . . . He procured a large room in Whitefryars near the Temple back gate, and made a large raised box for the musicians, whose modesty required curtaines. The room was rounded with seats and small tables, alehouse fashion. One shilling was the price, and call for what you pleased; there was very good musick, for Banister found means to procure the best hands in towne and some voices to come and perform there, and there wanted no variety of humour, for Banister himself did wonders upon a flageolet to a thro' bass, and the several masters had their solos. This continued full one winter, and more I remember not.

OPERA

Source: Roger North, *Memoirs of Musick.*

It had been strange if the gentlemen of the theaters had sate still all this while, seeing . . . a violent inclination in the towne to follow musick, and they not serve themselves of it. Therefore Mr. Betterton, . . . contrived a sort of plays, which were called Operas, but had been more properly styled Semi-operas, for they consisted of half musick, and half drama. . . . But nothing advanced musick more in this age then the patronage of the nobility, and men of fortunes, . . .

CHAPTER XI

PAINTING

Renaissance influence brought to England a new worldliness and an interest in luxurious decoration. With the accession of Henry VII Italian painters and sculptors began to be attracted to the English court, and much of what was produced in England was the work of foreigners. The Reformation excluded all church art and disapproved of sensuous painting, so for a long time portraiture was the only acceptable form of painting. Portrait painting was just a craft among other crafts, and a skilled portraitist had to spend much of his time on heraldic ornamentation, on book embellishment, and on decorations for royal revels and processions.

Holbein was of such a remarkable status that attention has tended to be drawn away from all his contemporaries: Eworth and Gheeraerts were fashionable portraitists. Miniature painting, called 'limning' reached an astonishingly high standard in the work of Nicholas Hilliard and his pupil Isaac Oliver.

In the seventeenth century foreign painters were still predominant in England. Rubens and Van Dyck introduced the baroque style of portraiture, while Samuel Cooper continued the tradition of miniature painting.

LIMNING

Source: Nicholas Hilliard, *A Treatise concerning the Arte of Limning* 1624.

... I wish it weare so that none should medle with limning but gentelmen alone, for that it is a kind of gentill painting of lesse subjection then any other; for one may leave when hee will, his coullers nor his work taketh any harme by it. Morover it is secreet, a man may usse it and scarsly be perseaved of his owne folke; it is sweet and cleanly to usse, and it is a thing apart from all other painting or drawing, and tendeth not to comon mens usse, either for furnishing of howsses or any patterns for tapistries, or building, or any other worke whatsoever, and yet it excelleth all other painting whatsoever in sondry points, in giving the true lustur to pearle and precious stone, and worketh

the metals gold or silver with themselfes, which so enricheth
and innobleth the worke that it seemeth to be the thinge itselfe.
. . .

. . . and as for an naturall
aptnes of or to painting after
the liffe, thosse surly which
have such a guift of God
ought to rejoyce with humble thankfulnes, and to be
very wary and temperat in
diet and other government,
least it be sone taken from
them againe by some sudaine
mischance, or by their evell
coustomes their sight or
stedines of hand decay.

Then this exortation give I more that he be diligent, yea
ever diligent, and put his whole uttermost and best endeavors
to excell all other, for a stronge man that putteth not forth his
strength is often foyled by weaker, and the most perfect and
cuningest must doe the same diligence, or rather more, to effect
and performe his worke then hee did at the first in larninge.
For it cannot be sayd that a man, be he never so cunning by teaching or naturall inclination, yet it will growe out of him as haire
out of the head, or fall from him, whether he will or no, but with
great labour, and this comfort shall he have then above others,
even an heaven of joy in his hart to behould his own well doings
remaining to his credit for ever. Yea if men of worth did knowe
what delight it breedeth, how it removeth mallancoly, avodeth
evell occasions, putteth passions of sorrowe or greefe awaye,
cureth rage, and shortneth the times, they would never leave
till they had attained in some good meassur a more then comfort.
. . .
Heer must I needs incert a word or two in honore and praisse of
the renowned and mighty King Henry the eight, a prince of

exquisit judgment and royall bounty, soe that of cuning stranger even the best resorted unto him and removed from other courts to his, amongst whom came the most excelent painter and limner Haunce Holbean, the greatest master truly in both thosse arts after the liffe that ever was, so cuning in both together, and the neatest; and therewithall a good inventor, soe compleat for all three as I never heard of any better then hee. . . .

. . . as breefly and as plainly as I can, concerning the best waye and meanes to practice and ataine to skill in limning; in a word befor I exhorted such to temperance, I meane sleepe not much, wacth not much, eat not much, sit not long, usse not violent excersize in sports, nor earnest for your recreation, but dancing or bowling, or littel of either.

Then the fierst and cheefest precepts which I give is cleanlynes, and therfor fittest for gentlemen, that the practicer of limning be presizly pure and klenly in all his doings, as in grinding his coulers in place wher ther is neither dust nor smoake, the watter wel chossen or distilled most pure, as the watter distilled frome the watter of some clear spring, or frome black cherize, which is the cleanest that ever I could find, and keepeth longest sweet and cleare, the goume to be goume aarabeeke of the whitest and brittlest, broken into whit powder on a faire and cleare grinding stone, and whit sugar candy in like sort to be keept dry in boxes of ivory, the grinding-stone of fine cristall, serpentine, jasper or hard porfory; at the least let your aparell be silke, such as sheadeth lest dust or haires, weare nothing straight, beware you tuch not your worke with your fingers, or any hard thing, but with a cleane pencel brush it, or with a whit feather, neither breath on it, especially in could weather, take heed of the dandrawe of the head sheading from the haire, and of speaking over your worke. . . .

The second Rulle is much like the first, and conserning the light and place wher you worke in. Let your light be northward somewhat toward the east, which comonly is without sune shininge in; one only light, great and faire let it be, and without mpeachment or reflections of walls or trees, a free sky light, the dieper the window and farer the better, and no by-window, but a cleare story in a place wher neither dust, smoak, noisse nor steanche may ofend. A good painter hath tender sences, quiet and apt, and the culers themsellves may not endure some ayers, especially in the sulfirous ayre of seacole and the guilding of gowldsmithes; sweet odors comforteth the braine and openeth the understanding, augmenting the delight in limning. Discret talke or reading, quiet merth or musike ofendeth not, but short-neth the time and quickneth the sperit, both in the drawer and he which is drawne; also in any wisse avoyd anger, shut out questioners or busi fingers. . . .

Knowe also that parchment is the only good and best thinge to limne on, . . . It must be most finly drest, as smothe as any sattine, and pasted with starch well strained on pastbourd well burnished, that it maye be pure without speckes or staynes, very smoothe and white. . . .

When your cullors are drye in the shell you are to temper them with your ringe finger very cleane when you will usse therof, adding a littel gume if it temper not well and flowingly, but beware of to much; if any cullor crack to much in the shell, temper therwith a littele sugar candye, but a very littel, least it make it shine. . . . If a cullor will not take by reason that some sweaty hand or fattye finger hath touched your parchment therabout, temper with that cullor a very littel eare waxe, . . . Liqued goolde and sillver must not be tempered with the finger but only with the penssel, and with as little gume as will but bind it that it wype not of with every touch, and with a pretty little toothe of some ferret or stote or other willde little beast.

CHAPTER XII

RELIGION

Freedom of thought or of worship had never been permitted and but rarely sought when the Medieval Church ruled men's lives. The ecclesiastical authorities, Papal and English, were dictatorial and rigidly conservative, enjoying wealth and power and forbidding any doubts or criticism in matters of religious belief and practice.

Yet sceptics there must always have been and the stirring of new thought and learning during the fifteenth century caused a significant number of people to question accepted doctrine. These heretics were hunted down ruthlessly and, if possible, made to recant.

HERETICS

Source: Kingsford's *Chronicles of London.*

28*th April*, 1494. Also this yere, the 28th day of Aprill was brent in Smythfield an old woman, . . . called Johan Bowghton, which

BURNING A HERETIC.

was there brent for many heresies to the number of ix Articles of heresy. And never wold turne from the said heresies for noon exortacion, but in the said false and heronyous opynyons dyed.

May 1498. This yere in the begynnyng of Maii, the kyng beyng at Canterbury, was brent an heretyk, a prest, which by the kynges exortacion before his deth was convertyd from his erowys opynyons, and died a Christen man; wherof his grace gate grete honour.

16*th June*, 1499. This yere, the Sonday beyng the xvj day of Jun., stode at the Crosse of Powlis iiij heritikes beryng ffagottes; and upon the next Sonday folowyng stode there viij herytykes, which were all brent upon the left cheke, and upon their garmentes or gownes was set a Rede Crosse and á Brawderid ffagot, which said crosse and ffagot they were enjoyned to were all the tyme of their lyves upon payne of goyng to the fyre yf they were founde without the said conysaunce.

THE RECANTATION OF STEPHEN SWALLOW
3 JULY 1489

Source: Literae Cantuariensis, Rolls Ser., iii, 312.

In the name of God. Amen. By fore you moost reverend fadir in God, John by the grace of the same Archiebisshop of Caunterbury, of all England Primate, and of the Apostolique See Legate, I, Stephyn Swallow, layman, of the parisshe of Wyly in the diocese of London, of my pure hert and fre will, confesse and knowlege that I in tyme passid be fore this houre, that is to witt by the space of xxx yeres and moore, of the sacraments of the Churche and of the articules of the feith have otherwyse belevid, felid, holden, affermyd, and taughte, than the seid holy Churche of Rome and Universall Church of God techith, holdyth, and observyth; and many and divers open and damned errours and heresies, contrary to the trew Catholique feith and determinacion of Holy Churche, I have bothe secretly and openly holden, affermyd, and taughte, and among other errours and heresies folowyng, that is to witt: That in the sacrament of the Auter remaynyth the substaunce of materiall brede and in like wyse of wyne after the consecracion, and that Crist is not in the same sacrament realy in his owne bodely presence, and so in the sacrament is not the very body of Crist. Also that baptime, confirmacion, orders, penaunce, matrimony, and all sacraments of the Churche be voyde and of none effect. Also that the sacrament of baptyme is not necessary to the salvacion of a childe borne betwene a Cristen man and a Cristen woman, nor he nedeth not to be cristenid. Also that the sowle of a childe borne ded is as good as the sowle of a childe levyng cristenid. Also if a man be contrite in his hert, and make his confession secretely and inwardly to God, that than all outward confession by mowth is superflue and unprofitabill. Also that the Pope is a old hoore, sittyng upon many waters, havyng a cuppe of poyson in his hande. Also that the Pope is Antecrist, and all Cardinalls, Archebisshoppes, Bisshoppis, Prests, and Religious men be the disciples of Antecrist. Also that pardon grantid by the Pope, Cardinallis, Archebisshoppes, or Bisshoppis, avaylyth not mannys sowle; for the soule of a man or woman immediatly after it is departid oute of the body goith forth with unto Hevyn or to Helle, for there is no Purgatory. Also that the Churche of Rome is the Sinagoge of Sathan, and the Pope is not the Vicar of Crist. Also that if Archebisshop, Bisshop, or Prest, be in dedely synne, he hath no power to consecrate, to cristen, nor to minystre any other sacrament. Wherfore I Stephyn aforseid, confessyng and knowyng my self a miserable synner, and grevously to have synned in this behalf, and from the wey of errowr and derknes retornyng and comyng ayene to the wey and light of trouthe and to the unyte of Holy Churche, all the aboveseid errours and heresies and everych of thaym, and alle other heresies, and all other dampned opinions contrary and repugnant to the true Catholik feith and determinacion of Holy Churche beforeseid, revoke, renounce, and by the Holy Trinite and these Holy Evaungeles of God, openly and solemnly abjure; and ovir this of pure hert and not feynid, submittyng me to the correction of Holy Churche, and mekely askyng mercy and grace, in like manner promitt and swere that all suche penaunce and satisfaction as shalbe enjoyned to me by you or by your commaundement, by reason or occasion of my seid excesse and offense, I shall doo and performe obediently and effectually and that from this hour afterward I shall never favour in any wyse suche errours or heresies, or eny other, nor no persone being to my knowlege an heretike or suspect of heresy. And if it happen hereafter, which God defende, me to doo contrary to this myne abjuracion, promise, and othe, I submitt me to the rigour and severite of the Holy constitucions and lawes of the Churche; and in to feyth and witnesse of these premisses I make the signe of the crosse †.

USE OF THE MASS

Here is a letter from the Princess Mary to King Edward the Sixth upon receiving the prohibition to use the Mass in her household,

My dutye moste humbly remembred unto your Majestie. It maye please the same to be advertysed that I have by my servantes receaved your moste honorable Letter, the contentes wherof doe not a litle trouble me, and so much the more for that any of my servants should move or attempte me in matteres towching my sowle, which I thinke the meaneste subjecte within your Realme could evell beare at their servantes hande; havinge for my parte utterly refused heretofor to talke with them in such matteres, and of all other persones leaste regarded them therein; to whom I have declared what I thinke as she which trusted that your Majestie would have suffered me your poore humble sister and beadeswoman to have used the accustomed Masse, which the Kinge your father and myne with all his predecessores evermore used; wherin also I have been brought upp from my youth, and therunto my conscyence doth not only bynde me, which by noe meanes will suffer me to thinke one thing and do another, but also the promise made to the Emperore by your Majesties Counsell was an assurance to me that in so doinge I should not offend the Lawes, although they seeme now to quallefye and deny the thing.

And at my laste waytinge upon your Majestie I was so bould to declare my mynd and conscyence to the same, and desired your Highnes, rather then you should constraine me to leave the Masse, to take my life, whereunto your Majestie made me a very gentle answere. . . .

Your Majestie's moste

humble sistere

Mary.

SUPERSTITION

Superstition was also rife, witchcraft a power in the land, and their horrible persecution, encouraged by James I and his Parliament, reached a peak in the early years of the seventeenth century. It only receded when, in the Restoration era, the clergy and more rational governing classes became sceptical of the existence of witches. Judges on Circuit, who in previous reigns had encouraged panic and superstition, began to expose flimsy evidence and to obtain acquittals of suspected witches.

Source: A letter to Lord Cromwell from Elis Price, to know what he should do with the Image of Darvell Gathern. 1538.

That there ys an Image of Darvellgadarn, in whome the people have so greate confidence, hope, and truste, that they cumme dayly a pillgramage unto hym, somme withe kyne, other with oxen or horsis, and the reste withe money: in so muche that there was fyve or syxe hundrethe pillgrames . . . that offered to the saide Image the fifte daie of this presente monethe of Aprill. The innocente people hathe ben sore aluryd and entisid to worshipe the saide Image, in so muche that there is a commyn sayinge as yet amongist them that who so ever will offer anie thinge to the saide Image of Darvellgadern, he hathe power to fatche hym or them that so offers oute of Hell when they be dampned. . . .
Writen in Northe Wales the vj. daye of this presente Aprill

Your bedman and dayelie

orator by dutie

Elis Price.

Source: The Autobiography of Thomas Whythorne, c. 1576. Ed. J. M. Osborn, 1961.

. . . concerning the temptors, the Devils I mean who will not omit anything that may work unto man's destruction, it is not one devil only that doth it, but it is divers and especially seven of them. They be accounted and named the seven principal or captain devils, because they have always borne a great sway amongst men. The first is called Lucifer, the devil of pride and presumption. The second is called Belzebub, the lord of envy and malice. The third is called Sathan, the master of wrath and disdain. The fourth is called Abadan, who is the patron of sloth and idleness. The fifth is named Mammon, who is the father of covetousness and snudgery (i.e. miserliness). The sixth is named Belphegor, the God of gluttony and drunkeness. And the seventh is called Asmodius, the ruler of lechery and whoredom. And whosoever is infected with any of the said vices, be sure he is possessed with a great captain devil, which must of necessity be cast out, or else of force the man must perish. These in the time of our trouble, grief or sickness, and especially Sathan, . . . will put into our minds all that he may, to have a mistrust in our good God, and that we be not of the number of those that be predestinate and elect to be saved, so will he present unto us whatsoever we have done and committed against the commandments of God, and will put into our minds huge mountains, as it were, of sins, that by the outrageousness and greatness of them he may bring us into desparation, which do stagger and doubt of Gods mercy and pardon.

WITCHCRAFT

Source: Newes from Scotland, 1591.

Within the town of Trenent, in . . . Scotland, there dwelleth one David Seaton, who . . . had a maid called Geillis Duncane, who used secretly to absent and lie forth of her master's house every other night. This Geillis Duncane took in hand to help all such as were troubled or grieved with any kind of sickness or infirmity, and in short space did perform many matters most miraculous; which things, for as much as she began to do them upon a sudden, having never done the like before, made her master and others to be in great admiration, and wondered thereat: by means whereof, the said David Seaton had his maid in great suspicion that she did not those things by natural and lawful ways, but rather supposed it to be done by some extraordinary and unlawful means. Whereupon, her master began to grow very inquisitive, and examined her which way and by what means she was able to perform matters of so great importance; whereat she gave him no answer. Nevertheless, her master, to the intent that he might the better try and find out the truth of the same, did with the

Title-page of Gerard's 'Herball'—an illustrated book about plants. Notice the formal garden

PLATE 16

Woodcarving of a joiner's shop. One man is planing, the other is turning a table leg on the lathe

help of others torment her with the torture of the pilliwinks upon her fingers, which is a grievous torture; and binding or wrenching her head with a cord or rope, which is a most cruel torment also; yet would she not confess anything; whereupon, they suspecting that she had been marked by the devil (as commonly witches are) made diligent search about her, and found the enemy's mark . . . in the forepart of her throat; which being found, she confessed that all her doings were done by the wicked allurements and enticements of the devil, and that she did them by witchcraft. . . . She confessed that she took a black toad, and did hang the same up by the heels three days, and collected and gathered the venom as it dropped and fell from it in an oyster shell, and kept the same venom close covered, until she should obtain any part or piece of foul linen cloth that had appertained to the King's Majesty, . . . and she saith, that if she had obtained any . . . piece of linen cloth which the King had worn or fouled, she had bewitched him to death, and put him to such extraordinary pains, as if he had been lying upon sharp thorns and ends of needles.

PURITANS

Tolerance in religious matters was of slow growth. The Established Church followed in the footsteps of the Medieval and was equally intolerant. Subsequently many bewildering changes in the form of religion were prescribed by successive governments. Persecution, by both Protestants and Catholics, caused a deepening of the belief in many people's minds in the importance of individual judgment and conscience in matters of religion.

Many members of the Established Church began to criticize its tenets and to demand 'purification' of authoritarian, imposed views. Thus they were called 'Puritans', but not until the seventeenth century did the more extreme among them begin to form sects outside the Church and, in desperation, to emigrate in search of freedom of thought and worship.

English Protestants, who had long ceased to expect miracles from God, also by the end of the seventeenth century ceased to expect them from the Devil. It was the beginning of the idea that the Universe and everything in it was subject to laws that could be understood but not altered.

Source: Paul Hentzner, *Travels in England,* 1598.

. . . there is a certain sect in England, called Puritans: these, according to the doctrine of the church of Geneva, reject all

K

ceremonies antiently held, and admit of neither organs nor tombs in their places of worship, and entirely abhor all difference in rank among churchmen, such as bishops, deans, &c. they were first named Puritans by the Jesuit Sandys. They do not live separate, but mix with those of the church of England in the colleges.

DISSENTERS

Source: The Journeys of Celia Fiennes, in 1697 *and* 1698.

The town (Scarborough) has abundance of Quakers in it, most of their best Lodgings were in Quakers hands, they entertain all people soe in Private houses in the town, by way of ordinary, so much a Meale, and their Ale every one finds themselves, there are a few Inns for horses only. I was at a Quakers Meeting in the town where 4 men and 2 women spoke, one after another had done but it seem'd such a confusion and so incoherent that it very much moved my compassion and pitty to see their delusion and ignorance, and no less excited my thankfullness for the Grace of God that upheld others from such Errors; I observ'd their prayers were all made on the first person and single, tho before the body of people, it seems they allow not of ones being the mouth of the rest in prayer to God tho' it be in the publick meetings; . . .

(Cullompton) . . . here was a large Meeteing of neer 4 or 500 people, they have a very good Minister but a young man, I was glad to see soe many tho' they were but of the meaner sort, for indeed its the poor receive the Gospell, and there are in most of the market towns in the West very good Meetings; this little place was one continued long streete, but few houses that struck out of the streete.

Ashburton is a poor little town, bad was the best Inn; its a Market town and here are a great many Descenters and those of the most considerable persons in the town, there was a Presbiterian an Anabaptist and Quakers meeting.

UPON THE SACRAMENTS

Source: John Bunyan, *Book for Boys and Girls*, 1686.

Two sacraments I do believe there be,
Baptism and the Supper of the Lord:
Both Mysteries divine, which do to me,
By Gods appointment, benefit afford:
But shall they be my God? or shall I have
Of them so foul and impious a Thought,
To think that from the Curse they can me save?
Bread, Wine, nor Water me no ransom bought.

RELIGIOUS TOLERATION

Source: E. Chamberlayne, *Angliae Notitia, or the Present State of England*, 1687.

Even since the beginning of our Reformation, there are some few families in several parts of England, have persisted in the Romish Religion, and are usually called Papists from Papa, the old usual name of the Bishop of Rome. Against these there are divers severe Laws still in force, but their number being not considerable, nor their Loyalty for many years last past questionable, those Laws have been more rarely put in execution; besides the clemency and gentle usage shewn to them here, begets in Romish States and Potentates abroad, the like gentle treatment of their Protestant Subjects, and of the English, living within their Dominions.

OLIVER CROMWELL ON RELIGIOUS TOLERATION

Source: Cromwell's Speech to the Second Protectorate Parliament, 17th Sept., 1656.

. . . I will tell you the truth: our practice since the last Parliament hath been, to let all this nation see that whatsoever pretensions to religion would continue quiet, peaceable, they should enjoy conscience and liberty to themselves;—and not make religion a pretence for arms and blood, truly we have suffered them, and that cheerfully, so to enjoy their own liberties. . . .

CHAPTER XIII

THE REFORMATION

The unity which the Roman Catholic Church had given to medieval Europe had worn thin by the late fifteenth century, as the laity became better educated and reading and thought extended mental horizons. Unity was shattered in the early sixteenth century by the exposures of Erasmus and the protests of Martin Luther and in England political differences between the King and the Pope aggravated an already critical situation.

Henry VIII summoned the Reformation Parliament in 1529, and over the next seven years passed a series of Acts destroying Papal authority in England. The monasteries remained the last stronghold of papal power and Thomas Cromwell and the King, between them, planned their destruction, which was carried out between 1536 and 1539.

Reactions to the confiscation of church property varied considerably. Wales and the northern counties were strongholds of conservatism and were conveniently further from London observers. In those areas royal commissioners often had to try to carry out their instructions against determined local opposition. In other areas there were fanatics only too ready to destroy things they disliked.

LETTERS TO LORD CROMWELL

Source: A letter from Dr. John London, one of the Visitors of Religious Houses, to Lord Cromwell. 1537.

. . . I have pullyd down the Image of our Ladye at Caversham wherunto wasse great pilgremage. The Image ys platyd over with sylver, and I have putte yt in a cheste fast locked and naylyd uppe, and by the next bardge that commythe from Reding to London yt shall be browght to your Lordeschippe. I have also pullyd down the place she stode in with all other ceremonyes, as lights, . . . , crosses, and imagies of wax hangyng abowt the chapel, and have defacyed the same thorowly. . . . Thys chapell dydde belong to Notley Abbey, and ther always wasse a chanon of that monastery wiche wasse callyd the Warden of Caversham, and he songe in thys chapell and hadde the offerings for hys lyving. He wasse acustomyd to schew many prety relyks, . . . All theese with many other, with the cots of thys image, her cappe and hair, my servant shall bring unto your Lordeshippe thys weke with the Surrendre of the Freers undre ther covent seale, . . . I have sent the chanon home agen to Notleye, and have made fast the doores of the chapell, wiche ys thorowly well covered with ledde: and if it be your Lordeships pleasur I shall se yt made suer to the Kings Grace's use. And if it be nott so orderyd, the chapell stondith so wildely that the ledde will be stolyn by night. . . . At Redinge xvij. Septembris.

At Caversham ys a propre lodginge wher the chanon lay, with a fayer garden and an orcherd mete to be bestowed upon som frynde of your lordeschips in thees parties; . . .

I beseech your gudde Lordeschippe to admytt me a poor suitor for thees honest men of Redinge. They have a fayer town and many gudde occupiers in ytt; butt they lacke that howse necessary, of the wiche for the mynystration of Justice thay have most nede of. Ther Town Hall ys a very small Howse and stondith upon the ryver, wher ys the commyn wasching place of the most part of the Town; and in the session dayes and other cowrt dayes ther ys such betyng with batildores, as oon man can nott here another, . . . The body of the Church of the Grey fryers, wiche ys selyd with laths and lyme, wold be a very commodoise rowme for them. . . .

Source: A letter from the Inhabitants of the Lordship of Holm Cultram in Cumberland, to Lord Cromwell, entreating for the preservation of the Abbey Church there. 1538.

Too the right honorable, ande our singler good Lorde mye Lord Prevye Seale.

Mooste humbly besechith your honorable Lordship, your poore Orators and Beedemen, beynge eightene hundred houselynge people[1] . . . th'Inhabitants of Holme Coltrane . . ., that it might please your Lordship to be a meane for us to our Soveraign Lorde the Kynge is Highenes for the preservacion and standynge of the Churche of Holme Coltrane before saide; whiche is not onelye unto us our parish Churche, and little ynoughe to receyve all us your poore Orators, but also a grete ayde, socor, and defence

[1] persons of age to communicate at the altar.

for us ayenst our neighbors the Scotts, withe out the whiche few
or none of your Lordshipps supplyants are able to do the King
is saide Hieghnes our bounden duetye ande service. . . .

Your humble and poore beedemen
th'inhabitants of the Lordship
of Holme Coltram.

Source: A letter from Edmund Knightley and three other Commissioners, to Secretary Cromwell, in favor of the Nunnery of Catesby
in Northamptonshire.

Right honorable after all humble recommendations theis shalbe
to advertyse you that we have byn yn execution of the Kyngs
Commission directed unto us, begynnyng at Chacumbe, wher we
accomplished all thyngs accordyng unto our Commyssion, and
frome thens we repayred to Assheby, where after on days tarreyng
we werre fayne to departe thens unto Catesby Nunrey by occasion
of sykenesse where we have also accomplisshed the Kyngs
Commyssion accordyng to his high commandement and our poore
discrecions. Which Howse of Catesby we founde in very perfett
order, the Priores a sure wyse, discrete, and very relygious woman,
with ix nunnys under her obedyencye, as religious and devoute,
and with as good obedyncye as we have in tyme past
seen, or belyke shall see. The seid Howse standyth in suech a
quarter, muche to the releff of the Kyngs people, and his Grace's
pore subjects their lykewyse mooe releved, as by the reporte
of dyvers worshypfull nere ther unto adjoynyng, as of all other,
yt ys to us openly declared. Wherfore yf yt shulde please the
Kyngs Highnesse to have eny remorse that eny suche relygous
House shall stande, we thynke his Grace cannot appoynt eny
House more mete to shew his most gracious charitie and pitey
on than on the seid Howse of Catesby. Ferther ye shall understande that as to her bounden dewtye towards the Kyngs Highnes
in theis his affayres, also for dyscrete entertaynment of us his
commyssioners and our company, we have not fownde nor
belyke shall fynde eny suche of more dyscretion. And lese
peraventure theyr may be labor made to her detryment and other
undoyng, before knowleg showlde cume to his Highnesse and
to yow frome us, yt may therfore plase yow to sygnify unto his

hyghnesse the effecte of theis our Letters, to th'entent his Grace may stay the Graunte theyrof tyll suche tyme we may ascerteyn yow of our full certyfycat and comparts in that behalfe accordyng. Frome Catesby the xij day off this present moneth off May, from the Kyngs Commyssioners at your commandement.

Edmond Knyghtley.   John Lane.   George Gyffard.
Robert Burgoyn.

DEMOLITION OF A CHURCH

Joseph Hall, Bishop of Norwich, wrote an account of the persecution of the Bishops by Parliament which gives a picture of the ungovernable fury of the Puritan iconoclasts. Here he describes in vivid terms the actual demolition of a cathedral church:

Source: Hard Measure, by Joseph Hall. 1647.

. . . There was not care and moderation used in reforming the cathedral church bordering upon my palace. It is no other than tragical to relate the carriage of that furious sacrilege, whereof our eyes and ears were the sad witnesses, under the authority and presence of Linsey, Tofts the sheriff, and Greenwood. Lord, what work was here, what clattering of glasses, what beating down of walls, what tearing up of monuments, what pulling down of seats, what wresting out of irons and brass from the windows and graves, what defacing of arms, what demolishing of curious stone work, that had not any representation in the world, but only the cost of the founder, and skill of the mason, what toting and piping upon the destroyed organ pipes, and what a hideous triumph on the market day before all the country, when, in a kind of sacrilegious and profane procession, all the organ pipes, vestments, both copes and surplices, together with the leaden cross, which had been newly sawn down from over the green yard pulpit, and the service books and singing books that could be had were carried to the fire in the public market-place; a lewd wretch walking before the train, in his cope, trailing in the dirt, with a service book in his hand, imitating, in an impious scorn, the tune, and usurping the words of the Litany, used formerly in the church; near the public cross all these monuments of idolatry must be sacrificed to the fire, not without much ostentation of a zealous joy in discharging ordnance to the cost of some who professed how much they had longed to see that day. Neither was it any news, upon this Guild day, to have the cathedral now open on all sides to be filled with musketeers, waiting for the major's return, drinking and tobaccoing as freely as if it had turned alehouse.

AN ACT AGAINST SUPERSTITION, 1550

And be it further enacted by the authority aforesaid, that if any person or persons of what estate, degree, or condition soever he, she, or they be, body politic or corporate, that now have or hereafter shall have in his, her, or their custody any books or writings of the sorts aforesaid, or any images of stone, timber, alabaster, or earth, graven, carved or painted, which heretofore have been taken out of any church or chapel, or yet stand in any church or chapel, and do not before the last day of June next ensuing deface and destroy or cause to be defaced and destroyed the same images and every of them . . . and be thereof lawfully convict, forfeit and lose to the King our Sovereign Lord for the first offence twenty shillings, and for the second offence shall forfeit and lose being thereof lawfully convict four pounds, and for the third offence shall suffer imprisonment at the King's will . . .

CHURCHES

Source: William Harrison, *A Description of England*, 1577.

As for our churches themselves, belles, and times of morning and evening praier, remaine as in times past, saving that all images, shrines, tabernacles, roodlofts, and monuments of idolatrie are remooved, taken downe, and defaced; onelie the stories in glasse windowes excepted, which for want of sufficient store of new stuffe, and by reason of extreme charge that should grow by the alteration of the same into white panes throughout the realme, are not altogither abolished in most places at once, but by little and little suffered to decaie, that white glasse may be provided and set up in their roomes. Finallie, whereas there was woont to be a great partition betweene the quire and the bodie of the church; now it is either verie small or none at all: and to saie the truth altogither needlesse, sith the minister saith his service commonlie in the bodie of the church, with his face toward the people, in a little tabernacle of wainscot provided for the purpose: by which means the ignorant doo not onelie learne diverse of the psalmes and usuall praiers by heart, but also such

PRAYERS FOR THE DEAD IN PURGATORY—A PRACTICE AGAINST WHICH STEPHEN SWALLOW PROTESTED. (*See p. 128.*)

as can read, doo praise togither with him: so that the whole congregation at one instant powre out their petitions unto the living God, for the whole estate of his church in most earnest and fervent manner. Our holie and festivall daies are verie well reduced also unto a lesse number; for whereas (not long since) we had under the pope foure score and fifteene, called festivall, and thirty Profesti, beside the sundaies, they are all brought unto seaven and twentie: and with them the superfluous numbers of idle waks, guilds, fraternities, church-ales, helpe-ales, and soule-ales, called also dirge-ales, with the heathnish rioting at bride-ales, are well diminished and laid aside. And no great matter were it if the feasts of all our apostles, evangelists, and martyrs, with that of all saincts, were brought to the holie daies that follow upon Christmasse, Easter, and Whitsuntide; and those of the virgine Marie, with the rest, utterlie remooved from the calendars, as neither necessarie nor commendable in a reformed church.

THE LITANY IN ENGLISH

Source: William Harrison, *Chronologie.*

1544. Upon the 18 of October, the Letany in thenglish toung is, by the kinges commaundement, song openly in Pawles at London; & commaundement geven that it should be song in the same toung thorow out all England. it was used in London, in some parish church, even sithens June in the yere expired; & the children of Pawles schole, whereof I was one at that time, inforced to buy those bookes, wherwith we went in generall procession, as it was then appointed, before the king went to Boulogne.

SINGING OF PSALMS

Source: Thomas Mace, *Musick's Monument*, 1676.

I shall not need to blazon it abroad in Print, how miserably the Prophet David's Psalms are (as I may say) tortur'd or tormented, and the Service of God dishonoured, made course, or ridiculous thereby: seeing the generall outcries of most Parochial Churches in the Nation are more than sufficient to declare and make manifest the same, so often as they make any attempt to sing at those Psalms . . .

'Tis sad to hear what whining, toting, yelling or screeking there is in many Country Congregations, as if the people were affrighted, or distracted.

CHARLES II ON THE ESTABLISHED CHURCH

Source: The Declaration of Indulgence, 15th March, 1672.

. . . we declare our express resolution, meaning and intention to be, that the Church of England be preserved, and remain entire in its doctrine, discipline, and government, as it now stands established by law: and that this be taken to be, as it is, the basis, rule and standard of the general and public worship of God, and the orthodox conformable clergy do receive and enjoy the revenues belonging thereunto; and that no person, though of different opinion or persuasion, shall be exempt from paying his tithes, or other dues whatsoever. And further, we declare that no person shall be capable of holding any benefice, living, or ecclesiastical dignity or preferment of any kind in this kingdom of England, who is not exactly conformable. We do in the next place declare our will and pleasure to be, that the execution of all and all manner of penal laws in matters ecclesiastical, against whatsoever sort of non-conformists, or recusants, be immediately suspended, and they are hereby suspended.

REMNANTS OF POPERY

Source: The Journeys of Celia Fiennes in 1698.

(Durham) . . . In the Vestry I saw severall fine embroyder'd Coapes, 3 or 4, I saw one above the rest was so richly embroider'd with the whole description of Christs Nativity Life Death and Ascention; this is put on the Deanes shoulders at the administration of the Lords Supper, here is the only place that they use these things in England, and severall more Cerimonyes and Rites retained from the tymes of Popery; there are many papists in the town and popishly affected, and dayly encrease. . . .

CHAPTER XIV

SUNDAY OBSERVANCE

The observance of the Sabbath as a day of rest and prayer was one of the most controversial issues during the whole of this period. The hours of work were very long by our present-day standards, so a rest on Sunday and on a large number of Saints' Days had for centuries been accepted custom and Church Courts exacted penance for work on these Holy Days.

After the Reformation the strict observance of the Sabbath was one of the main anti-catholic tenets, but Protestants differed considerably among themselves as to the correct approach:

IN HENRY VIII'S TIME

Source: The King's Book, 1543.

Men must have special care that they be not over scrupulous or rather superstitious in abstaining from bodily labour upon the holy day. For . . . it is not meant but we may, upon the holy day, give ourselves to labour for the speedy performance of the necessary affairs of the prince and the commonwealth, at the commandment of them that have rule and authority therein. And also in all other times of necessity, as for saving of our corn and cattle, when it is like to be in danger, or like to be destroyed, if remedy be not had in time.

(People who do not worship and exercise the holy works appointed for Sunday) should be better occupied labouring in their fields, and to be kept at plough, than to be idle at home. And women should better bestow their time in spinning of wool, than upon the Sabbath day to lose their time in leaping and dancing, and other idle wantonness.

IN THE TIME OF EDWARD VI

Source: Cranmer's Injunctions to the Clergy and Laity, 1547.

In our time God is more offended than pleased, more dishonoured than honoured upon the holy day, because of idleness, pride, drunkenness, quarrelling and brawling, which are most used in such days, people nevertheless persuading themselves sufficiently to honour God on that day, if they hear mass and service, though they understand nothing to their edifying.

(In future Sunday is to be kept) in hearing the word of God read and taught, in private and public prayers, in knowledging their offences to God, and amendment of the same, in reconciling themselves charitably to their neighbours . . ., in oftentimes receiving the communion of the very body and blood of Christ, in visiting of the poor and sick, in using all soberness and godly conversation.

IN ELIZABETHAN TIMES

Source: Homily of the Place and Time of Prayer, 1574.

It is lamentable to see the wicked boldness of those that will be counted God's people, who pass nothing at all of keeping and hallowing the Sunday. And these people are of two sorts. The one sort, if they have any business to do, though there be no extreme need, they must not spare for the Sunday, they must ride and journey on the Sunday; they must drive and carry on the Sunday; they must row and ferry on the Sunday; they must buy and sell on the Sunday; they must keep markets and fairs on the Sunday. Finally, they use all days alike, work-days and holy days all are one. The other sort is worse. For although they will not travel nor labour on the Sunday, as they do on the week-day; yet they will not rest in holiness, as God commandeth; but they rest in ungodliness and filthiness, prancing in their pride, pranking and pricking, pointing and painting themselves, to be gorgeous and gay; they rest in excess and superfluity, in gluttony and drunkenness, like rats and swine; they rest in brawling and railing, in quarrelling and fighting: they rest in wantonness, in toyish talking, in filthy fleshliness; so that it doth too evidently appear that God is more dishonoured, and the devil better served on the Sunday than upon all the days in the week beside.

Source: Stubbes, Anatomie of Abuses, 1585.

The Sabboth daie of some is well observed, namely, in hearing the blessed worde of God read, preached, and interpreted; in private and publique praiers; in singing of godly psalmes; in celebrating the sacraments; and in collecting for the poore and indigent, which are the true uses and endes whereto the Sabbaoth was ordained. But other some spende the Sabbaoth day (for the most parte) in frequenting of baudy stage plaies and enterludes; in maintayning lordes of misrule (for so they call a certaine kinde of plaie which they use), in Maie games, church ales, feastes, and wakesses; in pyping, dauncyng, dicyng, carding, bowlyng, tennisse playing; in beare baytyng, cocke fightyng, hawkyng, hunting, and suche like; in keeping of fayres and markettes on the Sabbaoth; in keepyng of courtes and leetes; in foote ball playing, and such other develish pastymes; in readyng of lascivious and wanton books, and an infinite nomber of suche like practises and prophane exercises used upon that day, whereby the Lorde God is dishonoured, his Sabaoth violated, his word neglected, his sacramentes contemned, and his people mervailously corrupted, and caried away from true vertue and godlines.

Source: A Statement to be presented to the Government, drawn up on behalf of the clergy of the diocese of Chester. *c.* 1590.

Fairs and markets in most towns are usually kept upon the Sabbath; by occasion whereof divine service in the afternoon is greatly neglected. . . . Wakes, ales, greenes, May-games, rushbearings, bear-baites, doveales, bonfires, all manner unlawful gaming, piping and dancing and such like, are in all places freely exercised upon the Sabbath. By occasion whereof it cometh to pass that the youth will not by any means be brought to attend the exercise of catechising in the afternoon; neither the people to be present at the evening service. So that it were hard for the Preacher to find a competent congregation in any church to preach unto.

Source: Orders issued by the J.P.s for Lancashire, 1616.

. . . Such persons as shall be found walking, talking or idle, standing either in the church-yard or market place in time of Divine Servuce shall pay 12d a piece and are to be bound to the good behaviour and to appear at the next assizes.

IN THE TIME OF JAMES I

Source: The Declaration of Sports, issued by James I, 1618.

... the general complaint of our people, that they were barred
from all lawful recreation, and exercise upon the Sunday's afternoon, after the ending of all divine service, which cannot but
produce two evils: The one, the hindering of the conversion of
many, whom their priest will take occasion hereby to vex,
persuading them that no honest mirth or recreation is lawful
or tolerable in our religion, ... The other inconvenience is,
that this prohibition barreth the common and meaner sort of
people from using such exercises as may make their bodies more
able for war, when we or our successors shall have occasion to
use them. ... For when shall the common people have leave to
exercise, if not upon the Sundays and holy days, seeing they must
apply their labour and win their living in all working days?

... Our pleasure is, That after the end of Divine Service, Our
good people be not disturbed, letted or discouraged from any
lawful recreation, such as dancing, either men or women, archery
for men, leaping, vaulting, or any such harmless recreation, nor
from having of May-games, Whitsun ales, and Morris dances,
and the setting up of May-poles and other sports therewith used,
so as the same be had in due and convenient time, without impediment or neglect of Divine Service: and that women shall
have leave to carry rushes to the church for the decorating of it
according to their old custom. But withall we do here account
still as prohibited all unlawful games to be used upon Sundays
only, as Bear and Bull-baitings, Interludes, and at all times in
the meaner sort of people by law prohibited, bowling.

... we bar from this benefit and liberty, all such known recusants
either men or women, as will abstain from coming to church or
Divine Service, being therefore unworthy of any lawful recreation
after the said service, that will not first come to the church, and
serve God; prohibiting in like sort the said recreations to any
that, though conform in Religion, are not present in the church at
the service of God, before their going to the said Recreations.

IN THE TIME OF CHARLES I

Source: Autobiography of Richard Baxter, 1615–1691.

In the village where I lived the reader read the Common Prayer briefly, and the rest of the day even till dark night almost, except eating time, was spent in dancing under a maypole or a great tree not far from my father's door: where all the town did meet together. And though one of my father's own tenants was the piper, he could not restrain him, nor break the sport; so that we could not read the Scripture in our family without the great disturbance of the tabor and pipe and noise in the street! Many times my mind was inclined to be among them, and sometimes I broke loose from conscience and joined with them; and the more I did it the more I was inclined to it. But when I heard them call my father Puritan, it did much to cure me and alienate me from them. . . .

Source: An Act for the further reformation of sundry abuses committed on the Lord's Day. 1627. (3 Charles I, C.1.)

Forasmuch as the Lord's Day, commonly called Sunday, is much broken and profaned by Carriers, Waggoners, Carters, Wain-men, Butchers and Drovers of Cattle to the great dishonour of God, and reproach of religion: Be it enacted . . . That no Carrier with any horse or horses, nor Waggon-men with any waggon or waggons, nor Carmen with any cart or carts, nor Wain-men with any wain or wains, nor Drovers with any cattle shall . . . travel upon the said day, upon pain that every person or persons so offending shall lose and forfeit twenty shillings for every such offence: or: if any Butcher, by himself or any other for him by his privity or consent, shall . . . kill or sell any victual upon the said day, that then every such Butcher shall forfeit and lose for every offence the sum of six shillings and eight pence.

UNDER THE COMMONWEALTH

Source: Parliamentary Ordinance, 8th April, 1640.

The Lords and Commons . . . do order and ordain . . . That all the laws enacted and in force, concerning the observation of the Lord's-day be carefully put in execution; and that all and singular person or persons whatsoever, shall in every Lord's day apply themselves to the sanctification of the same, by exercising themselves thereon, in the duties of piety and true religion, publicly and privately: and that no person or persons whatsoever shall publicly cry, shew forth, or expose to sale, any wares, merchandises, fruit, herbs, goods or chattels whatsoever, upon the Lord's day, or any part thereof; upon pain, That every person so offending, shall forfeit the same goods so cried, shewed forth, or put to sale: and that no person or persons whatsoever shall, without reasonable cause for the same, travel, carry burdens, or do any worldly labours, or work whatsoever, on that day, or any part thereof. . . .

The Lords and Commons do further order and ordain That all and singular May-poles that are, or shall be erected, shall be taken down and removed . . . that the King's Declaration concerning observing of Wakes, and use of exercise and recreation upon the Lord's Day; the Book entitled 'The King's Majesty's Declaration to his subjects concerning lawful Sports to be used'; and all other books and pamphlets that have been or shall be written, printed or published, against the morality of the fourth commandment, or of the Lord's Day, or to countenance the profanation thereof, be called in, seized, suppressed and publicly burnt . . .
Provided and be it Declared That nothing in this Ordinance shall extend to the prohibiting of dressing of meat in private families, or the dressing and sale of victuals in a moderate way in inns or victualling-houses for the use of such as cannot otherwise be provided for; or to the crying or selling milk (at certain hours) . . . it is further ordained That the Lord Mayor of the City of London and all Justices of the Peace . . . shall . . . cause all laws against rogues and vagabonds and beggars to be put in due execution; and take order that all rogues, vagabonds, and beggars do on every Sabbath day repair to some Church and chapel, and remain there soberly and orderly during the time of Divine-Worship.

Source: Parliamentary Ordinance, 1657.

Every person grinding or causing to be ground any corn or grain in any mills, or causing any fulling or other mills to work upon the day aforesaid; and every person working in the washing, whiting or drying of clothes, thread, or yarn, or causing such work to be done upon the day aforesaid; every person setting up, burning or branding beet, turf or earth, upon the day aforesaid; every person gathering of rates, loans, taxations, or other payments upon the day aforesaid (except to the use of the poor in the public collection); every chandler melting or causing to be melted, tallow or wax belonging to his calling; and every common brewer and baker, brewing and baking, or causing bread to be baked, or beer or ale to be brewed upon the day aforesaid; and every butcher killing any cattle, and every butcher, costermonger, poulterer, herb-seller, cordwainer, shoemaker, or other person selling or exposing or offering to sell any their wares or commodities upon the day aforesaid; all tailors and other tradesmen, fitting or going to fit, or carry any wearing apparel or other things; and barbers trimming upon the day aforesaid; all persons keeping, using, or being present upon the day aforesaid at any fairs, markets, wakes, revels, wrestlings, shootings, leaping, bowling, ringing of bells for pleasure, or upon any other occasion (save for calling people together for the public worship), feasts, church-ale, maypoles, gaming, bear-baiting, or any other sports or pastimes; all persons unnecessarily walking in the church or church-yards, or elsewhere in the time of public worship; and all persons vainly or profanely walking on the day aforesaid, and all persons travelling, carrying burdens, or doing any worldly labour or work of their ordinary calling on the day aforesaid, shall be deemed guilty of profaning the Lord's Day.

AFTER THE RESTORATION

Source: An Act for the better observation of the Lord's Day, 1677.

That all the Laws enacted and in force concerning the observation of the Lord's Day, and repairing to the Church thereon be carefully put in execution; and that all and every person or persons whatsoever shall on every Lord's Day apply themselves to the observation of the same by exercising themselves thereon in the duties of piety and true religion, publicly and privately; and that no tradesman, artificer, workman, labourer, and other person whatsoever shall do or exercise any worldly labour, business or work of their ordinary callings upon the Lord's Day, or any part thereof (works of necessity only excepted); and that every person being of the age of fourteen years or upwards, offending in the premises shall for every such offence forfeit the sum of five shillings; and that no person or persons whatsoever shall publicly cry, shew forth, or expose to sale any wares, merchandises, fruit, herbs, goods or chattels whatsoever upon the Lord's Day, or any part thereof, upon pain that every person so offending shall forfeit the same goods so cried or shewed forth or exposed to sale.

And it is further enacted that no drover, horse-courser, waggoner, butcher, higler, they or any of their servants, shall travel or come into his or their inn or lodging upon the Lord's Day or any part thereof, upon pain that each and every such offender shall forfeit twenty shillings for every such offence; and that no person or persons shall use, employ or travel upon the Lord's day with any boat, wherry, lighter or barge, except it be upon extraordinary occasion, to be allowed by some Justice of the Peace of the County. . . .

Provided that nothing in this act contained shall extend to the prohibition of dressing of meat in families, or dressing or selling of meat in inns, cooks' shops, or victualling houses, for such as otherwise cannot be provided, nor to the crying and selling of milk before nine of the clock in the morning and after four of the clock in the afternoon.

TYPICAL SUNDAYS

Source: Pepys's Diary.

Jan. 6th, 1661. (Lord's Day.) To church where, before sermon, a long Psalm was set that lasted an hour, while the sexton gathered his year's contribucion through the whole church.

Feb. 2nd, 1662. (Lord's Day.) To church in the morning, and then home and dined with my wife, and so both of us to church again, where we had an Oxford man give us a most impertinent sermon upon 'Cast your bread upon the waters,' &c. So home to read, supper, and to prayers, and then to bed.

PUNISHMENT FOR SABBATH-BREAKING
IN 1662

Source: History of the Life of Thomas Ellwood . . . by his own hand. (Ed. C. G. Crump.)

He was a very poor man, who lived by mending shoes and on a seventh-day night, late, a carman, or some other such labouring man, brought him a pair of shoes to mend, desiring him to mend them that night, that he might have them in the morning, for he had no other to wear. The poor man sat up at work upon them till after midnight, and then finding he could not finish them, went to bed, intending to do the rest in the morning. Accordingly he got up betimes and though he wrought as privately as he could in his chamber, that he might avoid giving offence to any, yet could he not do it so privately but that an ill-natured neighbour perceived it, who went and informed against him for working on the Sunday.   (The cobbler was sent to prison)

CHAPTER XV

EDUCATION AT HOME

It had long been the custom for early education to be carried out at home, under the care of the mother or, in grander households, the nurse, tutor or domestic chaplain. Children were taught their alphabet and some spelling by 'horn books'—small written or printed pages, mounted on wood, covered with a layer of horn and fastened down by a strip of metal so that they could not be easily destroyed.

During the sixteenth century a large number of books were published giving advice to parents, and also some written specifically for children.

INSTRUCTIONS TO CHILDREN

Source: The Young Children's Book—from the Ashmolean MS. 61 (Bodleian Library), *c.* 1500 A.D.

> Aryse be tyme oute of thi bedde,
> And blysse thi brest & thi forhede,
> Than wasche thi hondes & thi face,
> Keme thi hede, & Aske god grace
> The to helpe in All thi werkes;
> Thow schall spede better what so thou carpes.
> Than go to the chyrche, & here A messe,
> There aske mersy fore thi trespasse.
> To whom thou metys come by the weye,
> Curtasly 'gode morne' thou sey.
> When thou hast done, go breke thy faste
> With mete & drynke of gode repaste:
> Blysse thi mouthe or thou it ete,
> The better schalle be thi dyete.
> Before thi mete sey thou thi grace,
> Yt ocupys bot lytell space:—
> Fore oure mete, & drynke, & us
> Thanke we owre lord Jhesus:—
> A pater noster & Ave mary
> Sey fore the saulys that in peyne ly;

Than go labour as thou arte bownde,
And be not Idylle in no stounde:

. . . .

Wype thi mouthe when thou wyll drinke,
Lest it foule thi copys brinke;
Kepe clene thi fyngeres, lypes, & chine,
Fore thou may thi wyrschype wynne.
Yn thi mouth when thi mete is,
To drinke, or speke, or laugh, I-wys
Dame curtasy fore-bydes it the:

GETTING READY FOR SCHOOL

Source: F. Seager, *The Schoole of Vertue,* 1557.

Downe from thy chamber   when thou shalte go,
Thy parentes salute thou,   and the famely also;
Thy handes se thou washe,   and thy head keame,
And of thy rayment   se torne be no seame;
Thy cappe fayre brusht,   thy hed cover than,
Takynge it of   In speakynge to any man.
Cato doth councel thee   thyne elders to reverence
Declarynge therby   thy dutye and obedience.
Thy shyrte coler fast   to thy necke knyt;
Comely thy rayment   loke on thy body syt.
Thy gyrdell about   thy wast then fasten,
Thy hose fayre rubd   thy showes se be cleane.
A napkyn se that   thou have in redines
Thy nose to clense   from all fylthynes.
Thy nayles, yf nede be,   se that thou payre;
Thyne eares kepe cleane,   thy teath washe thou fayre.
If ought about thee   chaunce to be torne,
Thy frendes therof shewe   howe it is worne,
And they wyll newe   for thee provyde,
Or the olde mende,   In tyme beinge spyde,
This done, thy setchell   and thy bokes take,

And to the scole
But ere thou go,
That thou take with thee
For these are thynges
Forget not then
The souldiar preparynge
Leaves not at home
No more shulde a scoler
what he at scole
These thynges thus had,
Unto the schole

haste see thou make.
with thy selfe forthynke.
pen, paper, and ynke;
for thy study necessary,
with thee them to cary.
hym selfe to the fielde
his sworde and his shielde,
forget then truly
shulde nede to occupy.
Take strayght thy way
without any stay.

TEACHING GOOD MANNERS

Source: Hugh Rhodes, *The Boke of Nurture, or Schoole of good maners,* 1577.

There is fewe thinges to be understand more necessary then to teache and governe Children in learning and good manners, for it is a hye servyce to God, it getteth favour in the syghte of men, it multiplyeth goods, and increaseth thy good name, it also provoketh to prayer by whiche Gods grace is obtayned, if thus they bee brought up in vertue, good maners, and Godly learning. The cause of the world being so evill of lyving as it is, is for lack of vertue, and Godly bringing up of youth. Whych youth sheweth the dispositions and conditions of their Parentes or Maysters, under whome they have bene governed. For youth is disposed to take such as they are accustomed in, good or evill. For if the behavyoure of the governour be evill, needes must the Chylde be evill.

. . . . . .

It is also necessarye for Fathers and Maysters to cause their Chyldren and servantes to use fayre and gentle speeche, with reverence and curtesye to their Elders and Betters, rebuking as well their ydle talke and stammering, as their uncomly jestures in going or standing. And if yee put them to schoole, see that their maysters be such as feare God, and lyve vertuouslye, such as can punishe sharpely with pacience, and not with rygour, for it doeth oft times make them to rebell and run away, wherof chaunceth ofte tymes much harme. Also their Parentes must oft tymes instruct them of god and of his lawes, and vertuous instructions of hys worde, and other good examples, and such lyke. And thus by litle and litle they shall come to the knowledge of reason, fayth, and good Christen living. . . . And take good heede of anye newe servauntes that you take into your house, and howe yee put them in authorytye among your children, and take heede howe they spende that is given them: if they be tale tellers or newes caryers, reprove them sharpely, and if they will not learne nor amende, avoyde them thy house, for it is great quyetnesse to have people of good behaviour in a house. Apparell not your chyldren or Servauntes in sumptuous apparell, for it increaseth pryde and obstynacye, and many other evils, nor let your Chyldren go whether they will, but know whether they goe, in what company, and what they have done, good or evill. Take hede they speake no wordes of villany, for it causeth much corruption to ingender in them, nor shew them muche familiaritye, and see that they use honest sportes and games. Marke well what vice they are specially inclined unto, and breake it betymes. Take them often with you to heare Gods word preached, & then enquyre of them what they heard, and use them to reade in the Bible and other Godly Bokes, but especyally keepe them from reading of fayned fables, vayne fantasyes, and wanton stories, and songs of love, which bring much mischiefe to youth. For if they learne pure and cleane doctryne in youth, they poure out plentye of good workes in age. If any stryfe or debate bee among them of thy house, at nighte charytably call them togyther, and wyth wordes or strypes make them all to agree in one. Take heede, if thy servaunt or Chyld murmure or grudge agaynst thee, breake it betyme. And when thou hearest them sweare or curse, lye & fyght, thou shalte reprove them sharpelye. And yee that are friends or Kynne shall labour how to make them love and dreade you, as well for love as for feare.

INSTRUCTIONS TO SERVANTS AND CHILDREN

Source: Hugh Rhodes, *The Boke of Nurture, or Schoole of good maners,* 1577.

When that thou comest to the Church, thy prayers for to say,

See thou sleepe not, nor yet talke not, devoutly looke thou pray,
Ne cast thyne eyes to ne fro, as thinges thou wouldst still see;
So shall wyse men judge thee a foole, and wanton for to bee.
When thou are in the Temple, see thou do thy Churchly warkes;
Heare thou Gods word with diligence, crave pardon for thy fautes.

. . . . . .

Looke that your knyfe be sharp & kene to cut your meate withall;
So the more cleanlyer, be sure, cut your meate you shall.
Or thou put much bread in thy pottage, looke thou doe it assay:
Fill not thy spoone to full, least thou loose somewhat by the way.

. . . . . .

And sup not lowde of thy Pottage, no tyme in all thy lyfe:
Dip not thy meate in the Saltseller, but take it with thy knyfe.
When thou haste eaten thy Pottage, doe as I shall thee wish:
Wype clean thy spone, I do thee read, leave it not in the dish;
Lay it downe before thy trenchoure, thereof be not afrayde;
And take heede who takes it up, for feare it be convayde.
Cut not the best peece for thy selfe, leave thou some parte behynde:
Bee not greedye of meate and drinke; be liberall and kynde.
Burnish no bones with thy teeth, for that is unseemely;
Rend not thy meate asunder, for that swarves from curtesy;
And if a straunger syt neare thee, ever among now and than
Reward thou him with some daynties: shew thyselfe a Gentleman.
If your fellow sit from his meate and cannot come thereto,
Then cutte for him such as thou haste; he may lyke for thee doe.

. . . . . .

Scratche not thy head with thy fyngers when thou arte at thy
    meate;
Nor spytte you over the table boorde; see thou doest not this
    forget.
Pick not thy teeth with thy Knyfe nor with thy fyngers ende,
But take a stick, or some cleane thyng, then doe you not offende.

. . . . . .

Fyll not thy mouth to full, leaste thou perhaps of force must
    speake;
Nor blow not out thy crums when thou doest eate.
Fowle not the place with spitting whereas thou doest syt,
Least it abhore some that syt by: let reason rule thy wyt.

If thou must spit, or blow thy nose, keepe thou it out of sight,
Let it not lye upon the ground, but treade thou it out right.

A READY WAY FOR CHILDREN TO LEARN THEIR A. B. C.

Source: Sir Hugh Platt, *A Jewell House of Art and Nature*, 1594.

Cause 4 large dice of bone or wood to be made, and upon
every square, one of the small letters of the cross row to be graven,
but in some bigger shape, and the child using to play much
with them, and being alwayes told what letter chanceth, will soon
gain his Alphabet, as it were by the way of sport or pastime.
I have heard of a pair of cards, whereon most of the principall
Grammer rules have been printed, and the School-Master hath
found good sport thereat with his schollers.

LEARNING ARITHMETIC

Source: Pepys's Diary.

July 4th, 1662. . . . By and by comes Mr. Cooper, mate of the
Royall Charles, of whom I intend to learn mathematiques, and
do begin with him today, he being a very able man, and no
great matter, I suppose, will content him. After an hour's being
with him at arithmetique (my first attempt being to learn the
multiplication-table); then we parted till to-morrow.

July 9th, 1662. Up by four o'clock, and at my multiplication-
table hard, which is all the trouble I meet withal in my arithmetique.

July 14th, 1662. Up by 4 o'clock and to my arithmetique, and
so to my office till 8; . . .

In spite of some flourishing schools, many parents preferred to have
their children brought up at home under the guidance of a private
tutor. Sometimes he accompanied his charges to school and university
and if a young man went—as many did—on a tour abroad, he was
usually under his tutor's care.

WHAT A YOUNG NOBLEMAN LEARNT
IN HENRY VIII's TIME

Source: A letter written by Gregory Cromwell's tutor to his father, the Earl of Essex, the King's Secretary.

. . . And firste, after he hath herde Masse he taketh a lecture of a Diologe of Erasmus Colloquium, called Pietas Puerilis, whereinne is described a veray picture of oone that sholde be vertuouselie brought upp; and forcause it is so necessary for hime, I do not onelie cause him to rede it over, but also to practise the preceptes of the same, and I have also translated it into Englishe, so that he may conferre theime both to-githers, whereo (as lerned men affirme) cometh no smalle profecte . . . after that, he exerciseth his hande in writing one or two houres, and redith uppon Fabian's Chronicle as longe; the residue of the day he dothe spende uppon the lute and virginalls.. When he rideth (as he doth very ofte), I tell hime by the waye some historie of the Romanes or the Greekes, whiche I cause him to reherse agayn in a tale. For his recreation he useth to hawke and hunte, and shote in his long bowe, which frameth and succedeth so well with hime that he semeth to be therunto given by nature.

A PRECOCIOUS CHILD

Girls of good family were often very accomplished. Here the wife of a Puritan gentleman describes what she was taught in her youth.

Source: The Life of Mrs. Lucy Hutchinson, by herself—a fragment.

By the time I was four years old I read English perfectly, and having a great memory, I was carried to sermons; and while I was very young could remember and repeat them exactly, and being caressed, the love of praise tickled me, and made me attend more heedfully. When I was about seven years of age, I remember I had at one time eight tutors in several qualities, languages, music, dancing, writing, and needlework; but my genius was quite averse from all but my book, and that I was so eager of, that my mother thinking it prejudiced my health, would moderate me in it; yet this rather animated me than kept me back, and every moment I could steal from my play I would

employ in any book I could find, when my own were locked up
from me. After dinner and supper I still had an hour allowed me
to play, and then I would steal into some hole or other to read.
My father would have me learn Latin, and I was so apt that I
outstripped my brothers who were at school, although my
father's chaplain, that was my tutor, was a pitiful dull fellow.
My brothers, who had a great deal of wit, had some emulation at
the progress I made in my learning, which very well pleased

my father; though my mother would
have been contented I had not so
wholly addicted myself to that as to
neglect my other qualities. As for
music and dancing, I profited very
little in them, and would never practise my lute or harpsichords but when
my masters were with me; and for
my needle I absolutely hated it.

GIRLS' EDUCATION

Source: Hannah Woolley, *The Gentlewoman's Companion,* 1675.

The right Education of the Female Sex, as it is in a manner
everywhere neglected, so it ought to be generally lamented. . . .
Certainly Mans Soul cannot boast of a more sublime Original than
ours; they had equally their efflux from the same eternal Immen-
sity, and therefore capable of the same improvement by good
Education. Vain man is apt to think we were meerly intended
for the Worlds propagation, and to keep its humane inhabitants
sweet and clean; but, by their leaves, had we the same Literature,
he would find our brains as fruitful as our bodies. Hence I am
induced to believe, we are debarred from the knowledg of
humane learning, lest our pregnant Wits should rival th'towring
conceits of our insulting Lords and Masters.

. . . . . .

I cannot but complain of, and must condemn the great negligence of Parents, in letting the fertile ground of their Daughters
lie fallow, yet send the barren Noddles of their Sons to the
University, where they stay for no other purpose than to fill their

empty Sconces with idle notions to make a noise in the Country.

. . . . . .

There is no instruction more moving, than the example of your living. By that line of yours they are to conform their own. Take heed then lest the damp of your own life extinguish the light of your Childrens. As you are a kind Mother to them be a careful Monitor about them; and if your business will permit, teach them your self, with their letters, good manners. For there is an in-bred, filial fear in Children to their Parents, which will beget in them more attention in hearing, and retention in holding what they hear.

THE PLACE OF RELIGION IN EDUCATION

In this exceptionally Royalist family religious teaching and practice were foremost in the children's education:

Source: Autobiography of Anne, Lady Halkett.

She spared no expense in educating all her children in the most suitable way to improve them, and if I made not the advantage I might have done it was my own fault and not my mother's, who paid masters for teaching my sister and mee to write, speake French, play on the lute and virginalls, and dance, and kept a gentlewoman to teach us all kinds of needleworke, which shews I was not brought up in an idle life. But my mother's greatest care, and for which I shall ever owne to her memory the highest gratitude, was the great care she tooke that, even from our infancy, wee were instructed never to neglect to begin and end the day with prayer, and orderly every morning to read the Bible, and ever to keepe the church as offten as there was occation to meet herer either for prayers or preaching. So that for many yeares together I was seldome or never absent from divine service, at 5 a'clocke in the morning in the summer and 6 a'clocke in the winter, till the usurped power putt a restraint to that publick worship so long owned and continued in the Church of England; where I blese God, I had my education, and the example of a good Mother, who kept constantt to her owne parish church, and had allways a great respect for the ministers under whose charge she was.

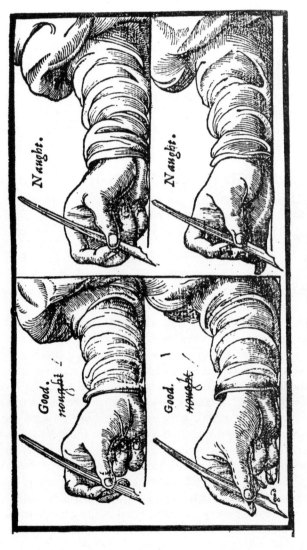

Howe you ought to hold your penne.

(A Newe Booke of Copies, 1574)

RVLES MADE BY E.B. FOR
Children to vvrite by.

TO make cõmon yncke, of wyne take a quarte,
Two ounces of gumme, let that be apart,
Fiue ounces of Galles, of copros take three,
Longe standing doth make it better to bee:
If wyne ye do want, rayne water is best,
And then as much stuffe as aboue at the least:
If yncke be too thicke, put vinegre in:
For water doeth make the colour more dimme,

To make yncke in haste.

In haste, for a shift when ye haue great neede,
Take woll, or wollen to stande you in steede,
Which burnt in the fire, the pouder beate small,
With vinegre, or water make yncke withall.

To keepe yncke longe.

If yncke ye desire to keepe longe in store,
Put bay salte therein and it will non hoare.

To make speciall blacke yncke.

If that common yncke be not to your minde,
Somne lampblacke thereto with g me water grinde:
Eche paynter can tell, how it shoulde be done
The cleaner out of your penne it will ronne:
The same to be put in horne or in leade,
No cotten at all, when longe it hath stayde,

The bottom will thicke put more common yncke
And it will be good well sturred, as I thinke.

To make staunche grayne.

Make staunche grayne of allume beaten full small,
And twise as much rosen beaten withall:
With that in a fayre clout knit very thinne,
Rubb paper or parchment, before ye beginne.

To chuse your quill.

Take quill of a goose that is some what rounde,
The thirde or fourth in wynge to be fownde:
And if at some tyme of those ye do want,
Take pinion as next, when Rauens quilie is skant,
And ryue it iust in the backe, as may bee.
For ragged your slitte else shall ye sice,
Amidde the slype that ronnes vpp the quill:
Were it of gander yee do it not spill,
The fether shaue of the quill do not pare,
The stronger your penne in hande ye may beare.

To make your penne.

Make clyft withoute teeth your penne good, & hard:
Thinner, an shorter, on right hand regarde:
The clyft somewhat long, the nebb not to shorte,
Then take it in hand in most comly sorte.

To holde your penne.

Your thumbe on your penne as hieſt beſtowe,
The forefinger next, the middle belowe:
And holding it thus in moſt comely wyſe,
Your Body vpright, ſtoupe not with your heade:
Your Breaſt from the borde if that you be wiſe,
Leaſt that ye take hurt, when ye haue well fed.

To make a good penne knife.

Your penneknife as ſtay in leaſt hand let reſt,
The mettle to ſofte nor to harde is beſt:
To ſharpe it maye be, and ſo cut to faſt,
Yfit be to dull a ſhrewd turne for haſt:
For whetſtone, harde touch that is very good,
Slate or ſhoo ſowle is not ill, but good.

How to ſit writing.

Your Body vpright, ſtoupe not with your head,
Your Breaſt from the borde when you haue well fed:
Incke allways good ſtore on right hand to ſtand,
Browne paper for great haſt, or elles box with ſand:
Dip Penne, and ſhake penne, and touch Pennes for heare:
Wax, quilles and penneknife ſee allwayes ye beare:
Whoſo that his paper doth blurre or elles blott,
Yealdes me a ſlouen it falles him by lotte:
In learning full ſlowe Write at beginning,
For great is your loſſe, and ſmall is your wynning.

If at the firſt tyme an ill touch, ye catche,
Vſe only is cauſe of ſpeedy diſpatche.

How to write faire.

To write very fayer, your Penne let be newe,
Diſh, daſh, longe tayle flye, falſe writinge eſchewe:
Nearely and cleanlie your hand for to frame,
Strong ſtawked penne vſe beſt of rauen.
And commelie to write, and geue a good grace,
Leaue betwene eche woorde ſmall (a) letters ſpace,
That fayre and ſeemely your hand may be redd,
Keepe euen your letters at foote, and at heade:
With diſtaunce a like betweene letter and letter.
One out of others ſhowes muche the better.

Scholer to learne it may doo you pleaſure,
To rule him to lynes iuſt of a meaſure:
Thoſe two lynes betweene to write very iuſt.
Not aboue or belowe write that he muſt:
The ſame to be done is beſt with blacke leade,
Which written betweene, is clenſed with bread.
Your penne from your booke but ſeldom remoue.
To followe, ſtrange hand with drie penne firſt proue.
Many one writeth the example lyeth by.
Who ſo one the ſame dooth neuer ſet eye:
But he that will learne with ſpeede for to write,
To marke his example muſt haue his delight,
                                                    Letter

Letter and title to make as the same,
And so shall the scholler be voide of all blame.

*Necessarie things belonging
to writing,*

And one thinge well marke, your selfe well to ease,
That non but best handes may alwayes best please:
Both farre of, and neare for faire handes doo seeke,
And them safe as golde, see that thou well keepe,

And neuer let rest thy hand for to frame,
Vntil that thou write as faire as the same
To writing belonges good things two or three,
As drawing and Painting, and eke Geometrie.
The which I would wish eche wight to obteyne,
But suerly to some it were to great payne.
So fare you well without booke well carne,
These fewe Rules I giue, which are as the sterne
To rule a good Scholler that doth his mind bend.
To followe good counsell and so I doe end.

E N D E

*Imprinted at London by Thomas Vautroullier, dwelling in the
Blackefriers by Ludgate.*

(*A Newe Booke of Copies, 1574*)

M

CHAPTER XVI

SCHOOLING

By a tradition coming down from the Middle Ages, the sons of the nobility and gentry were often sent away from home to learn manners and service in other houses—a practice which seemed heartless to many foreigners.

THE MANNER OF SERVING A KNIGHT, SQUYRE, OR GENTLEMAN

Source: Hugh Rhodes, *The Boke of Nurture, or Schoole of good maners,* 1577.

First yee must be dilligent to know your Maysters pleasure, and to knowe the order and custome of his house, for dyvers maysters are of sundry condicions and appetytes. . . .

When your Mayster will goe to his meate, take a towell aboute your necke, then take a cupbord cloth, a Basen, Ewer, & a Towell, to aray your cupbord: cover your table, set on bread, salt & trenchers, the salt before the bread, and trenchers before the salte. Set your napkyns and spoones on the cupbord ready, and lay every man a trencher, a napkyn, & a spone. And if you have more messes then one at your maisters table, consider what degree they be of, and thereafter ye may serve them: and then set down every thing at that messe as before, except your Carving knives. If ther be many Gentlemen or yomen, then set on bred, salt, trenchers & spoones, after they be set, or els after the custome of the house. . . . see ye have Voyders ready for to avoyd the Morsels that they doe leave on their Trenchours. Then with your Trenchour knyfe take of such fragmentes, and put them in your Voyder, and sette them downe cleane agayne. . . .

. . . then take up the salte, and make obeysaunce; and marke if your Mayster use to wash at the table, or standing: if he be at the table, cast a clean Towell on your table cloth, and set downe your basen and Ewer before your soveraigne, and take the ewer in your hand, and gyve them water. Then voyd your Basen and Ewer, and fold the bord cloth together with your towell therin, and so take them of the boord. And when your soveraygne shall wash, set your towell on the lefte hand of him, and the water before your soveraygne at dinner or supper; if it be to bedwarde, set up your basyn and towell on the cupbord agayne.

HOW TO ORDER YOUR MAYSTERS CHAMBER AT NIGHT TO BEDWARDE

Source: Hugh Rhodes, *The Boke of Nurture, or Schoole of good maners,* 1577.

. . . when your mayster intendeth to bedward, see that you have Fyre and Candell suffycyent. Ye must have clean water at night and in the morning. If your Mayster lye in fresh sheets, dry of the moystnesse at the fyre. If hee lye in a strange place, see his sheetes be cleane, then folde downe his bed, and warme his night Kercheife, and see his house of offyce be cleane, helpe of his cloathes, and drawe the Curteynes, make sure the fyre and Candles, avoyde the dogs, and shutte the dores; and at night or in the morning, your Mayster being alone, if ye have anything to say, it is good knowing his pleasure. In the morning if it be cold, make a fyre, and have readye cleane water, bring him his petticote warme, with his doublet, and all his apparell cleane brusht, and his shoes made cleane, and help to araye him, trusse his poyntes, stryke up his Hosen, and see all cleanlye aboute him; give him good attendance, and especyally among straungers, for attendaunce doth please Maysters very well. Thus doing wyth dillygence, God will preferre you to honour and good Fortune.

TREATMENT OF CHILDREN

Source: Italian Relations, p. 33.

The want of affection in the English is strongly manifested towards their children; for after having kept them at home till they arrive at the age of seven or nine years at the utmost, they put them out, both males and females, to hard service in the houses of other people, binding them generally for another seven or nine years. And these are called apprentices, and during that time they perform all the most menial offices; and few are born who are exempted from this fate, for every one, however rich he may be, sends away his children into the houses of others, whilst he, in return, receives those of strangers into his own. And on inquiring their reason for this severity, they answered that they did it in order that their children might learn better manners. But I, for my part, believe that they do it because they like to enjoy all their comforts themselves, and that they are better served by strangers than they would be by their own children.

A PAGE IN A NOBLE HOUSEHOLD

In the sixteenth and seventeenth centuries also, young boys of good family were sent as pages into noble households. They received no wages, but were clothed, fed and cared for.

In the household accounts kept by the Earl of Bedford's Steward the following entries refer to the cost of a page in that household.

1663–1664	For teaching the page on the fla-geolet	£2. 10s. 0d.
May 1670	To Mistress Abigail for two shirts for the little page	7s. 0d.
July 1670	To Mr. Freston for two periwigs for my lady's page, by direction from Mr. Taylor	£2. 0s. 0d.
November 1681	To the page, paid for twice cutting his hair	1s. 0d.
December 1681	To the page, for scouring his clothes	1s. 0d.
February 1682	For three pair of stockings for Lady Margaret's page	10s. 6d.
	For a hat and case for him	11s. 0d.
	For shoe buckles, buttons for his cuffs and a comb	3s. 4d.
March 1682	To the page, pocket-money	10s. 0d.
May 1682	For two pair of stockings for the little page	7s. 0d.

GRAMMAR SCHOOLS

The fifteenth century, for all its troubles, was a period of greatly increased educational opportunities for all classes except the poorest. Many Grammar schools were endowed by Bishops, Burghers and Municipal Guilds, and were intended for the free teaching of the poor, though very few of the labouring class were sent.

For the next two hundred years the cleverest boys of all classes were brought up together in Grammar Schools where they were taught to read, write and speak Latin and occasionally Greek and Hebrew, and to do a little mathematics. Methods of teaching were formal and dull, and punishments very severe, but in these schools the middle and upper classes came to understand each other, with great mutual advantage.

The child of a labourer or artisan did not usually go to a Grammar school, but nevertheless he was often taught to read the Bible, to write and to cast accounts. In some parishes there were endowments which enabled the parson or some other person to run a simple school. A census taken of the poor in Norwich in 1571 showed a surprising number of seven- and eight-year-old children who went to school.

Source: Harrison, *A Description of England,* 1577.

... there are great number of Grammer schooles through out the realme, and those verie liberallie indued, for the better reliefe of poore scholers, so that there are not manie corporat townes now under the queenes dominion, that hath not one Gramar schoole at the least, with a sufficient living for a maister and usher appointed to the same.

THE SEAL OF LOUTH GRAMMAR SCHOOL, SHOWING A BIRCHING

There are in like maner diverse collegiat churches as Windsor, Winchester, Eaton, Westminster ... and in those a great number of poore scholers, dailie mainteened by the liberalitie of the founders, with meat, bookes, and apparell, from whence after they have beene well entered in the knowledge of the Latine and Greeke toongs, and rules of versifieng (the triall whereof is made by certeine apposers yearelie appointed to examine them) they are sent to certeine especiall houses in each universitie, where they are received and trained up, in the points of higher knowledge in their privat hals, . . .

A CO-EDUCATIONAL BOARDING SCHOOL

Source: Thomas Platter, *Travels in England*, 1599.

. . . I saw Christ's Hospital . . ., founded by a great lady, and already in progress during her lifetime, which hospital finds food and drink and clothes for seven hundred young boys and girls, while reading and writing are taught in special schools in the same, and they are kept there until they are fit for some craft or service, when they are taken away and put out wherever they like, or opportunity offers, boys and girls alike; they are all fine children, taken from poor parents and put in here. They keep their hospital exceedingly clean—in the boys' long apartment are one hundred and forty beds in a row on either side, where they sleep two and two together, and by their beds they have low chests in which to keep their clothes. There are fewer girls in a smaller room.

SOME TEXTS FOR TRANSLATION INTO LATIN

Source: William Horman, *Vulgaria*, 1519.

Whereas a flint or another stone to smite fire cannot be got, it must be done with rubbing of two treen (i.e. wooden) pieces together.

I shall get me dry toadstools or fine linnen cloth, half burnt, to make tinder of.

Lay this flesh in the brine lest it be lost. (i.e. spoiled)

Peel some cloves of garlic and stamp them.

Wash all the greasy dishes and vessel in the lead cauldron or pan in hot water, and set them clean upon the scullery board.

Take a wisp of straw and ashes and scour this pot.

Set the earthen pot by him self for (i.e. to prevent) breaking.

These rags will serve for kitchen cloths.

TEACHING METHODS IN ELIZABETHAN TIMES

Source: Thomas Fuller, *The Worthies of England* (*Richard Mulcaster*), 1662.

His method of teaching was this. In a morning he would exactly and plainly construe and parse the lessons to his scholars; which done, he slept his hour (custom made him critical to proportion it) in his desk in the school; but woe to any scholar that slept the while. Awaking, he heard them accurately; and Atropos might be persuaded to pity, as soon as he to pardon, where he found just fault. The prayers of cockering mothers prevailed with him as much as the requests of indulgent fathers, rather increasing than mitigating his severity on their offending child. ... it may be truly said (and safely for one out of his school) that others have taught as much learning with fewer lashes. Yet his sharpness was the better endured, because unpartial; and many excellent scholars were bred under him. ...

CONTENTS IN GENERALL OF SUCH THINGS AS MAY (BY GODS BLESSING) BE EASILY EFFECTED IN OUR ORDINAIRE GRAMMAR SCHOOLES

An Elizabethan clergyman and schoolmaster, John Brinsley, was a devout puritan and an enthusiastic educational reformer. He carried out a great deal of research into the teaching methods of his day and published two books on the improvement of methods of instruction in the 'ordinarie' grammar schools. The first, *Ludus Literarius,* or The Grammer Schoole, appeared in 1612, the second, *A Consolation for our Grammar Schooles,* in 1622.

Celia Fiennes, in her Journal, mentions some interesting schools.

Source: John Brinsley, the Elder, *A Consolation for our Grammar Schooles,* 1622.

1. To teach scholars how to be able to reade well, and write true orthographie in a short time.

2. To make them ready, in all points of their Accidence and Grammar, to answer anie necessarie question therein.

3. To say without booke all the usuall and necessarie Rules, to construe their Grammar rules; to give the meaning, use, and order of the rules, to shew the examples, and to apply them: which being well performed, will make all other learning easie and pleasant.

4. . . . to construe truly, and in proprietie of words and sense, and also in pure phrase; to parse of themselves, and to give a right reason of everie word, why it must be so and not otherwise; and to deliver the English of the Lectures perfectly out of the Latine.

5. . . . to parse in Latine, looking onely upon the translation; and in all their Poets which they so learne: to do all this without books, which is farre the surest, viz. to repeate, construe, and parse with their booke under their arme.

6. To take their Lectures of themselves, except in the verie lowest Formes, . . . or to do it with verie little helpe, in some more difficult things.

7. To enter surely in making Latine, without danger of making false Latine, or using anie barbarous phrase.

. . . . . .

9. To make Epistles, imitating Tully and the best Authors in that kind, short and pithie, in pure Latine, and familiar.

10. To translate into English, according to proprietie both of words and sense; and out of the English to reade the Latine againe, to prove it, and give a reason of everie thing.

. . . . . .

12. To correct their faults of themselves, when they are but noted out unto them, or a question is asked of them.

. . . . . .

15. So to reade over so much of the chiefe Latine Poets, as Virgil, Horace, &c. and of other the best Authors, as shall be thought necessary, by that time, that by reason of their yeares they be in any measure thought fit, for their discretion, to go unto the University; and to be able to go thorough the rest of themselves, by ordinary helpes.

16. In Greeke to take their Lectures of themselves, to construe
    perfectly, and parse as in the Latine; to reade the Greeke
    backe againe, out of a translation, Latine, or English;
    also to construe, parse, and to proove it out of the same.

17. In the Hebrew to be able to construe perfectly, and to resolve
    so farre as is necessary for the Grammar-schoole; and to
    reade the Hebrew also out of the translation; . . .

18. To answer most of the difficulties in all classicall Schoole-
    Authors; as in Terence, Virgil, Horace, Persius, Juvenal.

    . . . . . .

20. To write Theames full of good matter, in pure Latin and with
    judgment, and how to invent matter of themselves.

21. To enter to make a verse with delight, without any bodging
    at all; and to furnish with copie of Poeticall phrase, out of
    the best Poets.

22. So to imitate and expresse Ovid or Virgil, as you shall hardly
    discerne, unlesse you know the places, whether the verses
    be of the Authors or the Scholars: and to write verses
    extempore of any ordinarie theame.

23. To translate forth of English or Latin into Greeke. Also to
    write theames or verses in Greeke.

24. To pronounce naturally and sweetly, without vaine affecta-
    tion; and to begin to do it from the lowest fourmes.

    . . . . . .

29. To write faire, in Secretarie, Romane, Greeke, Hebrue; as
    they grow in knowledge of the tongues.

    . . . . . .

31. To be acquainted with the grounds of Religion, and to have
    the summe, and all the chiefe Histories of the Bible. To take
    all the substance of the Sermons, if they be plainly and
    orderly delivered: and to set them downe afterwards in a
    good Latin style, or to reade them extempore into latin
    out of the English. To conceive and answer the severall
    points of the Sermons, and how to make a briefe repetition
    of the whole Sermon without booke.

    . . . . . .

33. To grow in our owne English tongue, according to their
   ages, and growths in other learning: to utter their minds in
   the same, both in propriety, and purity; and so to be fitted
   for divinity, law, or what other calling or faculty soever
   they shalbe after employed in.

. . . . . .

These things may be effected in good sort, . . . If the Maisters
. . . will take meete paines: and the Scholars being set to schoole,
so soone as they shall be meete, be kept to learning daily, without
loitering, having bookes and other necessarie helpes and en-
couragements: and by their parents care caused to do their
exercises at home, and be ever kept in meete awe, and submission
to their Maisters. . . . That so all scholars of anie towardnesse
and diligence, may be made good Grammarians, and everie way
fit for the Universitie by fifteene yeares of age, or at least by that
time that they shall be meete by discretion and government,
which is commonly sixteene or seventeene. And all this to be
done with delight and certaintie, both to Maisters and Scholars;
with strife and contention amongest the Scholars themselves,
without that usuall terrour and crueltie, which hath bene practised in manie places, and without so much as severitie amongest
good natures.

FREE SCHOOLS

Source: The Journeys of Celia Fiennes, 1697 and 1698.

(York) There is a very good free schoole for boys, they say the
best in England for learning and care, which makes it fill'd with
Gentlemens Sons besides the free Schollars from all parts;
provision being very cheape here.

(Shrewsbury) . . . here are three free Schooles together all built
of free stone, 3 large roomes to teach the children with severall
masters; the first has 150£ a year the second 100 the third 50£ a
year and teach children from reading English till fit for the
University, and its free for children not only of the town but
for all over England if they exceed not the numbers; . . . here
is a very good Schoole for young Gentlewomen for learning work
and behaviour and musick.

CHAPTER XVII

TEACHERS

There was no training for those who taught children, so parents and those endowing schools had to find the most suitable person they could. In this satire on Domestic Tutors the writer clearly shows us that a tutor is only a superior kind of servant. (A truckle bed was a small bed made to run under a larger one and generally used by a servant or attendant. This indulgence allowed to the pupil is the reverse of the rule practised in the Universities. In the statutes of Corpus Christi College at Oxford in 1516, students were ordered to sleep under the beds of the Fellows in a truckle-bed.)

DOMESTIC TUTORS

Source: Joseph Hall, *Satires,* 1597.

> A gentle squire would gladly entertain
> Into his house some trencher-chappelain;
> Some willing man that might instruct his sons,
> And that would stand to good conditions.
> First, that he lie upon the truckle-bed,
> Whiles his young master lieth o'er his head.
> Second, that he do, on no default,
> Ever presume to sit above the salt.
> Third, that he never change his trencher twice.
> Fourth, that he use all common courtesies;
> Sit bare at meals, and one half rise and wait.
> Last, that he never his young master beat,
> But he must ask his mother to define,
> How many jerks she would his breech should line.
> All these observed, he could contented be,
> To give five marks and winter livery.

TO TEACHERS

It is evident from the following that there were many complaints by parents about the incompetence and lack of interest shown by school-masters:

Source: John Brinsley, the Elder, *A Consolation for our Grammar Schooles.* 1622.

What a griefe may this justly be unto us, when one shall come, and crie out of us, to our faces: My sonne hath bene under you

six or seven years, and yet is not able so much as to reade English well; much lesse to construe or understand a peece of Latin, or to write true Latin, or to speake in Latin in any tolerable sort, which he might have bene well able to have performed, if that you had taken that course and those good paines with him which you might have done; for in such a schoole others much yonger than mine are able to do it. Another shall complaine: My sonne comes on never a whit in his writing. Besides that his hand is such, that it can hardly be read; he also writes so false English, that he is neither fit for trade, nor any employment wherein to use his pen. . . .

Moreover, how must this needs trouble us, when manie shall crie out of our severitie: some shall wish, I would my child had never known him. If he had not dealt so cruelly with my child, he had bene a scholar, whereas now he is undone. Or when our scholars coming to mans estate, shall curse us, for that by our blowes they were made dunses or deafe (though this often times unjustly) or to hate all learning. . . . Or when they shall thus complaine: Our Maister had not anie care of our govern-ment and manners. He never taught us the feare of the Lord, nor made the least conscience to plant anie Religion or grace in us.

VILLAGE SCHOOLMASTERS

Source: Autobiography of Richard Baxter (1615–1691).

In the village where I was born there was four readers succes-sively in six years, ignorant men, and two of them immoral in their lives, who were all my schoolmasters. In the village where my father lived, there was a Reader of about eighty years of age that never preached, and had two churches about twenty miles distant. His eyesight failing him, he said Common Prayer without book: but for the reading of the Psalms and chapters, he got a common thresher and day labourer one year, and a taylor another year: (for the clerk could not read well) and at last he had a kinsman of his own (the excellentest stage-player in all the country, and a good gamester and a good fellow) that got Orders and supplied one of his places. After him another younger kinsman, that could write and read, got Orders. And at the same time another neighbour's son that had been a while at school turned minister, and ... when he had been a preacher about twelve or sixteen years he was fain to give it over, it being discovered that his Orders were forged by the first ingenious stage-player. After him another neighbour's son took Orders. When he had been a while an attorney's clerk, and a common drunkard, and tipled himself into so great poverty that he had no other to live. . . . These were the schoolmasters of my youth (except two of them) who read Common Prayer on Sundays and holy days, and taught school and tipled on the week-days, and whipped the boys when they were drunk, so that we changed them very oft.

THE DUTY AND QUALIFICATION OF A GOVERNESS TO GENTLEMENS CHILDREN

Source: Hannah Woolley, *The Gentlewoman's Companion*, 1675.

They who undertake the difficult Employ of being an Instructress or Governess of Children, should be persons of no mean birth and breeding, civil in deportment, and of an extraordinary winning and pleasing conversation. They should not be harsh in expression, nor severe in correcting such as are under their charge, but instruct them with all mildness, cheerfully incouraging them in what they are injoin'd to perform; not suddenly striking, nor startling them with a loud rebuke, which causeth in some an aversness to what they should love, imbittering all the former delight they had in learning. . . .

A gentlewoman of my acquaintance, . . . being somewhat aged, and suspecting her strength was not able to grapple with active youth call'd up her maid to her assistance, with whose help she so cruelly chastised a young Gentlewoman for some fault she had committed, that with grief and shame she died in a little time after. . . .

As I must condemn the insolent severity of such a Governess, so I must not let pass without reproof the tyranny of some Mothers, whose presence makes their Children tremble, without the commission of a fault; by which means they many times with their imperiousness frighten their love into an abhorrency of their sight; to be sure they make them tell many a lye to excuse their negligence, . . . only that for that time they might escape the rigor of their punishment. Yet I would not have any mistake me . . . that I intend . . . overindulgence, . . . all that I would have a Mother do, is, that she would be moderate in the correction of an offence, . . . Be the incessant tormentor of her sloth, lest by proving burdensome to others, she at length becomes so to her self, by which means her understanding starves, and her body contracts an Hospital of Diseases. This you may remedy by suffering her not to sleep over long, lest the spirits be over-dull'd, as well as by too little rest.

If the season be dry, walk them in the fields; if not, some moderate exercise within doors, . . .

Letters undoubtedly is the first step to the perfection of knowledg, by which means they come to improve their own understandings by the help of others: Reading furnisheth them with agreeable discourse, and adapts them for the conversation of the most ingenious, . . . In the first place let them read some choice pieces of Piety, which may inflame their hearts with the love of God, . . . Some may imagine, that to read Romances after such practical Books of Divinity, will . . . be a vain thing, . . . I do believe such Romances which treat of Generosity, Gallantry, and Virtue, as Cassandra, Clelia, . . ., not omitting Sir Philip Sydney's Arcadia, are Books altogether worthy of their Observation. . . . Thus having qualified them for reading, you should so practice them in their pen, & all the Productions of the Needle, with all the curious devices of Wax-work, Rock-work, Moss work, Cabinet-work, Beugle-work, &c. and in due time let them know how to Preserve, Conserve, Distil; with all those laudable Sciences which adorn a compleat Gentlewoman.

CHAPTER XVIII

UNIVERSITIES

The two centres of learning in England were the universities of Oxford and Cambridge. These had flourished as monastic foundations during the Middle Ages, but after the Reformation they became mainly secular, encouraged and supported by the new class of lay administrators. Many of the students were sent up to obtain a liberal education rather than to study seriously. Organized games and athletics did not exist, sports were discouraged and there were many rules which seem to us more suitable to schoolboys than to undergraduates. Young men usually came up to the university at sixteen during Elizabeth's reign; some were two or even three years younger and many people thought this far too young. Here are two considerations delivered to Parliament on the matter in 1559.

Source: Hist. MSS. Com. MSS. of the Marquis of Salisbury, vol. I.

7. *Schoolmasters.*—None under the degree of baron to keep any schoolmaster in his house to teach children, for it is the decay of the universities and common schools.

8. *Education of the nobility.*—That an ordinance be made to bind the nobility to bring up their children in learning at some university in England or beyond the sea from the age of 12 to 18 at least; and that one-third of all the free scholarships at the universities be filled by the poorer sort of gentlemen's sons. The wanton bringing up and ignorance of the nobility forces the Prince to advance new men that can serve, which for the most part neither affecting true honour, because the glory thereof descended not to them, nor yet the common wealth (through coveting to be hastily in wealth and honour), forget their duty and old estate and subvert the noble houses to have their rooms themselves, etc.

CHILD STUDENTS

Source: Francis Bacon, *The Advancement of Learning.*

. . . a matter, which . . . I hold to be an error . . . is that scholars in universities come too soon and too unripe to logic and rhetoric

PLATE 17

Title-page of 'The English Gentleman'. Notice the various qualities illustrated

PLATE 18

Title-page of 'The English Gentlewoman'. Compare with Plate 17

arts fitter for graduates than children and novices . . . (so) that the wisdom of those arts, which is great and universal, is almost made contemptible, and is degenerate into childish sophistry and ridiculous affectation. And further, the untimely learning of them hath drawn on, by consequence, the superficial and unprofitable teaching and writing of them, as fitteth indeed to the capacity of children.

UNIVERSITY ENTRANCE

Source: Harrison, *A Description of England,* 1577.

. . . In my time there are three noble universities in England, to wit, one at Oxford, the second at Cambridge, and the third in London; of which, the first two are the most famous . . . in them the use of the toongs, philosophie, and the liberall sciences, besides the profound studies of the civil law, physicke, and theologie, are dailie taught and had: whereas in the later, the laws of the realme are onlie read and learned, by such as give their minds to the knowledge of the same. In the first there are not onelie diverse goodlie houses builded foure square for the most part of hard freestone (or bricke), with great numbers of lodgings and chambers in the same for students, after a sumptuous sort, through the exceeding liberalitie of kings, queens, bishops, noblemen and ladies of the land: but also large livings and great revenues bestowed upon them . . . to the maintenance onelie of such convenient numbers of poore mens sonnes as the severall stipends bestowed upon the said houses are able to support.

(Oxford and Cambridge). They were erected by their founders at the first, onelie for poore mens sons, whose parents were not able to bring them up unto learning: but now they have the least benefit of them, by reason the rich doo so incroch upon them. And so farre hath this inconvenience spread it selfe, that it is in my time an hard matter for a poore mans child to come by a felowship (though he be never so good a scholer, & woorthie of that roome.) Such packing also is used at elections, that not he which best deserveth, but he that hath most friends, though he be the woorst scholer, is alwaies surest to speed; which will turne in the end to the overthrow of learning.

N

In some grammar schooles likewise, which send scholars to these universities, it is lamentable to see what briberie is used; for yer the scholer can be preferred, such bribage is made, that poore mens children are commonlie shut out, and the richer sort received (who in time past thought it dishonor to live as it were upon almes) and yet being placed, most of them studie little other than histories, tables, dice, and trifles, as men that make not the living by their studie the end of their purposes, which is a lamentable hearing. Beside this, being for the most part either gentlemen, or rich mens sonnes, they oft bring the universities into much slander. For, standing upon their reputation and libertie, they ruffle and roist it out, exceeding in apparell, and banting riotous companie (which draweth them from their bookes unto an other trade.) And for excuse, when they are charged with breach of all good order, thinke it sufficient to saie, that they be gentlemen, which greeveth manie not a litle.

STUDENT LIFE AT OXFORD

A foreign visitor noticed the medieval vestiges in the routine and the clothes of students at Oxford in 1598.

Source: Hentzner, *Travels in England,* 1598.

These students lead a life almost monastic; for as the Monks had nothing in the world to do, but when they had said their prayers at stated hours, to employ themselves in instructive studies, no more have these. They are divided into three tables: the first is called the fellows table, to which are admitted earls, barons, gentlemen, doctors, and masters of arts, but very few of the latter; this is more plentifully and expensively served than the others: the second is for masters of arts, bachelors, some gentlemen, and eminent citizens: the third for people of low condition. While the rest are at dinner or supper in a great hall, where they are all assembled, one of the students reads aloud the bible, which is placed on a desk in the middle of the hall, and this office every one of them takes upon himself in his turn; as soon as grace is said after each meal, every one is at liberty either to retire to his own chambers, or to walk in the college garden, there being none that has not a delightful one. Their hábit is almost the same as that of the jesuits, their gowns reaching down to their ankles, sometimes lined with fur; they wear square caps; the doctors, masters of arts, and professors, have another kind of gown that distinguishes them: every student of any considerable standing has a key to the college library, for no college is without one.

A LETTER FROM LORD TREASURER BURLEIGH TO THE UNIVERSITY OF CAMBRIDGE, AS THEIR CHANCELLOR, FOR THE REFORMATION OF APPAREL

. . . no hatt be worne of any Graduate or Scholer within the University, except it be when he shall journey out of the Town, the same Graduate or Scholar having his name in any Table, or being in commons in any House of Learning in the said University; except in the time of his sicknes. And that all Scholers being Graduats upon the charges of any Howse, do wear a square cap of clothe, and lykewise scholers of Howses that be no Graduats, and all other Scholers that have taken no degree of Scholers, and do lyve upon their own charges, do weare in the said University a round clothe cap. Saving that it may be lawful for the sons of Noblemen, or the sons and heirs of Knights, to wear round caps of velvet, but not hats. And also that every such aforesaid Scholer, being a Graduate, shall wear abroad in the University, going out of his College, a gown and a hoode of clothe, according to the order of his Degree. Provided that it shall be lawfull for every Doctor of Divinity, and for the Master of any College, to weare a scarlett tippet, or a tippet of velvet, according to the antient customs of the realme, and of the said University: the which gown, tippet, and square cap, the said Doctors and Hedds shall be lykewise bound to weare when they shall resorte either to the Courte or to the City of London.

And that the excess of Shirtbands and Ruffs exceeding one inche and halfe (saving for the sonns of Nobelmen), the fashion and colore of other then white, be avoyded presently.

And no Scholer nor Fellowe of the foundation of any Howse of Learninge do weare either in the University or without, so long as he retaine the livings of a Fellowe or Scholer, any hose, stockings, dubletts, jackets, coats, or jerkins, or any other kinde of garment of velvet, satten, or silke, or in the faceing of the same shall have above one quarter of a yard of silke, or shall use any other light kynde of colore, or cutts, or gards, or fashion, which shall be forbidden by the Chancellors, . . .

And that no Scholer do weare any longe locks of heare upon his hedd, but that he be notted, polled, or rounded after the accustomed manner of the gravest scholers of the said University, under the pain of six shillings and eight pence for everye tyme that any graduate Fellow, Scholer, Pensioner, or Sizer shall offende in any of the foresaid Orders.

UNPROFITABLE STUDENTS

Many young gentlemen at the University evidently regarded their undergraduate career as a pleasant means of throwing away time and money with their friends.

Source: John Earle, *Micro-cosmographie*, 1628.

A young gentleman of the university is one that comes there to wear a gown, and to say hereafter he has been at the university. His father sent him thither, because he heard there were the best fencing and dancing schools; from these he has his education, from his tutor the over-sight. The first element of his knowledge is to be shewn the colleges, and initiated in a tavern by the way, which hereafter he will learn of himself. The two marks of his seniority is the bare velvet of his gown and his proficiency at tennis, where when he can once play a set, he is a fresh-man no more. His study has commonly handsome shelves, his books neat silk strings, which he shews to his father's man, and is loth to untie or take down, for fear of misplacing. Upon foul days, for recreation, he retires thither, and looks over the pretty book his tutor reads to him, which is commonly some short history, or a piece of 'Euphormio'; for which his tutor gives him money to spend next day. His main loitering is at the library, where he studies arms and books of honour, and turns a gentleman-critic in pedigrees. Of all things he endures not to be mistaken for a scholar, and hates a black suit though it be of satin. His companion is ordinarily some stale fellow, that has been notorious for an ingle to gold hatbands, whom he admires at first, afterwards scorns. If he have spirit or wit, he may light of better company and may learn some flashes of wit, which may do him knight's service in the country hereafter. But he is now gone to the Inns of Court, where he studies to forget what he learned before—his acquaintance and the fashion.

CHAPTER XIX

SCIENCE

Educated Englishmen had become familiar with the principal medieval scientific writings printed by the new continental presses. Interest became concentrated on the solution of concrete problems, and scientists tended increasingly to be concerned with physical rather than metaphysical problems and to insist on accurate observation and comparison. The universities in the seventeenth century were interested in much more than theology and classics. Robert Boyle set up his laboratory at Oxford in 1654 and Isaac Newton worked on optics at Cambridge and published his 'Principia' there in 1687.

Experimental methods and mathematical reasoning led to developments in such spheres as optics, statics, dynamics and mechanics. Instruments designed for closer observation and for more accurate measurement were designed at this time and were basic to later scientific developments. Great advances made in botany, anatomy, medicine,

SCIENTIFIC EXPERIMENTS.

zoology, and embryology were mainly due to a new precision of observation. The new direction of scientific thought was utilitarian—to gain power over nature. Francis Bacon wrote in the preface to his *Great Instauration*: 'I am labouring to lay the foundation, not of any sect or doctrine, but of human utility and power.'

It was not only scientists, however, who were interested in the new learning. A London businessman, Sir Thomas Gresham, founded and endowed Gresham College where, a little before 1660, a group of learned men began to meet once a week to discuss scientific subjects. This group was the forerunner of the Royal Society, of which King Charles II became patron in 1662.

WILLIAM HARVEY AND THE CIRCULATION OF THE BLOOD

Source: William Harvey, *Exercitatio Anatomica de Motu Cordis et Sanguinis in Animalibus*, 1628.

I began to think whether there might not be a motion, as it were, in a circle. Now this I afterwards found to be true; and I finally saw that the blood was forced out of the heart and driven by the beating of the left ventricle through the arteries into the body at large and into its several parts, in the same way as it is sent by the beating of the right ventricle through the arterial vein . . . into the lungs, and that it returns through the veins into the vena cava and so to the right ventricle, in the same way as it returns from the lungs through the venous artery . . . to the left ventricle. . . .

Since all things, both argument and ocular demonstration, show that the blood passes through the lungs and heart by the action of the ventricles, and is sent for distribution to all parts of the body, where it makes its way through the pores of the flesh into the veins, and then flows by the veins from the circumference on every side to the centre, from the lesser to the greater veins, and is by them finally discharged into the vena cava and right auricle of the heart, . . . it is therefore necessary to conclude that the blood in the animal body is impelled in a circle, and is in a state of ceaseless motion; that this is the act or function which the heart performs by means of its pulse; and that it is the sole and only end of the motion and contraction of the heart. . . .

Source: John Aubrey, *Life of Harvey.*

·I have heard him say, that after his booke of the *Circulation of the Blood* came out, that he fell mightily in his Practize, and that 'twas beleeved by the vulgar that he was crack-brained; and all the Physitians were against his Opinion, and envyed him; many wrote against him, . . . With much ado at last, in about 20 or 30 yeares time, it was received in all the Universities in the world; and, as Mr. Hobbes says in his book *De Corpore*, he is the only man, perhaps, that ever lived to see his owne doctrine established in his life-time.

FRANCIS BACON'S ATTITUDE TO SCIENCE

Source: Francis Bacon, *Novum Organum*, Book 1, aphorism 95.

Those who have handled sciences have been either men of experiment or men of dogmas. The men of experiment are like the ant; they only collect and use: the reasoners resemble spiders, who make cobwebs out of their own substance. But the bee takes a middle course, it gathers its material from the flowers of the garden and of the field, but transforms and digests it by a power of its own. Not unlike this is the true business of philosophy; for it neither relies solely or chiefly on the powers of the mind, nor does it take the matter which it gathers from natural history and mechanical experiments and lay it up in the memory whole, as it finds it; but lays it up in the understanding altered and digested. Therefore from a closer and purer league between these two faculties, the experimental and the rational (such as has never yet been made) much may be hoped. . . .

Source: Francis Bacon, *Novum Organum*, Book 2, aphorism 10.

Now my directions for the interpretation of nature embrace two generic divisions; the one how to educe and form axioms from experience; the other how to deduce and derive new experiments from axioms.

ISAAC NEWTON'S IDEAS ABOUT SCIENCE

Source: A letter written by Isaac Newton to Henry Oldenburg, the Secretary of the Royal Society, 2nd June, 1672.

For the best and safest method of philosophizing seems to be, first diligently to investigate the properties of things and establish them by experiment, and then to seek hypotheses to explain them. For hypotheses ought to be fitted merely to explain the properties of things and not attempt to predetermine them except in so far as they can be an aid to experiments. If any one offers conjectures about the truth of things from the mere possibility of hypotheses, I do not see how any thing can be determined in science; for it is always possible to contrive hypotheses, one after another, which are found rich in new tribulations. Wherefore I judged that one should abstain from considering hypotheses as from a fallacious argument, and that the force of their opposition must be removed, that one may arrive at a maturer and more general explanation.

THE ROYAL SOCIETY

Source: E. Chamberlayne, *Angliae Notitia, or The Present State of England,* 1687.

The design of the Royal Society is, in brief, to make faithful Records of all the Works of Nature, or of Art, which can come within their reach, so that the present Age and Posterity may be able to put a mark on the Errors which have been strengthened by long Prescription; to restore the Truths that have been neglected, to push on those which are already known to more various uses; to make the way more passable to what remains unrevealed, &c.

The business of their weekly Meetings is to order, to take account, consider, and discourse of Philosophical Experiments and Observations, to read, hear, and discourse upon Letters from all Parts, Reports, and other Papers containing Philosophical Matters; to view and discourse upon the Productions and Rarities of Nature and Art; to consider what to deduce from them, how they may be improved for the benefit of Mankind, which is their main aim.

In their discoursing they lay aside all set Speeches, and eloquent Harangues (as fit to be banish'd out of all Civil Assemblies, as a thing found by woful experience, especially in England, fatal to Peace and good Manners) and every one endeavours to express his opinion, or desire, in the plainest and most concise manner. . . .

The Royal Society then, since their first Institution, hath made a vast number of Experiments in almost all the Works of Nature; they have made particular Enquiries into very many things of the Heavens, as well as of the Earth, Eclipses, Comets, Meteors, Mines, Plants, Animals, Earthquakes, Fiery Eruptions, Inundations: Of Lakes, Mountains, Damps, Subterraneous Fires: Of Tides, Currents, and Depths of the Sea, and many hundred other things: They have composed many excellent short Histories of Nature, of Arts, of Manufactures, and of Works, whereof some are extreme curious. In a word, the Discoveries and Inventions made, should we say, but by some few Persons of this Society, if well considered, seem to surpass the Works of many foregoing Ages. . . .

The Coat of Arms granted by His Majesty to the Royal Society, is a Scutcheon with three Lyons of England, in chief, intimating, That the Society is Royal; the Crest is an Eagle, and the Supporters Hunting Hounds, Emblems of the quickest Sight and Smelling, to intimate the Sagacity, employed in Penetrating and searching after the Works of Nature.

BECOMING A FELLOW OF THE ROYAL SOCIETY

Source: F. N. L. Poynter, (Ed.) *Journal of James Yonge* (1647–1721), *Plymouth Surgeon.*

. . . I dined . . . once at Pontack's with the Royal Society. My friend Mr. Haughton, one of the fellows, was ordered by Sir J. Hoskins, vice president, to bring me to their meeting, which is every Wednesday at 4 afternoon in Gresham College. . . . Several philosophical things hapt to be discussed of, and when they broke up, which was about 6, the Secretary, Dr. Hook, and Dr. Tyson, with Mr. Haughton, told me I must be one of them. I told them it was an honour I could not pretend to, but without it would serve them what I could. Their president, observing what I said, told me it was a thing seldom offered, and seldomer refused. I said nothing more but what I said at first. Then he

invited me to dine at Pontack's with them next Wednesday, and
then give them my answer, . . .

The next Wednesday I dined with them at Pontacks, when
there were in all 16, several of them knights, doctors, &c.
I observed that they made no ceremony; every man sat as he came,
but the president placed me by him; the reckoning was 3s. 6d.
each and he paid for me. We went thence to the meetings, and
there I modestly accepted the fellowship they offered, and I was
then minuted down against next day of court and election. This
time I saw the famous Mr. Evlyn among them, . . .

UPON A PAIR OF SPECTACLES

Symptomatic of the new efficiency in scientific and technical matters
is the reference to spectacles in John Bunyan's *Book for Boys and Girls*,
published in 1686.

> Spectacles are for Sight, and not for Shew,
> Necessity doth Spectacles command;
> Was't not for need, there is but very few,
> That would for wearing Spectacles contend. . . .

THE PLEASURES OF OWNING A WATCH

Source: Pepys's Diary.

May 12th, 1665. . . . To the 'Change, and thence to my watch-
maker, where he has put it in order, and a good and brave piece
it is, and he tells me worth £14, . . .

May 13th, 1665. Lord! to see how much of my old folly and
childishnesse hangs upon me still that I cannot forbear carrying
my watch in my hand in the coach all this afternoon, and seeing
what o'clock it is one hundred times, and am apt to think with
myself, how could I be so long without one; though I remember
since, I had one, and found it a trouble, and resolved to carry
one no more about me while I lived.

ANATOMY

Source: The Journeys of Celia Fiennes, 1698.

I went to see the Barber Surgeons Hall (in Newcastle) . . .
there I saw a roome with a round table in it, railed round with
seates or benches for the conveniency in their disecting and
anatomiseing a body and reading lectures on all parts; there was
two bodyes that had been anatomised, one the bones were
fastned with wires the other had had the flesh boyled off and some
of the ligeaments remained and dryed with it, and so the parts
were held together by its own muscles and sinews that were
dryed with it; . . .

CHAPTER XX

AGRICULTURAL PROBLEMS

For centuries before Tudor times the 'enclosure' of open land had been going on for a variety of reasons. Now England was land-hungry and the movement for a more efficient use of land was accelerated. Waste land was being cleared and fenced for agricultural use and some commons on which the peasants had previously had rights of herding and harvesting were being enclosed; many landlords had taken over open-strip fields, fenced them and worked them more efficiently than the individual peasants had been able to do; the opportunities of the cloth trade encouraged many landowners to enclose arable land for sheep pasture. Opinions varied greatly about all these forms of enclosure. Some of the developments were approved of by everybody, others caused resentment and even rebellion among those who were likely to suffer inconvenience and loss.

Passions were deeply stirred on this complicated issue and many Acts of Parliament were passed in an attempt to stop the depopulation of the villages and hardship to the peasants. Preachers and writers protested also and, in extreme cases, direct action by those who felt themselves unjustly treated checked more serious abuses. But gradual change in agricultural methods was inevitable.

AN ACT FOR KEPYNG UP OF HOUSES FOR HUSBONDRY (4 Henry VII, c. 19—1489)

... the kyng ... remembreth that amonge all other thynges grete inconvenyences dayly doo encrease by desolation and pullyng downe and wylfull wast of houses and townes wythin this his reame, and leying to pasture londes whiche custumably have ben used in tylthe, wherby ydlenesse is growde and begynnyng of all myscheuous dayly dooth encrease. For where in some townes ii hundred persones were occupied and lived by their lawfull labours, now ben there occupied ii or iii herdemen, and the residue falle in ydlenes, the husbondrie whiche is one of the grettest comoditees of this reame is gretly decayed, chirches destroyed, the servyse of God wythdrawen, the bodies there beried not praied

for, the patrone and curates wronged, the defense of this londe
ayenst our enmyes outwarde febled and impeyred to the grete
displeysur of God, to the subversion of the policie and good rule
of this londe. . . .

THE COMMON OF YEVERNE AND THE USE THEROF

Source: Survey of Ewerne, 1553.

Also within the same mannor is a Common for wast grounde
lying open and not inclosed in the north-west parte of the uttermost borders of the lordshipp tewardes Farryndon, called
Yeverne Common; and conteyneth four-skore acres, wherin
all the tenaunts except the cotagers have common for ther
keyn and horses from the feast of Phillipp and Jacob unto the
feast of the Nativitye of our Lord God, and for ther sheape from
the feast of the Nativitye of our Lord God unto the myddle of
Marche, as hereafter shalbe declared.

Every tenaunt holinge one, two or thre tenements of the great
tenure shall keape upon the same common for every tenement
fyve kyne, two horses, and xxxv sheepe by the tenure of ther
londes, without any thinge payinge to the lorde for the same.

Every tenaunt holdinge too or thre tenements of the lesse
tenure shall keap upon the said common for every tenement two
kyne, one horse and xiij sheape, wythout any thinge paying for
the same.

The Pryor of Sont John's Jerusalem in Englond, as in the
right of his fre tenement, shall keap by custome upon the same
common two kyne and xxij shepe, without any thinge paying for
the same.

The person of Yeverne, as in right of his glebe, hath alwaies
been accustomed to keape eight beasts and one bull upon the
said common, without any thinge paying for the same.

No tenaunt or other person, or inhabitant, shall graunt a lyen,
or demyse his said common to any forener, but to suche as
inhabyte within the lordshipp of Y. by order of the courte,
as in the courte rolls of the same appereth . . .

The cotagers also, nor any other person (the tenaunts and freholders aforenamed excepted) have at any tyme within the remembraunce of any man lyving used or claymed any common or entercommon within the same common, otherwise than before declared. . . .

ENCLOSURES

Source: Hall's Chronicle in Henry VIII, by Edward Hall, ed. Charles Whibley (1904), Vol. I.

1514. Before this tyme the tounes about London, as Islyngton, Hoxston, Shordysh and other, had so enclosed the comon feldes with hedges and diches, that nother the young men of the citie myght shote, nor the auncient persons might walke for their pleasur in the feldes, except either the bowes and arrowes were broken or taken away, or the honest and substancial persons arrested or indited, saieng that no Londoner shold go out of the citie but in the hygh wayes. Thys sayeng sore greved the Londeners, and sodainly this yere a great nomber of the citie assembled them selfes in a morninge, and a turnar in a fooles coote came cryenge through the cytye, 'shovels and spades,' and so manye people folowed that it was wonder, and within a short space all the hedges about the townes were cast doune, and the diches filled, and every thyng made plain, the workemen were so diligent. The Kinges counsayll, hearyng of this assembly, came to the Gray Friers, and sent for the mayre and the counsail of the cytye to knowe the cause, whiche declared to them the noysance done to the Citezens, and their commodities and liberties taken from them, though they would not that the commonaltie and younge persones, whyche were dampnefyed by the noisaunce, would pluck up and remedy the same. And when the kinges counsayll had harde the aunswer, they dissimuled the matter, and commaunded the mayer to se that no other thynge were attempted, and to call home the citezens, which, when they had done their enterprice, came home before the kynges counsayll and the Mayre departed, without any harme more doing, and so after the feldes were never hedged.

Source: Seven Sermons before Edward VI, 1549, by Master Hugh Latimer.

My father was a Yoman, and had no landes of his owne, onlye he had a farme of iii. or iiii. pound by yere at the uttermost, and here upon he tilled so muche as kepte halfe a dosen men. He had walke for a hundred shepe, and my mother mylked xxx. kyne. He was able and did finde the king a harnesse, wyth hym selfe, and hys horsse, whyle he came to the place that he should receyve the kynges wages . . . He kept me to schole . . . He maryed my systers with v. pounde or xx. nobles a pece . . . He kept hospitalitie for his pore neighbours. And sum almes he gave to the poore, and all thys did he of the sayd farme. Wher he that now hath it, paieth xvi. pounde by yere and more, and is not able to do any thing for his Prynce, for himselfe, nor for his children, or geve a cup of drincke to the pore.

AN ACTE FOR THE MAINTENANCE OF HUSBANDRIE & TILLAGE, 1597–8 (39 Eliz. c. 2)

Whereas the Strengthe and florishinge Estate of this Kingdome hath bene allwayes and is greatly upheld and advaunced by the maintenaunce of the Ployghe & Tillage, beinge the Occacion of the increase and multiplyinge of People both for service in the Warres and in tymes of Peace, beinge allso a principall meane that People are sett on worke, and thereby withdrawen from Ydlenesse, Drunkenesse, unlawfull Games and all other lewde Practises and Condicions of Life; And whereas by the same meanes of Tyllage and Husbandrye, the greater parte of the Subjectes are preserved from extreame povertie in a competente Estate of maintenance and meanes to live, and the Wealthe of the Realme is kepte dispersed and distributed in manie handes, where yt is more ready to answere all necessary Chardges for the service of the Realme; And whereas allso the saide Husbandrie and Tillage is a cause that the Realme doth more stand upon it selfe, withowt dependinge upon forraine Cuntries either for bringinge in of Corne in tyme of scarsetye, or for vente and utterance of our owne Commodities beinge in over greate Abundance; And whereas from the xxvij yeare of Kinge Henry the Eighte of famous memory, untill the five & thirtiethe yeare of Her Majesties

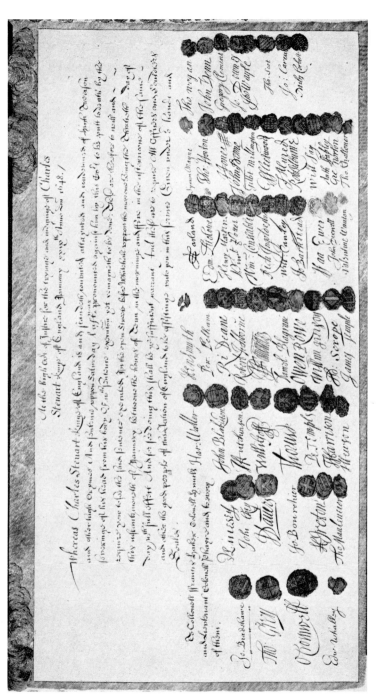

PLATE 19

The death-warrant of Charles I, with many signatures including that of Oliver Cromwell

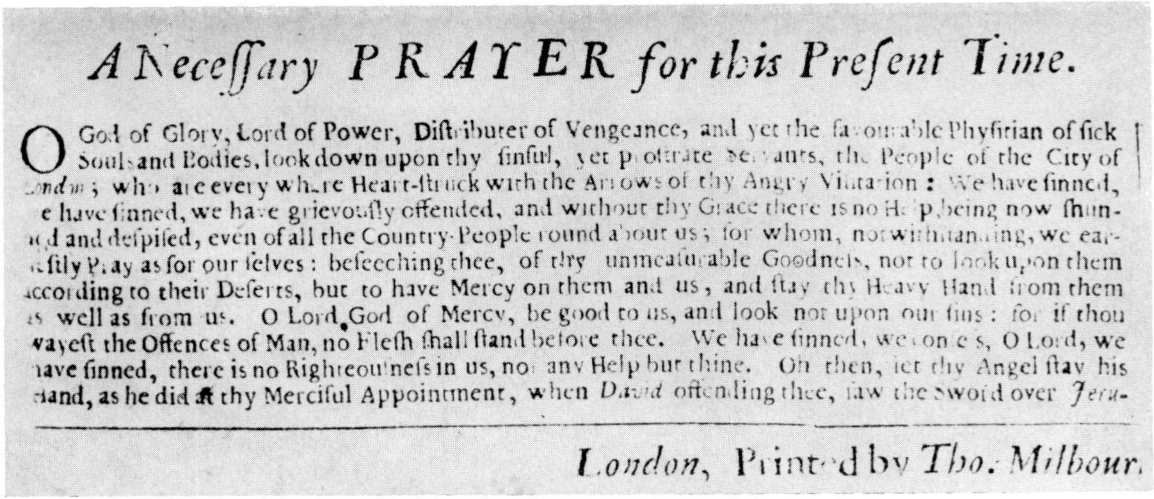

PLATE 20

A prayer for protection against the plague. Notice that plague was regarded as a visitation from God

moste happy Reigne, there was allwayes in force some Lawe whiche did ordeyne a conversion and continuance of a certayne quantitie and proporcion of Lande in Tillage not to be altered; and that in the laste Parliamente held in the said five and thirtiethe yeare of her Majesties Reigne, partlie by reason of the greate plentie & cheapnes of Graine at that tyme within this Realme, and partely by reason of the imperfection and obscuritie of the Lawe made in that case, the same was discontinued; since whiche time there have growen manie more depopulacions, by turning Tillage into Pasture, then at anie time for the like number of years heretofore: Be yt enacted . . . That wheras anie Landes or Growndes at anie tyme since the seavententh of November in the firste yere of her Majesties Reigne have been converted to Shepe Pastures or to the fattynge or grasinge of Cattell, the same Landes having bene tillable landes Feildes or Growndes such as have bene used in Tillage or for Tillage by the space of Twelve Yeares togither at the leaste nexte before suche conversion, according to the nature of the Soyle and course of Husbandrie used in that parte of the Country, all such Landes and Growndes as aforesaide shall before the firste day of May which shalbe in the yeare of our Lord God One thowsand five hundred nynetynyne, be restored to Tillage, or layde for Tillage in suche sorte as the whole Grownde accordinge to the nature of that Soile and course of Husbandrie used in that parte of the Countrie be within three yeares at the leaste turned to Tillage by the Occupiers and Possessours thereof, and so shall be contynued for ever.

II. And be yt further enacted by the aucthoritie aforesaide, That all Lands & Growndes which now are used in Tillage or for Tillage, having bene tillable Landes, Feildes or Growndes, such as nexte before the firste day of this presente Parliamente have bene by the space of Twelve Yeares togither at the leaste used in Tillage or for Tillage, accordinge to the nature of the Soyle & course of Husbandrie used in that parte of the Countrie, shall not be converted to any Shepe Pasture or to the grazinge or fattinge of Cattell by the Occupiers or Possessors thereof, but shall, accordinge to the nature of that Soyle and course of Husbandry used in that parte of the Countrie continue to be used in Tillage or for Tillage for Corne or Graine, and not for Woade.

o

VIII. And be yt enacted by the aucthority aforesaid, That if anie Person or Body Politique or Corporate shall offende againste the premisses, every suche Person or Body Politique or Corporate so offendinge shall loose and forfeyte for every Acre not restored or not contynued as aforesaide, the somme of Twenty shillinges for every yeare that he or they so offende; and that the saide Penaltyes or Forfeitures shalbe devided in three equall partes, whereof one thirde parte to be to the Queenes Majestie her Heires and Successors to her and there owne use, (and) one other thirde parte to the Queenes Majestie her Heires and Successors for Releife of the Poore in the Parishe where the Offence shall be committed . . . and the other thirde parte to such person as will sue for the same in anie Court of Records at Westminster. . . .

XIV. Provided allso, That this Acte shall not extende to any countyes within this Realme of Englande, but such onely as shall be hereafter specifyed; that is to say, the Counties of Northampton Leycester Warwicke Buckinham Bedford Oxforde Berkshire the Isle of Wighte Glocester Woorcester Nottingham Hampshire Wiltshire Somerset Dorsett. Derby Rutland Lincoln Hereford Cambridge Huntingdone Yorke Pembroke in South Wales and the Bishopricke of Durham, and Northumberlande, and the Counties of all Cities and Corporations lyinge situate and beinge within the Counties aforesaide, or confyninge to the same, and the Aynsty of the County of the City of Yorke. . . .

AN EPIGRAM, 1598

Source: Rev. Thomas Bastard, *Poems, English and Latin.*

Sheepe have eate up our medows and our downes,
Our corne, our wood, whole villages and townes.
Yea, they have eate up many wealthy men,
Besides widowes and Orphane childeren:
Besides our statutes and our iron lawes
Which they have swallowed down into their maws.
   Till now I thought the proverbe did but jest,
   Which said a blacke sheepe was a biting beast.

OFFENDERS AGAINST 39 ELIZ., c. 2

Source: Quarter Sessions Records of the North Riding of Yorkshire, ed.
J. C. Atkinson, Vol. I.

Helmsley 12 July 1608.

Jeffrey Milborne, Constable of Kyrkleatham, presenteth Raphe
Rockby of Marske, Esq. in the Constablery of Kirkleatham, for
converting and laying downe of 60 acres of arrable land into
pasture, viz. in a close called Wycar close xx acres or thereaboutes,
in Milflat close about xx acres, and in the Uperston and West
Yates about xx acres, contrary &c.

Will Marwood of Busby, Gentleman, for decaying of xxx
acres of arrable land or thereaboutes, and converting of xxx acres
of arrable land or thereaboutes, the same from tillage unto pasture
or meadowe, and tilled nothing in the same parish in lue thereof
contrary &c.; which said acres is lying in the fieldes of Carleton
called the Sike Close. . . .

Fr. Hall, of Worsall, thelder, for that he hath converted or layd
to pasture all the tyllage belonging to twoe oxganges of land at
Worsall; Rob. Metcalf of the same for the like decaye of tillage
belonging to five oxganges and (not) plowing any such quantitie
or qualitie in lieu thereof &c.

CHAPTER XXI

THE WOOL INDUSTRY

Trade in raw wool and woollen cloth had for long been the foundation of the English economy, and Tudor governments were concerned to maintain this.

The industry had moved gradually out of the towns into outlying rural areas, to escape municipal and guild regulations, and now State control allowed freer play to individual initiative. The settlement of foreign immigrants was encouraged and new skills and processes of manufacture were introduced. Thus the persecution of the Protestants in the Low Countries greatly helped the English wool trade, as repressive measures against French protestants later helped the silk trade.

Clothiers had for long been centred in East Anglia; Colchester and Norwich were busy and prosperous towns. In the seventeenth century the trade spread westwards to the Cotswolds, Somerset and Devon, and helped to build the wealth of the great merchant cities of Gloucester, Bristol, Exeter and Plymouth.

AN ACT RESERVING ENGLISH WOOL FOR ENGLISH CLOTHIERS (4 Henry VII. C. 11), 1489

For thencres and mayntenyng of Drapery and makyng of Cloth withyn this land, the Kynge oure Sovereigne Lord by thadvyse and assent of the Lordis spirituell and temporell and of the Comons in this present parliament assembled, and by auctorite of the same, hath ordeyned, establisshed and enacted that no maner of person, by himself or by eny othre, bye or bargeyn, from the first day of Marche that shalbe in the yere of our Lord mcccclxxxix, any wollez then unshorn, . . . of the growing of Berkshire, Oxenfordshire, Gloucestreshire, Herefordshire, Shropshire, Worcestirshire, Wilteshire, Somersetshire, Dorsetshire, Hampshire, Essex, Hertfordshire, Cambrigeshire, Northamptonshire, Suffolk, Kent, Surrey and Sussex, or any of them, afore the fest of the Assumpcion of our Lady then next ensuying; or bye or bargeyn any Wolles, or take promyse of bargeyn of any Wolles, that shall growe in any of the same Shires, in any yere or yeres to comme aftir the seid fest of the Assumpcion of our Lady, any tyme before the same fest of Assumpcion of our Lady that shalbe next after the Shering of the same Wolle or Wolles, but onely such persones as of the seid Wolles shall make or doo to be made Yarne or Cloth within this realme; upon peyn of forfeiture of the double value of all the Wolles bought or to be bargeyned or taken by promyse of bargeyn incontrarie to this ordenaunce; Nor that any marchaunt Straunger, by himself or by any othre persone, in any yere to come bye any Wolles before the fest of the purificacion of our Lady next aftir the clipping or sheryng of the same, upon like peyn of forfeiture; the one half of all suche forfeitures to be had to the Kingis use, and the other half therof to thuse of him that woll sue the partie that shall so breke the seid Ordenaunce: . . .

It is also ordeyned . . . that no maner of persone beyng sworn to be a wolle pakker, in any wise aftir the seid first day of Marche bye, bargeyn or gader any maner Wolle for any suche marchaunt Straunger within this realme, upon peyne of forfeiture of the same Wolle so bought bargeyned or gadered to thuse of any suche marchaunt Straunger: this ordenaunce to endure from the seid first day of Marche unto the end and terme of x. yeres next ensuyng.

A PROJECT FOR DYEING CLOTH IN ENGLAND, 1553

Source: The Request and Suite of a True-Hearted Englishman, written by William Cholmeley, Londyner, in the year 1553, ed. W. J. Thoms (Camden Soc., 1853).

. . . because that amonge oure commodities ther is none more nedefull to be wrought by us Englyshemen then woulle, forasmuch as of it are made boeth cloth and cappis, which every man muste necessarily weare, I have attempted to have the same wroughte and dyed within this realme by Englyshemen as substantyallye, truly, and perfectly well as ever it was, is, or can be done in Flanders, or in France, or any other parte of all the whole worlde.

And because the greatest difficultie, and only harde poynte of this myne attempted enterpryse, consisteth in the true and perfecte dying of cloth and cappis, with wodde and mader, I thought good to trye first what myght be done therein, not doubtyng to bryng all thinges easly to passe, if I mighte once attayne to the knowledge of the hardest poynt.

And to atchyve this my first purposed enterpryse, I sent to Anwarpe, and there procured for wages a man verye expert in the feate of dyinge, and wyllinge to serve in Englande, so that he myght sustayne no losse nor displeasure, if for lacke of water good for that purpose he could not performe the thinge that I requyred; for the dyars of Englande have raysed a foule slaunder upon the famouse river Temys, and all other waters of this your majesties realme, affyrmyng that the water therof wyll not serve to dye substanciall, true, and perfect colours withall, whear as no water in the whole worlde serveth better for the purpose then my workeman hath tryed the water of Temes to do.

To take awaye this let of this workman's connyng, I my selfe (beinge no man of great substance, and yet able to sustayne so muche losse if it had so chaunced) toke the whole adventure in hande, determinyng to put in hasarde so muche for the wealth of my contrey.

And susteyneyng no losse by the first adventure, but enjoyng a sufficient gayne, I conditioned with my sayde workeman for the term of x yeres, makyng a dyar of your majesties boroughe of Southwarke (who hath al maner implement to dying belongyng) halfe partnar with me duryng the tyme of the covenaunte made with my workeman, because that of my selfe I am not able (neyther hath it been my bryngyng up) to furnishe a dye house with all thinges thereto belongyng.

Thus have my partnar and I occupyed togyther the space of three yeres last past, either for us gayneing clearly by yere one hundred markes at the least upon the only dyinge of carsayes, broade clothes, and cappis, after the maner of the dyinge in Fraunce and Flaunders; which workemanship by my workeman done, and by the wearying tryed, is founde to be as good, substanciall, true, and perfect as any that hath ben or is dyed in the realme of France, Anwarp, or any other place beyonde the seas;

which thynge must nedis be very beneficiall to me and my
partnar, for as much as ther is none in all this realme that doeth
or can do the thing but only oure only workeman and suche as
have or shall learne it at his hande, which can be none but suche
as we must nedis have great commoditie by.

Notwithstanding, I for my parte, nothynge regardynge the
pryvate gayne that doeth and myght growe to me warde by the
meane of the singularitie of the feate, used by none other in all
this realme but by me and my partnar, have thought it my duitie
to make the thinge knowen to your majestie, that by thadvise
of your most honorable counsellours your auctoritie myght make
the feate common to all your loveing and faythfull subjectes,
not only the dyars of the citie of London, but of all other cities
and townes in al your majesties dominions; to the greate honoure
of this realme in the abandonyng of all desceytfull coloures, and
takyng away the reproche and shame of the Englysh nation,
which is reconned to be so grose wytted that they be not able to
attayne to the knowledge of the perfect workemanship of their
owne commodities; to the full contentation of your majestie
and of your nobles, who are or shall be delyted in the wearynge
of true and perfect good cloth trewly dyed at a reasonable pryce,
rejecting all vayne and unprofitable silkes which at this daye are
al to excessyve a pryce; and to the incomparable commoditie of
this your majesties realme and subjectes in that behalfe, wherby
the same maye in tyme be enryched with infinite treasure, . . .

INTRODUCTION OF STRANGERS FROM THE LOW COUNTRIES TO NORWICH, 1564

Source: Records of the City of Norwich, ed. Hudson and Tingey, Vol. II.

Master Thomas Sotherton, Maior of the Citye of Norwiche.
In the year of ower Lorde God 1564, the seveanthe year of the
reigne of ower Sovereign Ladye Elizabethe by the grace of God
of Englande Fraunce and Irelande Quene defender of the feythe,
etc. by reason that the comodities of woorsted makyinge is
greatelye decayed, by the whiche manye cittyzens bothe marchauntes and artizans that befor that tyme hadd (of the geyne
thereof) their whoale lyvinges, and great nombre of poore of

the cyttye were sette on worke by spinninge, weavinge, dyenge, callendringe and shearinge theseyde clothes which nowe were owte of estimation and vente, that the makers and woorkers

therof in all the exercises aforeseyde were fayne to geve themselves to other exercises and trades to maynteyne their families whiche was nothinge so proffytable, wherebye people become poore, manye lefte ther howses and dwelte in the countrye, that howses decayed for lacke of fearmes, and that they were letten at small prises, and the citye lyke to decaye yf prudente polici did not assyste the same. And after manye consultacons and devices what trades might be practized to redresse this poor state, was geven intelligence that dyverse strangers of the Lowe Countryes were nowe come to London and Sandwiche and had gotte lyscens of the Quenis Maiestye to exercize the makynge of Flaunders comodityes made of woolle, which straungers came over for refuge ageynste the persecution then raysed agaynste them by the power of the Duke Alva, principall for the Kynge of Spayne. And bycause the poore here might be excercized in theyr spynninge and woolle worke a motion was made to Thomas, then Duke of Norffolke, then lodged at his housse in this citye, that at his retorne to London he obtayned of the Quenis Maiestye, who of her gracious goodnes and mercifull clemencye havinge compassyon of the poore state of this her highnes citye, dyd tollerate and admytte to be and inhabite within this her highnes Citye of Norwiche thirtye master workemen, to have eyther of them tenne servauntes to exercize the makynge of those comodityes with warraunte to the Maiour and citezns to permitte them so to do. Whiche being done under her highnes lettres pattents (at seyde Duke his charges) was sente downe to the fore-seyde Maiour to be putte in execution.

ADVANTAGES RECEIVED BY NORWICH FROM THE STRANGERS, c. 1575

Source: S.P.D. Eliz., Vol. XX, No. 49. Printed in W. J. C. Moens, *The Walloons and their Church at Norwich* (Huguenot Soc. of London, 1887–8), App. XIX.

In primis they brought in grete comoditie thether, viz., the makinge of bayes, moccados, grograynes, all sorts of tuftes, etc., which were not made there before, wherby they do not onely set on worke their owne people but do also set on worke our owne people within the cittie as also a grete nomber of people nere xx myles aboute the cittie, to the grete relief of the porer sorte there.

Item—by their meanes our cittie is well inhabited, and decayed houses reedified and repaired that were in rewyn and more wolde (be), and now good rentes (are) paide for the same.

Item—the marchauntes by their comodities have and may have grate trade as well within the realme as withoute the realme beinge in good estimacion in all places.

Item—it cannot be but whereas a number of people be, but the one receyve comoditie of theother aswell of the citie as men of the contrie.

Item—they be contributors to all payments as subcedies, taskes, watches, contrubusions, mynisters wagis, etc.

Item—our owne people do practice and make suche comodities as the strangers do make, whereby the youthe is set on worke and kepte from idlenes.

Item—they digge and delve a nomber of acres of grounde and do sowe flaxe, and do make it out in lynen clothe which set many on worke.

Item—they digge and delve a grete quantite of grounde for rootes, which is a grete succor and sustenaunce for the pore bothe for them selves as for all others of citie and contrie.

Item—they live holy of them selves without charge, and do begge of no man, and do sustaine all their owne poore people.

And to conclude, they for the moste parte feare God, and do diligently and laborously attende upon their severall occupations, they obey all magistrates and all good lawes and ordynaunces, they live peaceablie amonge themselves and towarde all men, and we think our cittie happie to enjoye them.

UNEMPLOYMENT

Source: Shakespeare, *King Henry VIII*, Act 1, Scene 2.

Queen Katherine:
    I am solicited, not by a few,
And those of true condition, that your subjects
Are in great grievance. There have been commissions
Sent down among 'em, which hath flawed the heart
Of all their loyalties: wherein, although,
My good lord Cardinal, they vent reproaches
Most bitterly on you, as putter-on
Of these exactions, yet the King our master,—
Whose honour Heaven shield from soil!—even he escapes not
Language unmannerly; yea, such which breaks
The sides of loyalty, and almost appears
In loud rebellion.

Duke of Norfolk:
    Not 'almost appears,'—
It doth appear; for upon these taxations,
The clothiers all, not able to maintain
The many to them longing, have put off

The spinsters, carders, fullers, weavers; who,
Unfit for other life, compelled by hunger
And lack of other means, in desperate manner
Daring the event to the teeth, are all in uproar,
And Danger serves among them.

EXTRACTS FROM LETTERS WRITTEN BY REFUGEE STRANGERSS AT NORWICH TO THEIR FRIENDS AND RELATIONS AT YPRES, 1567

Source: Translated from H. Q. Janssen, 'De Hervormde vlugte-lingen van Yperen In Engeland' (Middleb. 1857) in W. J. C. Moens, *Register of Baptisms in the Dutch Church at Colchester* (1905). The letters are from the Archives of Ypres.

(1) *Clais van Wervekin* (hatmaker) *to his wife.* 21 *Aug.*, 1567.

. . . You would never believe how friendly the people are together, and the English are the same and quite loving to our nation. If you come here with half our property, you would never think of going to live in Flanders. Send my money and the three children. Come at once and do not be anxious. When you come, bring a dough trough for there are none here. . . . Bring also our long hooks to hang your linnen cords on. Buy two little wooden dishes to make up half pounds of butter; for all Nether-landers and Flemings make their own butter, for here it is all pigs fat. . . .

(3) *Clement Baet to his Wife* (5 *Sept.*, 1567).

. . . There is good trade in bays and I will look after a house as quickly as I can to get into business, for it will be easy to make money. I will get ready the gear for making bays against your coming. Bring all your and your daughter's clothing, for people go well clad here. . . . I let you know that we are merry and happy with each other. May God give you the same loving peace and riches as we have here at Norwich. It is very dear to hear the word of God peacefully.

THE ORGANIZATION OF THE WOOLLEN
INDUSTRY, 1615

Source: S.P.D., James I, Vol. lxxx.

These wools are usually converted by four sorts of people.

1. The rich clothier that buyeth his wool of the grower in the wool countries, and makes his whole year's provision beforehand and lays it up in store, and in the winter time hath it spun by his own spinsters and woven by his own weavers and fulled by his own tuckers, and all at the lowest rate for wages . . . many of them . . . sell again very much, if not most, of the wool they buy.

2. The second is the meaner clothier that seldom or never travels into the wool country to buy his wool, but borrows the most part of it at the market, and sets many poor on work, clothes it presently, and sells his cloth in some countries upon the bare thread, as in Devonshire and Yorkshire, and others dress it and sell it in London for ready money, and then comes to the wool market and pays the old debt and borrows more. Of this sort there are great store, that live well and grow rich and set thousands on work; they cannot miss the wool chapman, for if they do they must presently put off all their workfolk, and become servants to the rich clothier for 4*d.* or 6*d.* a day, which is a poor living.

3. The third sort are such clothiers that have not stock enough to bestow some in wool and some in yarn, and to forbear some in cloth as the rich clothiers do, and they buy but little or no wool, but do weekly buy their yarn in the markets, and presently make it into cloth and sell it for ready money, and so buy yarn again; which is weekly brought into the markets by a great number of poor people that will not spin to the clothier for small wages; but have stock enough to set themselves on work, and do weekly buy their wool in the market by very small parcels according to their use, and weekly return it in yarn, and make good profit thereof, having their benefit both of their labour and of the merchandise, and live exceeding well. These yarn-makers are so many in number that it is supposed by men of judgement that more than half the cloths that are made in Wilts, Gloucester, and Somersetshire is made by the means of these yarn-makers

and poor clothiers that depend weekly upon the wool chapman, which serves them weekly with wool either for money or credit.

4. The fourth sort is of them of the new drapery, which are thousands of poor people inhabiting near the ports and coasts from Yarmouth to Plymouth and in many great cities and towns, as London, Norwich, Colchester, Canterbury, Southampton, Exeter and many others. These people by their great industry and skill do spend a great part of the coarse wools growing in the kingdom, and that at as high a price or higher than the clothiers do the finest wools of this country.

FULLING AND DYEING

Source: The Journeys of Celia Fiennes, 1698.

Exeter is a town very well built the streets are well pitch'd[1] spacious noble streetes and a vast trade is carryd on; as Norwitch is for coapes callamanco and damaske soe this is for Serges— there is an increadible quantety of them made and sold in the town; their market day is Fryday which supplys with all things like a faire almost; the markets for meate fowle fish garden things and the dairy produce takes up 3 whole streetes, besides the large Market house set on stone pillars which runs a great length on which they lay their packs of serges, just by it is another walke within pillars which is for the yarne; the whole town and country is employ'd for at least 20 mile round in spinning, weaveing, dressing, and scouring, fulling and drying of the serges, it turns the most money in a weeke of anything in England, one weeke with another there is 10000 pound paid in ready money, sometymes 15000 pound; the weavers brings in their serges and must have their money which they employ to provide them yarne to goe to work againe; there is also a Square Court with penthouses round where the Malters are with mault, oat meal, but the serge is the chief manufacture; there is a prodigious quantety of their serges they never bring into the market but are in hired roomes which are noted for it, for it would be impossible to have it altogether.

[1] pitch'd = paved.

The carryers I met . . . with their loaded horses, they bring
them all just from the loome and soe they are put into the fulling
mills, but first they will clean and scour their roomes with them—
which by the way gives noe pleasing perfume to a roome, the
oyle and grease, and I should think it would rather foull a roome
than cleanse it because of the oyle—but I perceive its otherwise
esteemed by them, which will send to their acquaintances that are
tuckers[1] the dayes the serges comes in for a rowle to clean their
house, this I was an eye witness of; then they lay them in soack
in urine then they soape them and soe put them into the fulling-
mills and soe worke them in the mills drye till they are thick
enough; then they turne water into them and so scower them;
the mill does draw out and gather in the serges, its a pretty
divertion to see it, a sort of huge notch'd timbers like great teeth,
one would thinke it should injure the serges but it does not,
the mills draws in with such a great violence that if one stands
neere it, and it catch a bitt of your garments it would be ready
to draw in the person even in a trice; when they are thus scour'd
they drye them in racks strained out, which are as thick set one
by another as will permitt the dresser to pass between, and huge
large fields occupy'd this way almost all round the town which is
to the river side; then when drye they burle them picking out all
knotts, then fold them with a paper between every fold and
so sett them on an iron plaite and screw down the press on them,
which has another iron plaite on the top under which is a furnace
of fire of coales, this is the hott press; then they fold them exceeding exact and then press them in a cold press; some they dye but
the most are sent up for London white.

I saw the severall vats they were a dying in, of black, yellow,
blew, and green—which two last coullours are dipp'd in the
same vat, that which makes it differ is what they were dipp'd in
before, which makes them either green or blew; they hang the
serges on a great beame or great pole on the top of the vat
and so keep turning it from one to another, as one turns it off
into the vat the other rowles it out of it, soe they do it backwards
and forwards till its tinged deep enough of the coullour; their
furnace that keepes their dye panns boyling is all under that roome,

---

[1] tuckers = fullers or cloth-finishers.

made of coale fires; there was in a roome by it self a vat for the scarlet, that being a very chargeable dye noe waste must be allowed in that; indeed I think they make as fine a coullour as their Bow dyes are in London; these rolers I spake of; two men does continually role on and off the pieces of serges till dipp'd enough, the length of these pieces are or should hold out 26 yards.

SEALING OF CLOTH

Source: The Journeys of Celia Fiennes, 1698.

. . . they have beside the Town Hall (in Norwich) a hall distinct which is the Sealeing hall where their stuffs are all measured, and if they hold their breadth and lengths they are sealed, but if they are defective there is a fine layd on the owner and a private marke on the stuff which shews its defficiency.

CHAPTER XXII

MINING

Mining of all kinds expanded greatly during the sixteenth century.
It tended to be a part of the normal working of an estate under which
the coal or ore lay; the labourers who worked the fields were trans-
ferred to the mines in off-seasons. In some areas there were groups of
working miners who, by licence from the crown, worked a local mine:
tin in Cornwall, lead in Somerset, coal in the Forest of Dean. But
Elizabethan landlords tended more and more to encroach on these
ancient privileges.

THE COLLIER OF CROYDON, 1550

Source: One and Thyrtye Epigrammes, in Select Works of Robert Crowley,
ed. J. M. Cowper (E.E.T.S., 1872).

It is sayde, that in Croydon there dyd sometyme dwell
A Colier, that dyd all other Coliers excell.
For hys riches thys Colier myght have bene a knight;
But in the order of knighthode he hadde no delyght.
Woulde God all our knightes dyd minde colinge no more,
Than this Colier dyd knyghting, as is sayde before!
For when none but pore Colyars dyd wyth coles mell,
At a reasonable price they dyd theyr coles sell;
But sence oure Knyght Colyars have had the fyrste sale,
We have payed much money and had fewe sackes to tale.
A lode that of late yeres for a royall was solde,
Wyll coste nowe xvi s. of sylver or golde.
God graunt these men grace theyr pollyng to refrayne,
Or els bryng them backe to theyr olde state agayne.
And especially the Colyar that at Croydon doth sell;
For men thyncke he is cosen to the Colyar of Hell.

212

PLATE 21

Learning to walk. The mass of clothes must have helped the baby to balance—but how difficult to walk in!

PLATE 22

A needlework portrait

LETTER FROM THE QUEEN TO LORD SCORPE AND THE JUSTICES OF CUMBERLAND AND WESTMORLAND, ORDERING THEM TO PROTECT THE GERMAN MINERS, 1566

The Queen granted mining monopolies to favoured courtiers or to new joint-stock companies financed from London. The Company of the Mines Royal opened up new copper and lead mines in Cumberland, Wales and Cornwall, in order to help the munition supplies in time of war. Skilled foreign miners were imported to direct much of the work, and labour troubles inevitably followed.

Source: S.P.D., Eliz., Vol. XL, No. 87.

Wheras certayn Almaynes privyleged by our lettres patents under our great seal of england with ther great travaill, skyll and expenses of monyes, have of layte to there great commendacon recovered out of the montaynes and Rocks within our Countyes of Westmorland and Comberland great quantitye of myneralls, with ther full intencon to have furder proceded abowt the sayme, have of layte bene as we are credibly informed ympetched and assalted, Ryotouslye and contrarye to our peace and lawes, by a great nomber of disordered people of our said counties, wherupon manslaughter and murder of one of the said Almaynes hath ensuyd, to the lyklye discoragement of all ther sayd companye. We will therfore and straightlye charge and command you to apprehend and saiflye to Retayn in ward so manye as were occasyons eyther of the said tumult or murder, untyll we or our consell may be therof furder informed, and ye theruppon shall understand furder of our pleasure, that by example in theym, others may forbear to offend in the lyke.

PART OF A LETTER FROM DANIEL HOCHSTETTER TO JOHAN LOWVER ABOUT DIFFICULTIES AT THE KESWICK MINES, OCT. 10, 1566

Source: S.P.D., Eliz., Vol. XL, No. 81.

... As concerninge the tumulte or disquietnes that hathe ben, I send youe hearwithe thexaminacion of certayne of owre men. And I doe fynd the matter so to fall out, that if there be no

P

other order taken with the offendours, then hetherto hathe ben, I feare me we shall not be Able to kepe owre men Longe, unlesse it be to owre extreame costs and chardgies, for that they will not hasard theire Lyves in souche sorte, consideringe that they have no more wagies heare (with this danger) then they might have at home with quyetnes, ffor the offendours goe heare daylie up and downe before oure facies, bragginge and thretninge oure men of furder mischiefe, especiallye that naughtie man ffissher whoe hath ben the Ringleader and chiefe occasion of the villanous murderinge of Leonarde Stoultz, who defended him selfe a Longe space against xx of them, untill the Sonne of John a woode stroke him upon the Arme with a Staffe, that he could not any longer lyfte up the same for his defence, And then they fell all upon him and pitiously murdered him, the chefe occasion whereof was the sayd ffissher. This notwithestandinge the next day after being Sunday, there came a couple of men to Gresmor and did beat one of oure chiefe men, callyd Matfeller, And when he wolde have defendid him selfe, there came upon a Sodayne about the number of fyvetie Englishe men, and wold have ben upon them, And if Mr fflemynge had not chaunced to have comen by at that verie instante there had surelye great murder ben don.

IRON WORKS IN SUSSEX AND WASTAGE OF TIMBER, 1548-49

The new industries were a serious drain on the timber resources of the country and coal became increasingly used for domestic purposes in place of wood. The transport of the timber that was available was a serious problem and work had often to be moved to forest areas, so that sufficient wood was near at hand. The difficulty of carriage limited the use of coal to regions near the pits or close to navigable water, and lent increasing importance to coastwise trade. Newcastle became the centre of the export of 'sea-cole' to London and there were inevitable protests at her monopoly of the trade.

Source: Hist. MSS. Com. MSS. of the Marquis of Salisbury, Vol. XIII.

Petition to the Duke of Somerset, for a new commission. Articles to be enquired of by virtue of the King's commission to be directed to certain men of Sussex concerning the hurts done by iron mills and furnaces made for the same.

1. How many iron mills and furnaces for the same be now in Sussex?

2. How much great wood by estimation is yearly destroyed by the said mills and furnaces?

3. How much the price of a load of wood is already enhanced in divers places in Sussex by occasion of the said mills and furnaces?

4. Whether the said iron mills and furnaces be occasion of great detriment as well to the inhabitants in the towns of Calais and Guisnes, Bullen (Boulogne), etc., as also to the inhabitants of many towns and parishes in Sussex concerning their fuel.

5. If the said iron mills and furnaces be suffered to continue, then whether thereby there shall be great lack and scarcity of timber and wood in the parts near the mills for the making of houses, ships, etc. All the wood now standing within the county is not able to satisfy the ordinary occupations and necessary fuel wood for the poor commons the space of 20 years.

6. What number of towns are like to decay if the iron mills and furnaces be suffered to continue?

7. What number of persons are like to want livings if the iron mills, etc., be suffered to continue?

8. What hurts and harms have been done by occasion of the mills? And what be like to follow if they continue?

9. Whether notwithstanding the great number of mills iron is of a more greater price than it was at before there were so many?

10. How many of the iron mills and furnaces may conveniently be suffered to continue?

The presentment of the . . . jury concerning the annoyances of the iron mills in Sussex exhibited at Lewes January 12 in the year 2 Edward VI., as hereafter ensueth:

1. . . . . that there be within the shire of Sussex to the number of 53 iron mills and furnaces.

2. . . . that a hammer and a furnace spendeth yearly a 1000 loads of coal, which amounteth to 3000 loads of wood, besides the waste, which we be not able to answer unto.

3. . . . that within 15 years last past upon the downs a load of wood was commonly bought and sold for 14d., and now by occasion of the mills and furnaces every load is enhanced to 2s. 8d. and 3s. And in the Weald among the woods a load of wood was commonly brought and sold for 4d., and now by occasion of the mills every load is inhanced to the sum of 12d.

4. . . . the mills and furnaces do damnify and hurt as well the inhabitants of the towns of Calais, Guisnes, Boulogne and other beyond the sea as the inhabitants of Sussex.

5. . . . if the mills and furnaces be suffered to continue, whereas now all manner of timber and wood for all occupations as well for the sea as for the land is very scanty already, by the said mills and furnaces hereafter should be scarcity and almost none to be gotten.

6. . . . if the mills and furnaces be suffered to continue all the towns and villages upon the downs between Lewes and Bramber are within a short while like to decay and not to be inhabited for lack of timber and fuel.

7. . . . all the inhabitants of the towns and villages abovesaid shall be driven to seek their living in other places and there utterly to forsake their dwelling, whose number we be not able to express, if the mills and furnaces be suffered to remain.

8. . . . What hurts and harms hath been done by occasion of the mills and furnaces we cannot express, it is so great, and what will follow hereafter, we be not able to say.

9. . . . before so great a number of these furnaces, and iron mills were erected and set up iron was at £3 the ton, now it is inhanced to £8 the ton and upward.

10. . . . if the mills should be suffered to continue, then within short time tanners should not be able to occupy their tanning for lack of tan, because they fell the woods out of

season. . . . we think there may no iron mills and furnaces continue and remain within the space of 20 miles of the sea.

COAL-MINES

Source: Harrison, *A Description of England,* 1577.

Of colemines we have such plentie in the north and westerne parts of our Iland, as may suffice for all the realme of England: and so must they doo hereafter in deed, if wood be not better cherished than it is at this present. And to saie the truth, notwithstanding that verie many of them are caried into other countries of the maine, yet their greatest trade beginneth now to grow from the forge into the kitchin and hall, as may appeere alreadie in most cities and townes that lie about the coast, where they have but little other fewell, except it be turffe and hassocke. I marvell not a little that there is no trade of these into Sussex and Southhampton shire, for want whereof the smiths doo worke their iron with charcoale. I thinke that far carriage be the onelie cause, which is but a slender excuse. . . .

COMPLAINT OF THE LORD MAYOR OF LONDON AGAINST THE NEWCASTLE COAL MONOPOLY, c. APRIL, 1590

Source: Lansdowne MSS. 65, No. 11.

Touching the prices of Seacole: It is verie apparent that before the making of the grand Lease the price of Seacole of the best sorte was at 4s. the Chaldron; After the assignacion of the said Lease to one Mr. Sutton the price was enhaunced to vi s. the Chalder and soe contynued during the tyme that the said Mr. Sutton enjoyed the Lease; but, being once assigned over to the Towne of new Castle, the price of Seacole beganne to encrease to an excessive rate . . . and is now growen to ix s. the chaldren, nether can so be had except the Buyers be content to take of both sortes, viz: the good and bad cole together. . . .

Whereas the Inhabitantes were wonte to digge upp and have before hande great stoare of Seacole readie for caryadge, now they dyett and feede the shipp maisters and marchantes with such scarscitie as maie best serve for theire advantage; Albeit the said mynes will affored great plentie without feare of future want of the commodite. . . .

The inhabitantes of new Castle to prevent more plentie of Seacole which might rebate and bringe downe the price, restraine the owners and possessors of such (other) mynes from ladeing theire cole at anie other place save before the said Towne. . . .

The said . . . , to the end they maie utter theire worse sorte of cole, which serveth onlie for the Smythes forge and such other uses, in greatter plentie, and at as highe a rate as the verie best cole, use to put of and delaie the merchauntes and Masters of Shipps some tymes, 4, 5, or 6 weekes together, whereby they inforce them to take a thirde parte, and sometymes an halfe of the worse sorte of cole at as deare a rate as they doe the best cole, or els to staie for the ladeing theire shipps at theire owne pleasures;
. . .

SUGGESTED REMEDIES

Source: Lansdowne MSS. 65, No. 11.

. . . that noe forreine Bottom shalbe laden with anie Seacole at the towne of New Castle or anie other place uppon the River of Tyne, till the Englishe shippes (if anie be present) have their full lading.

That noe straunger or Englishe be permitted to transporte beyond the sea anie of the best sorte of cole, but of the seconde or third sorte onlie, as they were wonte and accustomed to doe by order taken by the Towne of New Castle.

. . . that all other owners or farmers of Cole Mynes, as well as . . . the inhabitantes of New Castle maie open their mynes, and make sale of theire coles at a reasonable rate, not exceeding . . . vij s. the chalder, and to lade the same at most opportune places without anie restreint.

RULES TO BE OBSERVED BY MINERS AT WOLLATON, NOTTS., c. 1600

Source: Hist. MSS. Com. MSS. of Lord Middleton.

This is our master's commandment that all you stovers of the feild shalle make your just acount unto your undermen everye nowne and every nyght what you have gett and sould. For every tyme that you do mys, you must losse 3s. 4d.

And for every bourdenne of colles that you do sowfer to be borne from the feild you must losse 12d.

And for every bordenne of wood the like 12d.

And that you shale make just messeures betwene the lord and the countre, . . .

And if aney one be takene with aney of the pit candels bearing whome to his house, 3s. 4d.

And if aney one be takene with ane of the pit towles in his house, to losse 3s. 4d.

And if aney one be taken cutting of aney of the pit rowpes or with aney in his howse, to lowse 6s. 8d.

And for every of these defaultes whosoever he is, it must be taken up of his wages the next Seterday after.

More, if aney mann do take ane of the lordes money without the comand of him or his officers, to losse 10s. and so to departte the towne and the feyld.

WORKING CONDITIONS IN MINES

Source: The Journeys of Celia Fiennes in 1697.

Here we entred Darbyshire and went to Chesterffield 6 mile, and came by the Coale Mines where they were digging; they make their mines at the Entrance like a well and so till they come to the Coale, then they digg all the ground about where there is Coale and set pillars to support it and so bring it to the well, where by a basket like a hand-barrow by cords they pull it up, so they let down and up the miners with a cord. . . .

Thence to Buxton, 9 mile over those craggy hills whose bowells are full of Mines of all kinds of black and white and veined marbles, and some have mines of Copper, others Tinn and Leaden mines in which is a greate deale of Silver; . . . they digg down their mines like a well, for one man to be let down with a rope and pulley and so when they find ore they keep digging under ground to follow the ore, which lies amongst the stone . . . they generally look very pale and yellow that work Underground, they are forced to keep lights with them and some tymes are forced to use Gunpowder to break the stones, and that is sometymes hazardous to the people and destroys them at the work.

CHAPTER XXIII

WORKING CONDITIONS

In the Middle Ages questions of wages and working conditions had been decided in each locality by members of the town council and of the craft guilds. By the sixteenth century many towns had decayed, industry had spread into the surrounding countryside and craft guilds were much less powerful. Wages and working conditions were now controlled by Justices of the Peace and permission was liberally given for the settlement of foreign immigrants if it could be shown that they could bring new skills and new knowledge into England. Justices of the Peace also controlled the conditions of apprenticeship, though conditions varied greatly from district to district and from one master to another.

A PRINTING SHOP.

COMPLAINT OF THE SHOEMAKERS OF NORWICH AGAINST THEIR JOURNEYMEN

Source: Records of the City of Norwich, ed. Hudson and Tingey, 1910. Vol. II.

Assembly on the Feast of St. Matthew 6 H. vii (21 Sept. 1490)

It is agreed that the bill of the Shomakers craft shall be enacted according to the effect of that bill. And whosoever of the said craft shall act to the contrary, he shall forfeit six shillings and eight pence, and they shall be divided in this form, viz. one part to the Community and the other part to the craft. Which same bill, word for word, follows:

To our right honourable Mastres, the Meire and his Brethren Alderman, and to our good mastres and weelwillers of the Common Cownsell of the Cite, Sheweth to your grete discrecions the poor Artificers and craftymen of Shomakers of the seid cite, that wher dyvers jornymen and servaunts of the seid crafte gretly disposed to riot and idelnes, whereby may succede grete poverte, so that dyvers dayes wekely whan them luste to leve ther bodyly labour till a grete parte of the weke be almost so expended and wasted, ayenst the avauntage and profight werely of them self and of ther Mastres also. And also contrary to the lawe (of) god and good guydyng temporall, they labour qwikly toward the Sondaye and festyuall dayes on the Saterdayes and vigils ffro iiij of the clock at after none to the depnes and derknes of the nyght foloweng. And not onely that synfull disposicion but moche warse so offendyng in the morowynggs of such festes, and omyttyng the heryng of ther dyvyne servyce; Wherfor prayeth the seid artificers hertyly, that the rather forgoddys cause and also that vertuous and true labour myght help to the sustentacion of the seid crafte, that by your generall assent may be ordeyned and enacted for a laudable custume, that none such servaunt or jornyman from hensforth presume to occupye nor werke after the seid howre in vigeles and Saterdayes aforesaid, upon peyne by your discrecions to be sette for punyshment alsweel of the seid artificers for ther favoryng and supportyng, as for the seid jornymen so werkyng and offendyng.

BOND OF APPRENTICESHIP TO A BAKER, FEB. 24, 1531

Source: Records of the Borough of Leicester, ed. M. Bateson, Vol. III.

This indenture made the xxiiiith day of Februare, in the raene of our Soverand lorde Kyng Henry the VIIIth the xxiith, wyttunes that John Harbarde late of Truvystun, dosse bynd hym selfe prentes to Wylliam Tebbe then beyng Maere of Leicester to the bakares krafte for the terme of vii yaere and the viiith yaere gorneman; also the said Wylliam dosse bynde him be this indenture to gyff to the seid Jhon for the terme of vii yaere every yaere viii d. and the viiith yaere every weke vj d. and to be dobull araede bothe for the hallyday and the warke daye att hys cumyng furthe, and to be kepyd as a prentes schud be, that is to saye maete and drynk, hosse and shoys, lyllyn, wollyn, and hys krafte to be toghtt him and nothyng to be hyd frome hym therof: also the seid John dosse bynd hymselfe be thys indenture to be trw servand for thoes yaeres and that he schall nott stelle none of is Masters gudes, nott be vi d. in the yaere, and that he schall nott wse no gamyng, nor he schall nott make no promys of wedloke exsep is Master gyff hym leffe, nor he schall nott bye or sell exsep ytt be for is masters profytt, and he schall kyepe is masters consyll in all maner of thynges that is lefull. In wyttines here of Wylliam Tebbe, Thomas Kattelyn baelle, John Westes, Thomas Bette, Justes of the paesse, Thomas Howytt, Wylliam Fowollar, Klarke with other mo.

MUNICIPAL REGULATIONS OF HOURS AND WAGES BY THE COMMON COUNCIL OF LONDON, 1538

Source: Guildhall Journal, Vol XIV.

For certayn reasonable & necessary consideracions it ys enactyd establysshed & ordeyned at thys present commen Counsell by the aucthoritye of the same, that from hensfurth Almaner of Carpenters masons joyners tylers plasterers Briklayers gardeners laborers & all other hand crafty men whiche shall fortune to worke by the day with any person or persones withyn the libertyes of thys Citye, shall from the feast of the

Natyvytue of our lady untyll the feast of thannunciacion of oure blessyd lady contynually begynne hys dayes woorke at the howre of vj of the clok yn the mornyng & so to contynue untyll ix of the clok then next ensuyng. And than to goo to hys brekefast & to tary therat but onely one quarter of an howre, & than immedyatly to resorte ageyn unto hys sayd worke & there to contynue untyll the howre of xij of the clok, and then to goo to hys dynner & to resorte ageyn unto hys worke by the howre of one of the clok at after noone at the farthest, & there to contynue untyll the houre of iiij of the clok at after noone, and than to have libertye to goo to hys drynkeyng by the space of one quarter of an houre onely, and than immedyatly to resorte ageyn to hys seyd woorke & there to contynue untyll the howre of vj of cloke at nyght, & to have none other houres or vacant tyme yn the hole day other than as ys aforesayd, And to take for hys dayes woorke from the sayd feast of the Natyvytye of our lady untyll the feast of thannunciacion of our blessyd lady yerely but onely vij d. by the day.

Item yt ys further enacted by auctorytie aforesayd that every of the sayd Craftsmen and others whyche shall fortune to woorke by the day, shall from hensfurth, from the feast of the Annunciacion of oure blessyd lady untyll the feast of the Natyvytie of oure lady, contynually begynne hys dayes worke at the howre of v of the clok yn the mornynge & so to contynue untyll viij of the clok then next ensuyng, & then to goo to hys brekefast & to tary therat but onely one quarter of an houre. And than immedyatly to resort ageyn to hys seyd woorke & there to contynue untyll the houre of xij of the clok, & then to goo to hys dynner & to resort ageyn unto hys worke at the howre of one of the clok in the after noone at the farthest, & there to contynue untyll the houre of vij of the clok at after noone, and yn the meanetyme to have no more than a quarter of an howre for hys drynkyng tyme. And to have none other houres or vacant tyme yn the hoole day than as ys aforesayd, & to take no more for hys hole dayes woorke from the sayd feast of thannunciacion of oure blessyd lady untyll the feast of the Nativytie of oure blessyd lady saynt mary the vrygyn, but onely viij d. by the day & no more.

And bycawse that the sayd artyficers must of necessytie occupye brykks tyles lyme lome gravell & sande, and the same ys not so good & well made as hath bene accustomed nor kepyng measure as of olde tyme hathe bene used. It ys nowe enactyd by the aucthorytie aforesayd that tyles brykkes lyme gravell & sand shalbe as well made & kepe the measure as hathe bene accustomed at any tyme withyn theys fowerty yeres nowe last past, upon payne of forfaiture for every suche defaut iij s. iiij d. to be payed by the owner of the same, whiche shalbe recovered by accion of dett byll playnt or Informacion yn any of the kynges courts withyn thys Cytye, in whiche accions & suytes or any of theym the defendant shall not be receyvyd to wage or doo hys lawe nor any proteccion to be allowed yn the same.

Item yt ys enactyd by aucthorytye aforesayd that none of the sayd crafts men or others aforesayd shall take any other wages by day or otherwyse for any of theyre apprentices duryng the first ij yeres of apprenticehod of theyre sayd apprentice, but onely as laborers do & have usually takyn, & not to take as a Crafts man or Journeyman, and that after any apprentyce of any suche Crafts man afore remembred hath served ij yeres of hys apprenticehod, that than the maister of suche apprentice to take onely suche wages for such apprentices as shalbe admytted & appoynted by the Chamberlayn of London for the tyme beyng And by the Wardeyns of the said occupacion as they shall thynke convenyent by theyre dyscrecions, And that yf any freeman of the sayd citye breke any poynt or article conteyned yn thys present ordynaunce & refuse to obey the same, That than he so offendyng shall lose hys freedom. Provyded alwayes that gardyners and laborers shall yn all thynges observe & kepe the ordynaunce aforesayd yn all degrees except onely that they nor any of theym shall take any more for hys dayes woorke than fyve pence stirlyngs & not above.

A BAKERS' STRIKE AT CHESTER, 1557

Source: R. H. Morris, *Chester in the Plantagenet and Tudor Reigns.*

Memorandum that on Saturday the xiiii[th] daye of November Ao 1557, John Webester, then maire of the Citie of Chester, did caule before hym in the pentice of the said citye Richard Danold and Edward Smith, then stewards of the occupacions of bayckers of the said citie, and conserning which tyme of the pryse of whete soulde in the markyt of the said citie the same daye, which was for xlvi s. the quarter of Chester meesure the derist, and ther opon appoynted unto them for the assize the weke folowing to baycke the half penye whyte loufe vi ounces and haulefe, and so of all kynds of bred ratable after the same assise, which the said stewards then refused and desierid ryspyt unto the Monday next folowing to speeke with ther hole occupacion. Upon which Mondaye the said stewards gave an answer unto the said mayre in the name of the hole occupacion that they would not consent to baycke after that assise but utterly refused the same, wherupon the tewesday next insuing, videlicet the xvii[th] of November, at an assemble in the comon haule of the said citie the said assise was examenyd reasouned and debatyd, conserning the measure of the brason houpe of the saide citie with the measure and assise appoyntyd by the statute of this realm and allso with the mesure and assyese then used in London and the pryces of corne; accordinglye yt was therby the said mayre, aldermen, sheriffs and comon counsell of the same cytye fully agreid and concludyd that the same assise afore appoyntyd by the said mayre was laufull nessesary and suffycyent for the Bayker to lyve upon, and that from thensfourth the said bayckers should observe and kepe the said rite of assises accordinge to the pryces of corne as the markyt shall faule or ryse, upon the payne before tyme appoyntyd by the statutes of this realme.

And then the same mayor eftsones sent for the said stewards and diverse other of ther company and occupacion and shewed them the mynde and hole determynacion of the hole counsell of this cite, and requiered them to baycke therafter according to ther dutye that ther should be no want of brede within this said citye, but they in no wyse would therto consent, by resone wherof ther was grete wante of brede within this saide citie, wherupon the mayre by the advyse of his brethern aldermen shiriffs and other of the comon counsell the xxi[th] daie of the saide November made open proclamacion as folowith: 'For as much as the comon bayckers of this citie being manye tymes by the Mayre admonyshed and comandyd to baycke brede after the assise by hym raisonably geven according to his office, presentlie do refuse to backe brede for the sustenance of the inhabytants of the same citie and others therto resorting, be reasone wherof the saide citizins be lycke to be at grete hynderaunce for lacke of brede, for spedye remedye therin to be had Mr Mayre by virtue of his office and by thadvise of his worshipfull bretherne the aldermen of the same citye, do requier all loving citizens to make necessary provicion for this presente tyme for suche brede as theye shall occupye, and that yt shalbe lawfull to all persones as well of the cytye as the countrye to baycke good and holsome brede for the sustenance of the said citizens after a resonable sorte, and to bringe the same from tyme to tyme into the markyt, wher they shall not have onely redye monye for ther brede with hartye thankes, but allso be discharged from all sute procurid by the comon bayckers of this citie or any other person or persones in ther names; and to thentent the premysses may be well accomplyshed Mr Mayre do the moste hartyly dysier all the said loving citiznes to be good and loving neighbors in doing and setting forward of the same as they tender the comon welthe and state presentlie of this citie.

THE STATUTE OF APPRENTICES, 1563

Source: Statues of the Realm, iv. 1.

II. That no manner of person (after 30th Sept. next) . . . shall be retained hired or taken into service . . . to work for any less . . . term than for one holy year, in any of the sciences . . . or arts of clothiers . . . shoemakers . . . pewterers, bakers, brewers, . . . saddlers. . . .

XI. That the Justices of Peace of every Shire . . . shall have authority by virtue hereof, within the limits . . . of their several commissions to . . . rate and appoint the wages. . . .

XXIV. That . . . it shall not be lawful to any person . . . other than such as do now lawfully . . . exercise any craft . . . to set up . . . any craft . . . except he shall have been brought up therein seven years at least . . . nor to set any person on work in such mystery . . . being not a workman at this day, except he shall have been apprentice as is aforesaid, or else having served as an apprentice . . . will become a journeyman. . . .

XXX. That the Justices of Peace of every county . . . shall yearly . . . make a special and diligent enquiry of the branches and articles of this Statute . . . and where they shall find any defaults, to see the same severely corrected and punished.

A TANNER'S APPRENTICE THREATENED WITH COMPULSORY SERVICE IN HUSBANDRY, 1563

Source: Norwich Municipal Archives. Depositions taken before the Mayor and Aldermen of Norwich, 1549–67, ff. 53–53b.

Robart Myller, of the cittie of Norwich, Tanner, of the age of xvi yeares or ther abowte, examined before Mr William Farrow, Mayor of the Cittie of Norwich, W. Mingay Henry Croke Henry Bacon Jo. Aldrithe, Justices of the peace, on Wdenesdaye the xiiii th of Aprrell, Anno 1563, sayth: That he was in servyce with one William George of Hempton, Tannor, and dwelte with hym by the space of Thre yeares, And upon a tyme aboute sevenight before candlemas Last paste the wyfe of the sayde William George ded falloute with this examinate and Rebuked hym for his worke very moche, And this examinate sayed unto hys dame: I am sory that I cannot please you, but yf my Sarvice maynot please you, yf you and my Master Will give me Leave to departe I shall provide me of a service in some place, I truste. And heruppon his sayde dame declaryd un to her husbonde the same night that the sayde Robart Myller coulde be content to go from hym and to place hym selfe in some other survice. And therupon he callyd this examinate unto hym and askyd hym whether he wolde go from hym or not, and he sayde: for that my survice cannot please you nor my dame If you will geve me Leve to departe I canbe contentyd to departe, and then the sayde William George his Master sayde: with a good will you shall departe and provide yourselfe of a Master so well as you can. And there upon he drewe to his purse and payed to this examinate seven shillings in mony that he ought hym for certeyne calve skynnys that he had solde of his. And on the Sundaye mornyng this examinate came to his sayde Master to take his leve, And then his sayde Master sayde unto him seyng: you will go a waye, you shall not go owte of the hunderde, but you shall serve eyther Mr Clyfton or ells Mr

PLATE 23

The visit of the wet-nurse. Notice the baby being swaddled and bed-curtains being drawn

PLATE 24

The schoolmistress. Notice the relaxed and homely atmosphere

Raymer in husbondry. And this deponent sayed: Master, I have served thes thre yeares in your occupacion and can no skyll in husbandry and I wilbe lothe to lose all this tyme that I have served in the occupacon. And then the sayed William George sayde: Tarry tyll Sondaye and you shall have a new payer of shoos; and so this examinate tarryed styll ther with the sayde William George tyll the Tewesdaye next followyng, and in that tyme he had understandyng that ther was a warrant procured for hym to serve in hosbondry, and thereupon he cam from his sayde Master thesayde Tewesday, And so cam strayght to Norwich and placed hym selfe in the service of one Richarde Smethe, Tanner. And further this examinate saythe that the sayde Richarde Smythe sent hym from Norwiche to Elmeham Fayer on our laydys daye with certeyne lether to sell, And there the sayde William George met with this examinate and sayde unto hym: How sayest thou Robyn? hadest not thou as good to have served me for thre yeares as to serve where thou doest serve for vii yeares? for now thou arte bounde thou cannest not get owte of the Cittie nowe. And thou beste wyse thou mayest saye that thou receyved of that vi d. that I toke of the at Burreham Markett for the rent of thy howse, that I lete it the for to reteyne the with vi yeares, or ells thou canst never get owte of the cittie; and further he sayeth not.

COMPLAINT OF THE CITIZENS OF LONDON AGAINST ALIENS, 1571

Although the government controlled immigration and frequently encouraged it in order to introduce new techniques into industry, there were still complaints about it and in 1571 the citizens of London protested:

Source: S.P.D. Eliz., Vol. LXXXI, No. 29.

The Subiettes of England and Cittizens of London find themselves greeved at two sortes of straungers settlers here amongst us.

    1. marchants.   2. handycraftesmen.

Against marchant strangers there are six speciall provisions
Q

by the lawes of the land, and the charters of the citty. All which are offended by theis straungers.

1. As first they ought not to take any lodgings or houses within the citty but to abide at the tables of freehostes, and to dwell in noe other place . . . Contrary heerunto the marchant straungers take uppe the fairest houses in the Citty, devide & fitt them for their severall uses, take into them several lodgers & dwellers. . . .

2. Secondlie they ought to sell their merchaundize within six weekes after the landing thereof.

Contrary heerunto they keepe their Marchandizes soe long as they list, feed the markettes with them at their pleasure, take all times of advantage for the utterance of their commodities, . . .

3. Thirdlie they ought not to sell any merchaundizes by Retayle, Contrary heerunto many of their merchaunts are Retaylers also; keepe shoppes inward, and private chambers, and therein sell be whole sale and retayle, send to every mans house, serve chapmen, send to fayres, and utter their commodityes many other wayes.

4. They ought to imploye the money taken for the commodities of their countrys upon the commodityes of this Kingdome, which they doe not; for whereas they have halfe the trade of this Kingdome in importe they imploy not a twentieth part thereof, but transport the money or make it over by Exchange, and keepe the Exchange within their own handes, . . .

5. They ought not to buy and sell merchandizes one to another, which they doe freely amongst themselves, and colourably deale by others procuring some poore freeman to beare the name, but they have the benefitt, and have ingrossed almost all the newe draperie into their handes. . . .

6. They ought not to be in companies or Societyes, Contrary thereunto they are a common wealth within themselves, trade in partner shippe with strangers, and as factours for whole cittyes, commerce with us for nothing that they can have of their owne nacion, though they be demized or borne heere amongst us, yett they keepe themselves severed from us in church, in a government, in trade, in language and marriage. . . .

7. The custome of the citty, and Acts of Councell in the citty are that no man being a straunger to the liberties of the citty shall use by handicraftes within the cittie.

Contrary heerunto the straingers use all the severall craftes and occupacions that any man of this kingdome doth use and theis handicraftesmen save all things to their owne nacion whollee, and much to the (harm of the) better sort of our nacion.
. . . And by the statute of 5 Elizabeth, cap. 4, thoughe they were persons borne within the realme, yet ought not to exercise any manuall trade within this kingdome except they were brought uppe seven yeares apprentice to the trade according to that statute, which none or very few of them have beene.

And thus both Alliens, Denizens, and Natives bee they merchantes or Artisans are provided against by the lawes of the land, and charters of the Cittye, which wee desire that after a fitt tyme of warninge may bee put in execucion, or such other remedy applyed as to the wisedome of hir Majestie and this state seeme most fitt and convenient.

REGULATION OF WAGES BY JUSTICES OF THE PEACE, 1591–2

Source: W. J. Hardy, Hertford Session Rolls, 1581–1698. 1906.

Reaping, binding and laying of wheat or rye in shocks well grown and not ledged by the acre .	iid.
Labourers from the Annunciation of our Lady until Michaelmas not to have more by the day than with meat and drink	iiid.
And without (meat and drink)	viiid.
Masons, carpenters, joiners, wheelwrights, plough-wrights, bricklayers, tilers, and plasterers, being masters of the said occupations, or of the best sort shall not have more by the day than with meat and drink.	viiid.
The same of the second sort shall not take more by the day than with meat and drink	vid.
A man servant (of husbandry) of the best sort shall not have more by the year than with a livery . .	xls.

The best sort of women servants shall not have more by the year than with a livery   .   .   .   .   . xxis.

A shoemaker servant of the best sort being married to have without meat and drink for every dozen of shoes   .   .   .   . xxiid.

A LETTER TO THE MAIOUR AND JURATES OF THE TOWNE OF SANDWICH, ASKING FOR THE RELAXATION OF THE STATUTE OF ARTIFICERS, 1593

Source: Acts of the Privy Council, New Series, Vol. XXIV.

There is one Repent Hubbard of that towne whoe (as we are given to understand) hathe bene heretofore a man of good sub-staunce and habillytie and become very poore by great losses at sea and otherwyse, and not being hable to followe his trade which before his decaie he did use, havinge (as yt should seeme) a very honest care to lyve to maintaine him selfe, his wyfe and children hathe betaken him selfe to the occupacion of a baker and hath used baking allmoste for these two yeeres, and because he was never bownde apprentice to that science he ys threatened (as ys alledged unto us) to be sued uppon the statute made in the 5th yeere of her Majesty's raigne concernyng apprentices. Wee have thought good, consideringe this poor gentleman hath an honest intent to lyve by his handy labour and not meanynge to chardge or burthen the town with his wyfe or children, to praie you to call soche persons before you that have or shall have at anie tyme hereafter any purpose to sue him uppon the foresaid statute, and to intreate and require them in our names that they wilbe con-tented to tollerate him and not to trouble or molest him by course of lawe, but that in respect of his great losses he maie be permitted to use the said facultie, whereby he may be batter hable to main-taine him, his poore wyfe and children. And so not doubtinge but they will shewe them selves herein conformable, beinge for so charytable a cause as this ys, wee bidd, etc.

CONDITIONS IN A WEAVING FACTORY

Source: Thomas Deloney, *The Pleasant History of Jack of Newbury,* 1596.

Within one room being large and long,
There stood two hundred looms full strong:
Two hundred men the truth is so,
Wrought in these looms all in a row.

And in another place hard by
An hundred women merrily,
Were carding hard with joyful cheer,
Who singing sat, with voices clear.
And in a chamber close beside,
Two hundred maidens did abide
In petticoats of stammell red
And milk-white kerchers on their head.

These pretty maids did never lin
But in that place all day did spin:
And spinning so with voices meet,
Like nightingales they sung full sweet.
Then to another room came they,
Where children were in poor array:
And everyone sat picking wool,
The finest from the coarse to cull.

A dye-house likewise had he then,
Wherein he kept full forty men;
And likewise in his fulling mill,
Full twenty persons kept he still.

HOURS OF WORK

Source: Richard Baxter, *The Divine Appointment of the Lord's Day Proved.*

The tyranny of many masters maketh the Lord's Day a great mercy to the world: for if God had not made a law for their rest

and liberty, abundance of worldly impious persons would have
allowed them little rest for their bodies, and less opportunity for
the good of their souls. . . . Tenants and labourers, carters and
carriers, and abundance of tradesmen are so poor, that they can
hardly spare any proportion of time: much less all their children
and servants, whose subjection, with their parents' and masters'
poverty, restraineth them. Alas! they are fain to rise early and
hasten to their work and scarce have leisure to eat and sleep as
nature requireth: and they are so toiled and wearied with hard
labour, that if they have at night a quarter of an hour to read a
chapter and pray, they can scarce hold open their eyes from
sleeping.

CHAPTER XXIV

THE REGULATION OF TRADE

Prices and the conditions under which a particular trade could be carried on had for long been locally controlled, but during the sixteenth century municipal control was gradually replaced by state control. Justices of the Peace could grant the right to set up trade and the influence of the Crown in these matters was considerable. During the seventeenth century the control of commercial affairs passed to Parliament and those who wanted to bribe or beg for benefits went to Westminster and no longer to Whitehall.

ORDERS OF THE JUSTICES OF CORNWALL FOR THE REFORMATION OF THE UNREASONABLE PRICES OF VICTUALS IN MARKETS, 1550

Source: Strype, *Ecclesiastical Memorials* (1822), Vol. II.

FIRST, That the said justices within their circuits and limits to them appointed, do treat with the best and most honest personages of any market-towns within their said limits; and to know of them the names of those which were wont to serve the markets, and such as now be hable to serve the same markets, of grain; which of butter and cheese; which of flesh; and whether they, or any of them, have withdrawn, or not.

Item, After that taken and entred in a book, then to know of them what the names of those were that have sold the same at excessive prices, sithence the late commandment.

Item, That every justice in their limits do send for the said sellers, and do take their answers, and the proofs of the said town-dwellers. And if it shal then appear they have offended, then to give them day under sureties to appear before them to receive their deserts.

Item, If they accuse others that make sale of the same to them at excessive prices, that then those be sent for, and put under like sureties.

. . . that they that were accustomed to serve the markets with butter and cheese, and other victuals, do serve the same, if they have wherewith, at the Kings price.

Item, That the butcher, having beefs, muttons, and al other victuals at his graziers hands, at the Kings price, shal be compelled to sel the same to the Kings people according to that rate, by the orders of the mayors and chief officers of the market-town, at the commandment of the justices.

Item, That if any ambiguity rise betwixt the butcher and the grazier in making the price, having regard to the largeness of the beast, that the same be appealed, and adjudged by the justice of peace next adjoyning.

Item, That every victualler bring the hide of every the beasts that shal be killed weekly to the markets, and there make sale of them in open market, at such prices as the justices of peax shal appoint.

Item, That henceforth no fisher make sale of any kind of fish upon the sea, nor elsewhere, but upon the strand; and that the same remain upon the strand during one whole hour, to be sold to al comers of the country, at such prices as one of the said fishers and one of the landmen will appoint. And in case none of the country be there to buy the said fish, or any part thereof, by the space of one hour, that then the said fishers shal be at liberty to sel the same . . . to their most advantage, as they and the buyers may agree.

AN ACTE TO RESTRAYNE CARRIENG OF CORNE VICTUALS AND WOOD OVER THE SEA
(1 and 2 Philip and Mary, c. 5), 1555

. . . That notwithstanding, many and sundrye covetous and unsatiable persons seking their onely lucers and gaynes, hathe and dayly dothe carye and convey innumerable quantitie aswell of Corne Chese Butter and other Victuall, as of Wood, out of this Realme into the parties beyonde the Seas; By reason wherof, the sayd Corne Vyctuall and Wood arre growen unto a wonderfull dearthe and extreame pryses, to the greate detryment of the Common wealthe of this your Highnes Realme and your faithefull

subjectes of the same: For Remedie wherof, It may please your
Highnes that it may be enacted . . . That no maner of person
or persons after the xx^th daye of Januarye next comming, shall
carye and transporte out of this Realme, by any Shippe, Craier
or other Vessell whatsoever, into any place in the parties beyonde
the Seas or into the Realme of Scotlande, any Wheate Rie Barley
or other Corne or Grayne growing within this Realme, or any
Maulte made within the same, or any Bere Butter Chese Hearing
or Wood, . . . without sufficient and lawfull aucthoritie so to doo,
upon the paines and penalties hereafter ensuing; that ys to saye,
thowner and owners of the sayd Shippes . . . to forfaite the said
Shippes . . . wherin the said Corne Butter Chese Hearing Victuall
or Wood shall be so transported and caried; and the Owners . . .
of the said Corne Butter Chese Hearing and Woodd to forfeite
the doble value of the same so caryed and conveied, and the
Master and Mareners of the said Shippes . . . for evrey suche
Offence to forfeite all their Gooddes, and to be imprisoned by
the space of one whole yeare without Baile or Maynprise.

OFFENCES OF TRADESPEOPLE, 1564

*Source: Records of the City of Norwich, ed. Hudson and Tingey, Vol. II.
The enquest for the Clarke of the Markett (4 March, 6 Eliz.)*

Fyrst they ffynde that the Cittie hathe neyther common beame,
ballaunces nor waightes.

Also they do ffynd that John Fayerclyff, miller, doth kepe
pullery as hennys, duckes, pygges, and swyne contrary to ther
charge.

Item they ffynde that the comon bakers viz. John Pye (and
eleven others) do bake ther brede under the syse (assize) and
contray to ther charge.

Also they do ffynde that the comon alebrewers viz. Edwarde
Pye, Wedow Geywoode, John Lawrewoode, Ralphe Stephanson
and (blank) Glaven do brewe ther ale not holsome for mans
body and that they have no taster according to ther charge.

Also they do ffynde that the comon berebrewars viz. Thomas
Narford (and eight others) brew beare not holsome for mannes
body.

Item they do ffynde that coummon inholders viz. Mr. Norgate, Mr. Hed, Aldermen, John Clarke (and thirty-five others) do sell ther bottelles of hay not contaynyng wayghte.

Also they do ffynde that wynsellers viz. Mr. Norgate, Mr. Hed, Aldermen (and seven others) do sell ther wyne contray to the Statute.

Also they do ffynde that bochars viz. Mr. Grene, Alderman, (and eighteen others) do kyll ther bulls unbayted and kene (cows) with calfe.

Also they do ffynde that the fysshemongers viz. Mr. Warden Alderman (and eight others) do sell their ffysshe not well wateryd.

Also they do ffynde that the typlers viz. Alys Broune, Margery Dinglow, Thomas Moyes (and twenty others) do sell ther ale and beare with pottes unsyzed and sealyd and also they do not sell a quart of the best ale or beare for a halfpenny.

Also they do ffynde that the whight lether tawers viz. Vincent Tesmonde (and six others) do tewe calve skynnes.

nye sprats, nye great sprats

FISH SELLER.

ORDERS ISSUED BY THE J.P.'s FOR LANCASHIRE, 1616

1. First that there be no wares nor victuals sold or shewed upon any Sunday (necessary victuals only excepted) and that no butcher sell any flesh upon any Sunday after the second peal ended to morning prayer nor yet at any time in the afternoooon upon the Sabbath day and that every person so offending presently be brought by the Constable before some justice of the peace to be bound by him to the good behaviour and to appear at the next assize after he is so bound.

2. That no Householder after the beginning of the last peal to morning prayer suffer any person (not being of the household) to eat, drink, or remain in their house in time of Divine service but shall shut their doors up to the end that all persons within the said house may go to the church: if any be found in any alehouse in time of Divine service the said alehouse to be put down and henceforth not to be licensed again.

PAPER-MAKING. NOTICE MOULDS BEING DIPPED IN RAG PULP AND THE SHEETS LAID OUT TO DRY.

NEW INDUSTRIES

Source: Stowe: *Annales*, 1592.

The first making of Venice glasses in England began at the Crotched Friars in London about the beginning of the reign of Queen Elizabeth, by one Jacob Venaline, an Italian.

The cutting of iron bars in a mill for the ready use of smiths, to make long rods and all sorts of nails, was brought first into England in the year 1590, by Godfrey Box of the Province of Liege. He likewise set up the first mill for the making of copper plate. And upon the same river, called Dartford River, not long before, was set up a mill to make white paper, by Master John Spilman (a German); this was the first mill in England, wherein fine paper was made. In the reign of King James coarse paper (commonly called brown paper) was first made in divers places, serving grocers and such like.

USURY

As a gradually increasing proportion of people were engaged in trade and industry, where a ready flow of money was necessary, the medieval view of the wickedness of usury changed and the lending of money was legalized by Act of Parliament in 1571. Many prosperous merchants turned financiers and had great power, for legal limits to the rate of interest were hard to enforce, and trade, though flourishing, was often precarious. *The Merchant of Venice* was enjoyed by audiences only too familiar with Antonio's predicament.

In the early seventeenth century it was customary for merchants to keep their gold and silver in the Tower mint, but fear that Charles I would seize it to pay his debts caused them to begin to deposit the money with the goldsmiths. These then began to act as bankers for the public by accepting deposits of money, for which a receipt was issued, giving the depositor an opportunity of drawing cash. From these early notes our present-day paper money has evolved.

Source: Harrison, *A Description of England*, 1587.

... usurie, a trade brought in by the Jewes, now perfectlie practised almost by everie christian and so commonlie, that he is accompted but for a foole that dooth lend his monie for nothing.

INTERVENTION OF THE PRIVY COUNCIL IN A CASE OF USURY, 1601

Source: Acts of the Privy Council, Vol. XXXI.

A letter to the Lord Byshopp of Exceter, Sir Thomas Denys and Sir Robert Bassett, knights, John Drakeland, and Thomas Revell, esquires.

There hath an humble petition bene exhibited unto us by divers poore men, inhabitants of the County of Devon, informynge us of very hard dealinge by usury and other extreame courses used by one John Hamlyn of Exwicke nere unto the cytty of Exceter against them, tendinge to theire utter impoverishment and undoinge, which greivances are more particulerlie declared in theire inclosed peticion. Wee have therefore thought good uppon this theire humble suite made unto us to recomend the same unto your Lordship and the rest, and hereby do praie and require you to send for the said John Hamlyn before you and dulie to heare and examine all the informacions of thes poore men that doe complaine against him, and thereuppon yf you fynde those accusacions to be true to advyse him to a more Christian and charytable consideracion of thes his neighbours, whome yf you shall not be able to bringe to better conformytie, then wee praie you to certyfie us of your proceeding and what uppon due examinacion of theire complaint you conceve of his hard dealinge.

CURRENCY

Source: Journal of Frederick, Duke of Wirtemberg, 1592.

. . . the kings and queens of England have had gold and silver coins struck for payment. A double rose-noble is worth thirty-two English shillings, that is, eighteen French francs, or eight thalers or rix-dollars; a rose-noble half as much. An angel, having on it the knight St. George . . . is worth ten shillings, or five francs, or three German florins; an Hungarian ducat, worth six shillings and eight pence, is equal to two florins; a French crown, or crown of the sun=six shillings, or twenty-seven batzen, as in France; a Spanish pistole just as much. Of silver coins, which the Queen has had struck of pure good silver, a shilling is equal to four and a half batzen; half-a-shilling, to two batzen one kreutzer. Twelve pennies go for a shilling, or two for three kreutzers.

CHAPTER XXV

TRAVEL

By present day standards, travel was slow, uncomfortable and dangerous, so that an important foreigner would find it worth while to provide himself with a pass from the sovereign. Yet the roads were busy and no traveller can have felt bored for long, for adventures of all kinds were frequent. There were, of course, no police, and it was as well not to trust anyone unless you knew him personally. Safe arrival, of either goods or persons, was matter for relief or even surprise, though the postal service was considerable.

THE STATE OF THE ROADS

Source: Harrison, *A Description of England,* 1587.

Now to speak generally of our common highways through the English part of the isle . . ., you shall understand that in the clay or cledgy soil they are often very deep and troublesome in the winter half. Wherefore by authority of parliament an order is taken for their yearly amendment, whereby all sorts of the common people do employ their travail for six days in summer upon the same. And albeit that the intent of the statute is very profitable for the reparations of the decayed places, yet the rich do so cancel their portions, and the poor so loiter in their labours, that of all the six, scarcely two good days' work are well performed and accomplished in a parish on these so necessary affairs. Besides this, such as have land lying upon the sides of the ways do utterly neglect to ditch and scour their drains and water-courses for better avoidance of the winter waters . . ., whereby the streets do grow to be much more gulled than before, and thereby very noisome for such as travel by the same. Sometimes also, and that very often, these days' works are not employed upon those ways that lead from market to market, but each surveyor amendeth such by-plots and lanes as seem best for his own commodity and more easy passage unto his fields and pastures. And whereas in some places there is such want of stones, as thereby the inhabitants are driven to seek them far off in other soils, the owners of the lands wherein those stones are to be had, and which hitherto have given money to have them borne away, do now reap no small commodity by raising the same to excessive prices, whereby their neighbours are driven to grievous charges, which is another cause wherefore the meaning of that good law is very much defrauded. Finally, this is another thing likewise to be considered of, that the trees and bushes growing by the streets' sides do not a little keep off the force of the sun in summer for drying up of the lanes. Wherefore if order were taken that their boughs should continually be kept short, and the bushes not suffered to spread so far into the narrow paths, that inconvenience would also be remedied, and many a slough prove hard ground that yet is deep and hollow. Of the daily encroaching of the covetous upon the highways I speak not. But this I know by experience, that whereas some streets within these five and twenty years have been in most places fifty foot broad according to the law, whereby the traveller might either escape the thief, or shift the mire, or pass by the loaden cart without danger of himself and his horse; now they are brought unto twelve, or twenty, or six and twenty at the most, which is another cause also whereby the ways be the worse, and many an honest man encumbered in his journey. But what speak I of these things whereof I do not think to hear a just redress, because the error is so common, and the benefit thereby so sweet and profitable to many by such houses and cottages as are raised upon the same.

A PASS

Source: The Journal of Frederick, Duke of Wirtemberg, 1592.

Theras this noblman Connte Mombeliard is to passe over Contrye us England in to the lowe Contryes. Thise Schalbe to wil and command you in heer Majte. name for such, and is heer plensure to see him fournissed With post horses in his travail to the sen side, and there to soecke up such schippinge as schalbe fit for his transportations, he pay nothing for the same, forwich

PLATE 25

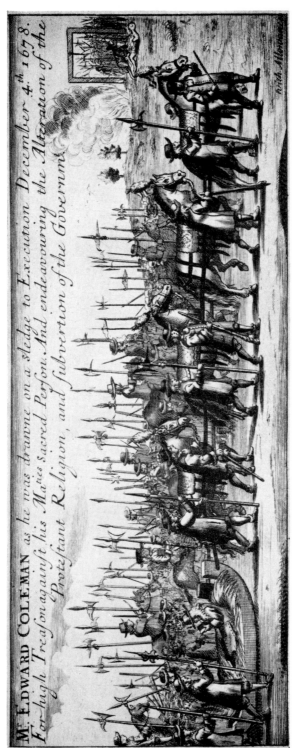

On the way to the execution. Note the three crimes he was charged with

PLATE 26

Etching of the last horse-race run before King Charles II at Windsor. 1687. Notice the grand *stand*!

tis schalbe your sufficient warranti soo see you faile noth therof
at your perilles.

> From Bifleete, the 2. uf September 1592.
>> Yur Friend
>>> C. Howard.

(Locus Sigilli)

To al Justices of peace Maiors Bayliffes and al other her Majte.
officiers. in especial to my owne officiers of te admyraltye.

A PLEA FOR WATER TRANSPORT

The early seventeenth century saw a steady increase in heavy wheeled
traffic on the roads, with the result that they were badly cut up and
often impassable for carts and wagons. If pack horses had to be used,
the expense was considerable. There were many people who urged
the use of waterways for transport but there were also many whose
interests were against this development. For example, certain farmers
who bred draught-oxen for drawing iron-shod two-wheeled carts
did their best to encourage the use of the roads for transport. They
accused the boatmen of damaging fences and crops when towing their
boats upstream.

One writer lists over two hundred towns in weekly communication
with London by carriers' carts and wagons, so that the wear and tear
on the main post-roads must have been considerable. He maintained
that the use of waterways for transport would not only save the roads,
but save labour.

Source: Carriers' Cosmography, by John Taylor. 1634.

> In common reason all men must agree
> That if these rivers were made clean and free
> One barge, with eight poor men's industrious pains
> Would carry more than forty carts or wains.
> And every wain to draw them horses five
> And each two men or boys to guide or drive
> Charge of two hundred horse and eighty men
> With eight men's labour could be saved then.

THE INTRODUCTION OF COACHES

Source: Stowe, Annales, 1615.

In the year 1564 Guylliam Boonen, a dutchman, became the
queene's coachmanne, and was the first that brought the use of

R

coaches into England. And after a while, divers great ladies, with as great jealousie of the queene's displeasure made them coaches, and rid in them up and downe the countries to the great admiration of all beholders, but then by little and little they grew usual among the nobility and others of sort, and within twenty years began a great trade of coach making. And about that time began long wagons to come into use, such as now come to London from Canterbury, Norwich, Ipswich, Gloucester, &c. with passengers and commodities. Lastly, even at this time, 1605, began the ordinary use of caroches.

A CHARIOT WITH SPRINGS

Source: Pepys's Diary.

Sept. 5th, 1665. . . . After dinner comes Colonell Blunt in his new chariot made with springs, and he hath rode, he says, now this journey, many miles in it with one horse, and outdrives any coach, and out-goes any horse, and so easy, he says. So for curiosity I went into it to try it, and up the hill to the heath, and over the cart-rutts and found it pretty well, but not as easy as he pretends.

ARGUMENTS AGAINST COACHES

Coaches were not allowed to ply for hire in the streets of London until 1634 when permission was granted for a rank by the maypole in the Strand. But a great many people objected to the use of coaches, whether privately owned or for hire. A pamphlet against coaches was published in 1679:

Coaches and sedans (quoth the waterman), they deserve both to be thrown into the Theames, and but for stopping the channel I would they were, for I am sure where I was woont to have eight or tenne fares in a morning I now scarce get two in a whole day: our wives and children at home are readie to pine and some of us are faine for meanes to take other professions upon us. . . .

Before these coaches were set up, travellers rode on horse-back, and men had boots, spurs, saddles, bridles, saddlecloths and good riding-suits, coats and clokes, stockings and hats:

whereby the wool and leather of the kingdom was consumed
and the poor people set at work by carding, combing, spinning,
knitting, weaving and fulling. And you cloth-workers, drapers,

tailors, saddlers, tanners, curriers, shoe-makers, spurriers,
lorimers and felt-makers had a good employ: were full of work,
got money, lived handsomely, and helped with their families,
to consume the provisions and manufactures of the kingdom:
but by means of these coaches, these trades, besides many others
depending upon them, are become almost useless: and they,
with their families, reduced to great necessity: insomuch that
many thousands of them are cast upon the parishes, wherein
they dwell, for a maintenance.

Besides, it is a great hurt to the girdlers, sword-cutlers, gun-
smiths, and trunk-makers: most gentlemen, before they travelled
in their coaches, used to ride with swords, belts, pistols, holsters,
portmanteaus, and hat-cases: which, in these coaches, they have
little or no occasion for. For, when they rode on horseback,
they rode in one suit and carried another to wear, when they came
to their journey's end; or lay by the way: but in coaches, a silk
shirt and an Indian gown with a sash, silk stockings and beaver-
hats men ride in, and carry no other with them, because they
escape the wet and dirt, which on horseback they cannot avoid:
whereas, in two or three journeys on horseback these clothes
and hats were wont to be spoilt: which done, they were forced to

have new very often, and that increased the consumption of the manufactures, and the employment of the manufacturer: which travelling in coaches doth no way do. And if they were women that travelled, they used to have safeguards and hoods, side-saddles and pillions, with strappings, saddle and pillion-cloths, which, for the most part, were either laced or embroidered: to the making of which there went many several trades: seeing there is not one side-saddle with the furniture made, but, before it is furnished, there are at least thirty-seven trades have a share in the making thereof: most of which are either destroyed, or greatly prejudiced by the abatement of their trade: which being bred unto, and having served seven years' apprenticeship to learn, they know not what other course to take for a livelihood. . . .

Men do not travel in these coaches with less expence of money or time than on horseback. . . . For instance: from London to Exeter, Chester or York, you pay forty shillings a-piece in summer-time, forty-five shillings in winter, for your passage: and as much from these places back to London. Besides, in the journey, they change coachmen four times and there are few passengers that give twelve-pence to each coachman at the end of his stage . . . and at least three shillings comes to each passenger's share to pay for the coachman's drink on the road: so that in the summer-time the passage backward and forward to any of these places costs four pounds eleven shillings, in the winter five pounds one shilling. And this only for eight days riding.

WRONGFUL ARREST

Thomas Ellwood, the Quaker son of an Oxfordshire squire, was returning one day in 1661 from visiting a friend at Chalfont St. Peter's. He was at the time in disgrace with his father on account of his religious beliefs and had been lent a horse by his host. Relinquishing the horse at Beaconsfield and dismissing the groom who had accompanied him, he proceeded homeward on foot. These two stories told in his autobiography illustrate some of the dangers of seventeenth-century travel.

Source: History of the Life of Thomas Ellwood by his own hand.

Before I had walked to the Middle of the Town, I was stopt

and taken up by the Watch. I asked the Watchman What Authority he had to stop me, travelling peaceably on the Highway. He told me he would shew me his Authority; and in order thereunto, had me into an House hard-by, where dwelt a Scrivener whose Name was Pepys. To him he gave the Order which he had received from the Constables, which directed him to take up all Rogues, Vagabonds and sturdy Beggars. I asked him, For which of these he stopped me; but he could not answer me.

I thereupon informed him what a Rogue in Law is, viz. One, who for some notorious Offence was burnt on the Shoulder; and I told them, they might search me if they pleased, and see if I was so branded. A Vagabond, I told them was One that had no Dwelling-house, nor certain Place of abode; but I had, and was going to it; and I told them where it was. And for a Beggar I bid them bring any one that could say, I had begged or asked Relief.

This stopt the Fellow's Mouth, yet he would not let me go; But, being both weak-headed and strong-willed, he left me there with the Scrivener, and went out to seek the Constable, and having found him, brought him thither. He was a young man, by Trade a Tanner, somewhat better mannered than his Ward man, but not of much better Judgment.

He took me with him to his House. And having settled me there, went out to take Advice, as I supposed, what to do with me; leaving no Body in the House to guard me, but his Wife, who had a young Child in her Arms.

She enquired of me, upon what Account I was taken up; and seeming to have some Pity for me, endeavoured to perswade me not to stay, but to go my way; offering to shew me a Back-way from their House, which would bring me into the Road again beyond the Town, so that none of the Town should see me, or know what was become of me. But I told her I could not do so.

Then having sate a while in a muze, she asked me, If there was not a Place of Scripture which said, Peter was at a Tanner's House? I told her there was such a Scripture, and directed her where to find it.

After some Time she laid her Child to sleep in the Cradle, and stept out on a sudden; but came not in again in a pretty while.

I was uneasy that I was left alone in the House, fearing lest, if any Thing should be missing, I might be suspected to have taken it; yet I durst not go out to stand in the street, lest it should be thought I intended to slip away.

But besides that, I soon found Work to imploy myself in; for the Child quickly waking, fell to crying, and I was fain to rock the Cradle in my own Defence, that I might not be annoyed with a noise, to me not more unpleasant than unusual.

At length the Woman came in again, and finding me nursing the Child, gave me many Thanks, and seemed well pleased with my Company.

When Night came on, the Constable himself came in again, and told me, Some of the Chief of the Town were met together, to consider what was fit to do with me; and that I must go with him to them. I went, and he brought me to a little nasty Hut, which they called a Town-house (adjoining to their Market-house) in which dwelt a poor old Woman whom they called Mother Grime, where also the Watch used by Turns, to come in and warm themselves in the Night.

When I came in among them, they looked (some of them) somewhat sourly on me, and ask'd me some impertinent Questions; to which I gave them suitable answers.

Then they consulted one with another, how they should dispose of me that Night, till they could have me before some Justice of the Peace, to be examined. Some proposed That I should be had to some Inn, or publick House, and a Guard set on me there. He that started this was probably an Inn-keeper, and consulted his own interest. Others objected against this, That it would bring a Charge on the Town. To avoid which, they were for having the Watch take charge of me, and keep me walking about the Streets with them till Morning. Most voices seemed to go this Way; till a third wished them to consider, Whether they could answer the doing of that, and the Law would bear them out in it? And this put them to a Stand. I heard all their Debates, but let them alone, and kept my Mind to the Lord.

Whiel they thus bandied the Matter to and fro, one of the Company asked the rest, If any of them knew who this young Man was, and whither he was going? Whereupon the Constable, (to whom I had given both my Name, and the Name of the Town where I dwelt) told them my Name was Ellwood, and that I lived at a Town called Crowell in Oxfordshire.

Old Mother Grime, sitting by and hearing this, clap'd her Hand on her Knee, and cry'd out, I know Mr. Ellwood of Crowell very well. For when I was a Maid I lived with his Grandfather there, when he was a young Man. And thereupon she gave them such an Account of my Father, as made them look more regardfully on me; and so Mother Grime's Testimony turned the Scale, and took me off from walking the Rounds with the Watch that Night.

The Constable hereupon bid them take no further Care, I should lie at his House that Night, and accordingly took me home with him, where I had as good Accommodation as the House did afford. Before I went to Bed, he told me, that there was to be a Visitation, or Spiritual Court (as he called it) holden next day at Amersham, about four Miles from Beaconsfield, and that I was to be carried thither.

In the Morning . . . the other Constable came, and I was called down.

This was a budge Fellow, and talked high. He was a Shoemaker by Trade, and his Name was Clark. He threat'ned me with the Spiritual Court. But when he saw I did not regard it, he stopt, and left the Matter to his Partner, who pretended more kindness for me, and therefore went about to perswade Clark, to let me go out at the Back-door, to slip away.

The Plot, I suppose, was so laid, that Clark should seem averse, but at length yield, which he did; but would have me take it for a Favour. But I was so far from taking it so, that I would not take it at all; but told them plainly that as I came in at the Fore-door, so I would go out at the Fore-door. When therefore they saw they could not bow me to their Will, they brought me out at the Fore-door into the Street, and wished me a good journey. Yet before I went, calling for the Woman of the House I paid her for my Supper and Lodging, for I had now got a little Money in my pocket again.

A QUARREL
Source: Thomas Ellwood's Autobiography.

My Father being then in the Commission of the Peace, and going to a Petty Sessions at Watlington, I waited on him thither. And when we came near the Town, the Coachman seeing a nearer and easier Way (than the common Road) through a Corn-field, and that it was wide enough for the Wheels to run, without endamaging the Corn, turned down there. Which being observed by an Husbandman, who was at plow not far off, he ran to us, and stopping the Coach, poured forth a Mouthful of Complaints, in none of the best Language, for driving over the Corn. My father mildly answered him, That if there was an Offence committed, he must rather impute it to his Servant, than himself; since he neither directed him to drive that Way, nor knew which Way he drove. Yet added, that he was going to such an Inn at the Town; whither if he came, he would make him full Satisfaction for whatsoever Damage he had sustained thereby. And so on we went, the Man venting his Discontent, as he went back, in angry Accents. At the Town, upon Enquiry, we understood that it was a Way often used, and without Damage, being broad enough; but that it was not the common Road, which yet lay not far from it, and was also good enough; wherefore my Father bid his Man drive home that Way.

It was late in the evening when we returned, and very dark; and this quarrelsome Man, who had troubled himself and us in the Morning, having gotten another lusty Fellow, like himself, to assist him, way-lay'd us in the Night, expecting we would return the same Way we came. But when they found we did not, but took the common Way, they angry that they were disappointed, and loth to lose their Purpose (which was to put an Abuse upon us) coasted over to us in the dark, and laying hold on the Horses Bridles, stopt them from going on. My Father asking his Man, what the Reason was that he went not on, was answered, That there were two Men at the Horses Heads, who held them back, and would not suffer them to go forward. Whereupon my Father opening the Boot, stept out, and I followed close at his Heels. Going up to the Place where the Men stood, he demanded of them the Reason of this Assault. They said,

We were upon the Corn. We knew, by the Routs, we were not on the Corn, but in the common Way, and told them so. But they told us, They were resolved they would not let us go on any farther but would make us go back again. My Father endeavoured, by gentle Reasoning, to perswade them to forbear, and not run themselves farther into the Danger of the Law, which they were run too far into already; but they rather derided him for it. Seeing therefore fair Means would not work upon them, he spake more roughly to them, charging them to deliver their Clubs (for each of them had a great Club in his Hand, somewhat like those which are called Quarter-Staves). They thereupon, laughing, told him They did not bring them thither for that End. Thereupon my Father, turning his Head to me, said, Tom, disarm them. . . . Wherefore stepping boldly forward, to lay hold on the Staff of him that was nearest to me, I said, Sirrah, deliver your Weapon. He thereupon raised his Club, which was big enough to have knockt down an Ox, intending no doubt to have knockt me down with it, as probably he would have done, had not I, in the Twinkling of an Eye, whipt out my Rapier and made a Pass upon him. I could not have failed running of him through up to the Hilt had he stood his Ground; but the suddain and unexpected Sight of my bright Blade, glittering in the dark Night, did so amaze and terrify the Man, that slipping aside, he avoided my Thrust; and letting his staff sink, betook himself to his Heels for safety, which his Companion seeing, fled also. I followed the former as fast as I could, but . . . Fear gave him Wings, and made him swiftly fly; so that although I was accounted very nimble, yet the farther we ran, the more Ground he gain'd on me, so that I could not overtake him. . . . I was gone so far beyond my Knowledge, that I understood not which Way I was to go, till by hollowing, and being hollowed to again, I was directed where to find my Company.

A PADDER

Source: Abraham de la Pryme, *Diary.*

 . . . a great lusty man-servant . . . got a maggot into his head to turn padder, so he acquainted his master with his resolution, explaining that it would be a much easier and more profitable way of living. His master dissented, but all to no purpose. And so, next morning, away he went, with a good clubb in his hand; and being got in the London Road, somewhere about Newark or Grantham, there overtook him on the road, a genteel man on horseback. John letts him come up to him, and taking his advantage, he catches hold of his bridle, and bidds him stand and deliver. Upon which he of horseback, being a highwayman himself, he began to laugh that a thief should pretend to rob a thief! 'But', says he, 'harken, thou padder, I'm one of thy trade; but surely, thou'rt either a fool or one that was never at the trade before.' 'No, Sir', says John, 'I never was at this trade in my life before.' 'I thought so', says the highwayman; 'therefore, take my advice, and mind what I say to you. When you have a mind to robb a man, never take hold of his bridle and bid him stand, but, the first thing you do, knock him down, and, if he talk to you, hit him another stroke, and say, 'Sirrah! you rogue, do you prate?' and then', says the highwayman, 'you have him at your will.' . . . Thus they walk'd on for about a mile, the highwayman teaching the other his art; and as they were going a by way to a certain town, they comes to a badd lane. Says the padder to the other on horseback, 'Sir, I am better acquainted with this country than perhaps you are, this lane is very badd, and you'll indanger (of) lying fast, therefore you may go through this gate, and along the field side, and so miss all the ill way.' So he took his advice, and going that way the padder went the other way, and coming to the place where the highwayman should ride through a gapp into the lane again, this rogue, this padder, stands under the hedge, and as soon as ever he sees the highwayman near him, he lends him such a knock over the head that he brought him down immediately. Upon which he began to say, 'Sirrah, you rogue, is this your gratitude, for the good advice that I gave you?' 'Ah! you villain, do you prate?' And with that gave him another knock. And so, having him wholly at his mercy, he takes almost fifty pounds from him, and gets upon his horse, and away he rides home to his master, by another way, as fast as he could go, and being got home he goes to his master and tells him, saying—'Tash! master, I find this a very hard trade

that I have been about, as you sayd it would prove, and I am
resolved to go no more, but be contented with what I have gott.
I have a good horse here, and fifty pounds in my pocket, from a
highwayman, and I have considered that I cannot be prosecuted
for it, therefore I'll live at ease.' . . .

ON THE POST-BOY

Source: John Bunyan, *Book for Boys and Girls,* 1686.

> Behold this Post-boy, with what haste and speed
> He travels on the Road; and there is need
> That he so does, his Business call for haste.
> For should he in his Journey now be cast,
> His Life for that default might hap to go;
> Yea, and the Kingdom come to ruin too.
>   Stages are for him fixt, his hour is set,
> He has a Horn to sound, that none may let
> Him in his haste, or give him stop or stay.
> Then Post-boy blow thy horn, and go thy way.

OF THE OFFICE OF POST-MASTER GENERAL

Source: E. Chamberlayne, *Angliae Notitia, or The Present State of
England,* 1687.

The Profits of the said Office are setled by Act of Parliament,
on his Royal Highness the Duke of York; but his Majesty doth
constitute his Postmaster-General, by Letters Patents under the
Great Seal of England. This Office is now in the Hands of the
King, and is executed by Sir Philip Frowd, Esq.;

His Majesty keepeth one Grand, or General Office in the City
of London, from whence Letters and Pacquets are dispatched.

Every *Monday* to France, Italy, Spain, Flanders, Germany,
Sweden, Denmark, &c. and to Kent.

Every *Tuesday* to the United Netherlands, Germany, &c. and
to all parts of England, Scotland, and Ireland.

Every *Wednesday* to Kent only, and the Downs.

Every *Thursday* to France, Spain, Italy, and all Parts of England and Scotland.

Every *Friday* to the Spanish and United Netherlands, Germany, Sweden, Denmark, and to Kent.

Every *Saturday* to all parts of England, Scotland, and Ireland.

And the Answers of the said Letters and Pacquets are received in the said Office in due course; and from thence dispersed, and delivered according to their respective Directions, with all expedition.

The said Office is managed by a Deputy, and other Officers, to the number of Seventy seven persons, who give their actual Attendance respectively in the dispatch of the business.

Upon this Grand Office depends one hundred eighty two Deputy-Postmasters in England and Scotland; most of which keep Regular Offices in their Stages, and Sub-Postmasters in their Branches; and also in Ireland, another General Office for that Kingdom, which is kept in Dublin, consisting of Eighteen like Officers, and Forty five Deputy-Postmasters.

His Majesty keeps constantly for the transport of the said Letters and Pacquets:

Between England and
France, Two Pacquet-Boats.
Flanders, Two Pacquet-Boats.
Holland, Three Pacquet-Boats.
Ireland, Three Pacquet-Boats.

And at Deal, Two Pacquet-Boats for the Downs.

All which Officers, Postmasters, and Pacquet-Boats, are maintained at his Majesties own Charge.

And as the Master-piece of all those good regulations, established by the Postmaster General, for the better Government of the said Office, he hath annexed and appropriated the Market-Towns of England, so well to the respective Postages, that there is no considerable Market-Town, but hath an easie and certain Conveyance for the Letters thereof, to and from the said Grand Office, in the due course of the Males every Post.

Though the number of Letters missive in England, were not at all considerable in our Ancestors days, yet it is now so prodigiously great, (since the meanest People have generally learnt to write) that this Office was farmed at Forty or fifty thousand Pounds a year.

Note also, That letters are conveyed with more Expedition, and less Charges, than in any Foreign Countrey.

A Letter containing a whole Sheet of Paper, is conveyed 80 Miles for 2d., and two Sheets, 4d. and an ounce of Letters but 8d. and that in so short a time, by night as well as by day, that every 24 hours the Post goes 120 Miles; and five days an Answer of a letter may be had from a place 300 Miles distant from the Writers. Moreover, if any Gentleman desire to ride Post to any principal Town in England, Post-Horses are always in readiness (taking no Horse without the consent of his owner) which in other Kings Reigns was not duly observed; and only 3d. is demanded for every English Mile, and for every Stage to the Post-Boy 4d. for conducting.

Besides this excellent convenience of conveying Letters, and Men on Horseback, there is of late such an admirable commodiousness, both for Men and Women of better Rank, to travel from London to almost any great Town of England, and to almost all the Villages near this great City, that the like hath not been known in the World, and that is by Stage-Coaches, wherein one may be transported to any place, sheltered from foul Weather, and foul Ways, free from endamaging ones Health or Body by hard jogging, or over-violent Motion; and this not only at a low Price, as about a Shilling for every five Miles, but with such velocity and speed, as that the Posts in some Foreign Countries make not more Miles in a day; for the Stage-Coaches, called Flying-Coaches, make forty or fifty Miles in a day; as from London to Oxford or Cambridge, and that in the space of 12 hours, not counting the time for Dining, setting forth not too early, nor coming in too late. . . .

OF THE PENNY-POST

Source: E. Chamberlayne, *Angliae Notitia, or The Present State of England*, 1687.

. . . there is established another Post, call'd the Penny-Post whereby for one Penny any Letter or Parcel, not exceeding one

Pound weight, or Ten Pounds value, is most speedily and safely conveyed to, and from all parts within the Bills of Mortality, and to most Towns within Ten Miles round London, not conveniently served by the General Post. . . . And for the better carrying on this useful Design, there are Six General Offices kept at a convenient distance from one another, at all which, Officers do constantly attend from Morning until Night, every day, Sundays only excepted; and a very great number of Messengers are imploy'd, who have all given Security for the collecting and delivering of Letters, &c. Also five or six hundred Receiving Houses in London, and the other Towns; a List of which Towns will be delivered to any Person gratis at the General Offices . . .

. . . whatsoever Letters that come from all Parts of the World by the General Post, directed to Persons in any of those Countrey Towns to which the Penny-Post does go, are delivered by the Messengers thereof, the same day they come to London; and the Answers being left at their Receiving-Houses, are by them safely carryed every Night to the Office in Lombard-street. . . .

The Conveniences of . . . the Penny-Post, are as follow. All Gentlemen, Country-Chapmen, and others, may hereby speedily and cheaply give notice of their arrival at London; Shopkeepers and Tradesmen may send to their Workmen for what they want; Bills mey be dispersed for publication of any concern; Summons or Tickets conveyed to all parts; Brewers Entries safely sent to the Excise-Office; Appointments of Meetings among Men of Business; much time saved in solicitation for Money; Lawyers and Clients mutually correspond; Patients may send to Doctors, Apothecaries, and Chyrurgeons, for what they shall want; besides many other Advantages.

SIGN POSTS

With increasing use of the roads, signposts were becoming necessary and these were ordered by statute in 1697. The following year Celia Fiennes wrote:

. . . They have one good thing in most parts of this principality (Lancashire) . . . that at all cross wayes there are Posts with Hands pointing to each road with the names of the great town or market towne that it leads to. . . .

ICY CONDITIONS AT SEA NEAR NEWFOUNDLAND IN 1670

Source: F. N. L. Poynter (Ed.), *Journal of James Yonge* (1647–1721), *Plymouth Surgeon.*

March 14th. At two this morning the wind comes at North, and we make sail. It blows fresh and cold. At 8 it overblew, snowed, and freez'd, we had much ado to get down our sails, every rope grown exceeding big with ice. . . . We are in very desperate danger, not able for our lives to loose a knot of sail, all being frozen so stiff and fast with the ice. . . .

March 15th. . . . are in a sad fearful condition, all the ship like a lump of ice. We shipt two very dangerous seas; the water freezes as soon as it comes on the decks, not for our lives able to loose a knot of sail, all things are so frozen, . . . Towards evening, . . . after throwing kettles of hot water on the sails and ropes we made shift to set our mainsail, with a ruff in.

March 16th. Wednesday morning, we made shift to cut away an unmeasurable quantity of ice from our ship's bows, decks and ropes. . . . From Sunday evening to this day noon I kept myself warm in my bed, not rising but to the house of office, which was hard by and my lodging being in the great cabin. Here I made a resolution never to go this voyage more, nor to sea again, if I could find any reasonable incouragement. . . .

March 18th. . . . We are in a dangerous case, and the worse because our master and his mate were now both drunk. . . .

A FAKED BILL OF HEALTH

Source: F. N. L. Poynter (Ed.), *Journal of James Yonge* (1647–1721), *Plymouth Surgeon.*

When we came in (to Genoa), our merchants came by us but durst not come on board till we had prattick; we had no bill of health to certify the place not having the pest whence we came. Wherefore I set my wits and drew up one, as from a Governor of Newfoundland, and signed myself as Secretary. The seal was dominic plaster, hanging to a label, stampt between two leaves with the broad end of a leaden weight with some rude marks in it which were hid by the leaves. This passed for current, and prattick admitted, we lay there. . . .

A SHIP'S DOCTOR IN 1661

Source: F. N. L. Poynter (ed.) *Journal of James Yonge (1647–1721) Plymouth Surgeon.*

About the middle of May, my master . . . shipped me to go chyrurgeon's assistance of the 'Montague', a third-rate frigatt, mounted with 64 guns, 250 men, Captain Riches Utburs commander. I was under Mr. Robinson, an old chyrurgeon in the army in Scotland that came out with General Munk. A man he was of good skill in his profession, wholly ignorant of sea affairs, and understood little of physick. He was a morose, ill-natured man and hard to please. His chief mate was his eldest son, and another younger he had which went for his servant or cabin-boy. I am sure it proved a hard task for me, for I were a servant to them all, and in the whole voyage did all the drudgery. My own master was severe, but generous and ingenious, but this was cruel, not giving me the least favour, so that under the misery thereof I often wished myself dead. My great support was Mr. Richard Davies, who was chief mate and a friend of my father's. My life in this voyage is to be guessed when it's known I was perpetually working, was slenderly provided with clothes and necessaries, had no one to take care of me, were 13 months at short allowance, and in all the voyage heard not one line or received one penny from my father.

THE FATE OF SAILORS

Source: Pepys's Diary.

June 30th, 1666. . . . mightily troubled . . . about getting shipped some men that they have these last two nights pressed in the City out of houses: the persons wholly unfit for sea, and many of them people of very good fashion, which is a shame to think of; and carried to Bridewell they are, yet without being impressed with money legally as they ought to be. . . .

July 1st, 1666. . . . about the business of the pressed men, and

PLATE 27

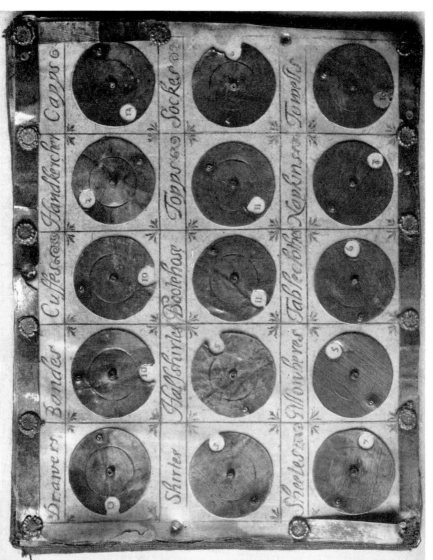

A washing tally of beechwood covered by a piece of horn. Below the name of each garment is a dial with a moveable indicator

PLATE 28

(*a*) Letter K from an album of ornamental writing

(*b*) Two sides of a silver horn-book. A thin piece of horn protected the printed letters from wear

late at it till twelve at night, shipping of them. But, Lord! how some poor women did cry; and in my life I never did see such natural expression of passion as I did here in some women's bewailing themselves, and running to every parcel of men that were brought, one after another, to look for their husbands; and wept over every vessel that went off, thinking they might be there, and looking after the ship as far as ever they could by moonlight, that it grieved me to the heart to hear them. Besides, to see poor patient labouring men and housekeepers leaving poor wives and families, taking up on a sudden by strangers, was very hard, and that without press-money, but forced against all law to be gone. It is a great tyranny.

Sept. 30th, 1665. . . . The great burden we have upon us at this time . . . is the providing for prisoners and sicke men that are recovered, they lying before our office doors all night and all day, poor wretches. Having been on shore, the captains won't receive them on board, and other ships we have not to put them on, nor money to pay them off or provide for them.

Oct. 7th, 1665. . . . the horrible crowd and lamentable moan of the poor seamen that lie starving in the streets for lack of money, which do trouble and perplex me to the heart; and more at noon when we were to go through them, for then a whole hundred of them followed us, some cursing, some swearing, and some praying to us. . . .

July 10th, 1666. To the office, the yarde being very full of women (I believe above three hundred) coming to get money for their husbands and friends that are prisoners in Holland; and they lay clamouring and swearing and cursing us, that my wife and I were afeared to send a venison-pasty that we have for supper tonight to the cook's to be baked, . . . But by and by the women got into the garden and come all to my closett window, and there tormented me; and I confess their cries were so sad for money, and laying down the conditions of their families and their husbands, and what they have done and suffered for the King, and how ill they are used by us, and how well the Dutch are used here by the allowance of their masters, . . . that I do most heartily pity them, and was ready to cry to hear them, but cannot helpe them. . . .

s

GUARDING THE COASTS

Source: Thomas Platter, *Travels in England,* 1599.

. . . it is extremely difficult to land in England, since there are only five ports in the whole realm, all very well and securely fortified to prevent any enemy from approaching. Thus, as soon as anything is sighted at sea, for battleships are always anchored at the ports keeping watch there, a signal is given at the ports with a burning pan of resin, and this is straightway observed inland, for the country is flat for the most part; and throughout the entire kingdom pans of resin are set up on little mounds, and watch kept there day and night, and as soon as a signal is given it travels over the whole country, so that roughly speaking, in a trice the report goes round of what is happening at sea.

The country has good soldiers, but they do not care to go abroad; when soldiers are required, and idlers are found loitering in the towns, they are given money, and whether they will or no, are forced to leave forthwith, and if they are caught deserting their case has been dealt with and justice done forthwith. For since this kingdom is surrounded by water on all sides, so that the only approach to or departure from it is by ship, the order is give out at all ports and harbours that no Englishman may leave without a passport.

RAISING MONEY FOR THE NAVY

Here is a letter of Privy Seal to Roger Columbell, requesting a loan, Jan., 1588; with receipt, April, 1588.

Source: Thomas Wright, *Queen Elizabeth and her Times,* 1838, vol. II.

Trustie and well-beloved, we greet you well. Whereas for the better withstanding of the intended invasion of this realme, upon the great preparation made by the Kinge of Spaine, both by sea and land the last yeare, the same having been such as the lyke was never prepared at any time agaynst this realme, we are now forced for the defence of the same, and of our good loving subjects, to be at infinite charges both by sea and land, especially for that the same intended invasion tendeth directly to the conquest of this realme, and fynding also by such intelligences as we dayly receive that the lyke preparations are nowe making for the lyke intent the next yere, by the said Kynge, for the withstanding whereof it shall be necessarie for us to prepare bothe by sea and land, which cannot be performed without great charges: we have therefore thought it expedient, having alwaies our good and loving subjects most ready upon such lyke occasion to furnish us by way of loane of some convenient portions of money, agreable with their estate, (which we have and mynde always to repaye), to have recourse unto them in lyke manner at this present.

And therefore, having made choyce in the several parts of our realme of a number able to do us this kind of service, which is not refused between neighbour and neighbour, amongst the number we have also particularly named you, Roger Columbell, for your ability and good-will you beare to us and our realme, to be one; wherefore we require you to paye to our use the sum of fyve-and-twentie pounds to such person as by our lieutenant of that countie shall be named to you by his hand wryting. And these our letters of privy seale, subscribed by the partie so named, by our lieutenant that shall receive the same, confessing the time of the receipt thereof, shal be sufficient to bynd us, our heires, and successors, duly to repaye the said summe to you or your assignes, at the end of one yere, from the 26th day of January, in the thirty first yere of our raigne.

Thos. Kery

Received of Mr. Roger Columbell, the 12th daye of Aprill, for her Majestie's use, the above said sum, twenty and five poundes, at Haddon, by me.

John Maners,

Clerk in Engham.

SHIP MONEY LEVIED ON INLAND TOWNS, 1596

Source: Acts of the Privy Council, Vol. XXV.

(25 February, 1596.) A letter to the Bailifs, etc., of Tewkesbury. Whereas her Majestie hath thowght yt very expedient forthwith to set to seas her Navy Royall for the defence of her realm, and

for the better execucion hereof hath given order to sondry of her subjects to furnish owt and put in readiness a convenient nomber of ships to attend on her said Navy, of which nomber of ships the citty of Bristoll is to prepare three, and in contribucion to this charge the Maiour and Aldermen of the cittie of Gloucester are required and have yielded to contribute two hundred pounds, which wowld be overburthensom for them to bear but by th' assistance of that town of Tewkesbury, which taketh benefite by trafficke to the seas and not far from the port of Gloucester, and therefore ought to yeild supply herein as uppon like occacions yt formerly hath don in the year 1588. Wee have therefore thowght good and accordingly do require you forthwith to impoze and levie of th' inhabitantes of that town of Tewkesbury the somme of fortie pounds, and the same withowt delay to pay to the hands of the Maiour of Gloucester towards the making up of the said somme of two hundred pounds, which wee doubt not but you will have care forthwith to accomplish, that the intended service be not through your default hindred, being of so great importance and concerning the safetie of your selfes and the realm in generall.

CHAPTER XXVI

INNS

English hospitality was renowned and excellent inns on the better roads helped to offset the dangers and difficulties of travelling. But there were hazards even there and the inn-keeper and his servants might well be in league with the highwaymen.

Source: Harrison, *A Description of England,* 1577.

Those towns . . . . . . have great and sumptuous innes builded in them, for the receiving of such travellers and strangers as passe to and fro. The manner of harbouring wherein, is not like to that of some other countries, in which the host or goodman of the house dooth chalenge a lordlie authoritie over his ghests, but cleane otherwise, sith everie man may use his inne as his owne house in England, and have for his monie how great or little varietie of vittels, and what other service himselfe shall thinke expedient to call for. Our innes are also verie well furnished with naperie, bedding, and tapisterie, especially with naperie: for beside the linnen used at the tables, which is commonlie washed dailie, is such and so much as belongeth unto the estate and calling of the ghest. Ech comer is sure to lie in cleane sheets, wherein no man hath beene lodged since they came from the landresse, or out of the water wherein they were last washed. If the traveller have an horsse, his bed dooth cost him nothing, but if he go on foote he is sure to paie a penie for the same: but whether he be horsseman or footman if his chamber be once appointed he may carie the kaie with him, as of his owne house so long as he lodgeth there. If he loose oughts whilest he abideth in the inne, the host is bound by a generall custome to restore the damage, so that there is no greater securitie anie where for travellers than in the gretest ins of England. Their horsses in like sort are walked, dressed, and looked unto by certaine hostelers or hired servants, appointed at the charges of the goodman of the house. . . .

Certes, I believe not that chapman or traveller in England is robbed by the waie without the knowledge of some of them: for when he commeth into the inne, & alighteth from his horsse, the hostler forthwith is verie busie to take down his budget or capcase in the yard from his sadle bow, which he peiseth slilie in his hand to feele the weight thereof: or if he misse of this pitch, when the ghest hath taken up his chamber, the chamberleine that looketh to the making of the beds, will be sure to remoue it from the place where the owner hath set it, as if it were to set it more convenientlie some where else, whereby he getteth an inkling whether it be monie or other short wares, & therof giveth warning to such od ghests as haunt the house and are of his confederacie, to the utter undoing of manie an honest yeoman as he journeth by the waie. The tapster in like sort for his part dooth mark his behaviour, and what plentie of monie he draweth when he paieth the shot, to the like end: so that it shall be an hard matter to escape all their subtile practices. Some thinke it a gay matter to commit their budgets at their comming to the good-man of the house: but thereby they oft bewraie themselves. For albeit monie be safe for the time that it is in his hands (for you shall not heare that a man is robbed in his inne) yet after their departure the host can make no warrantise of the same, sith his protection extendeth no further than the gate of his owne house: and there cannot be a surer token unto such as prie and watch for those booties, than to see anie ghest deliver his capcase in such maner.

Source: Thomas Platter, *Travels in England*, 1599.

There are a great many inns, taverns, and beer-gardens scattered about the city, where much amusement may be had with eating, drinking, fiddling, and the rest, as for instance in our hostelry, which was visited by players almost daily. And what is particularly curious is that the women as well as the men, in fact more often then they, will frequent the taverns or ale-houses for enjoyment. They count it a great honour to be taken there and given wine with sugar to drink; and if one woman only is invited, then she will bring three or four other women along and they gaily toast each other; the husband afterwards thanks him who has given his wife such pleasure, for they deem it a real kindness.

In the ale-houses tobacco or a species of wound-wort are also obtainable for one's money, and the powder is lit in a small pipe, the smoke sucked into the mouth, and the saliva is allowed to run freely, after which a good draught of Spanish wine follows. This they regard as a curious medicine for defluctions, and as a pleasure, and the habit is so common with them, that they always carry the instrument on them, and light up on all occasions, at the play, in the taverns or elsewhere, drinking as well as smoking together, as we sit over wine, and it makes them riotous and merry, and rather drowsy, just as if they were drunk, though the effect soon passes—and they use it so abundantly because of the pleasure it gives, that their preachers cry out on them for their self-destruction, and I am told the inside of one man's veins after death was found to be covered in soot just like a chimney. The herb is imported from the Indies in great quantities, and some types are much stronger than others, which difference one can immediately taste; . . .

Source: Fynes Moryson, *Itinerary*, 1617.

. . . the World affoords not such Innes as England hath, either for good and cheape entertainement after the Guests owne pleasure, or for humble attendance on passengers; yea, even in very poor villages. . . . For assone as a passenger comes to an Inne, the servants run to him, and one takes his horse, and walkes him till he be cold, then rubs him and gives him meate, yet I must say that they are not much to be trusted in this last point, without the eye of the Master or his servant to oversee them. Another servant gives the passenger his private chamber, and kindles his fier; the third puls of his bootes, and makes them cleane. Then the Host or Hostesse visit him; and if he will eate with the Host, or at a common table with others, his meale will cost him sixe pence, or in some places but foure pence (yet this course is lesse honourable, and not used by Gentlemen); but if he will eate in his chamber, he commands what meate he will, according to his appetite, and as much as he thinkes fit for him and his company, yea, the kitchin is open to him, to command the meat to be dressed as he best likes; and when he sits at Table, the Host or Hostesse will accompany him, or, if they have many Guests, will at least visit him, taking it for curtesie to be bid sit downe; while he eates, if he have company especially, he shall be offred musicke, which he may freely take or refuse; and if he be solitary, the musitians will give him the good day with musicke in the morning. It is the custome, and no way disgracefull, to set up part of supper for his breakefast. In the evening or in the morning after breake-fast, (for the common sort use not to dine, but ride from breake-fast to supper time, yet comming early to the Inne for better resting of their Horses) he shall have a reckoning in writing, and if it seeme unreasonable, the Host will satisfie him either for the due price, or by abating part, especially if the servant deceive him any way, which one of experience will soone find . . . I will onely adde, that a Gentleman and his Man shall spend as much as if he were accompanied with another Gentleman and his Man; and if Gentlemen will in such sort joyne together to eate at one Table, the expences will be much diminished. Lastly, a Man cannot more freely command at home in his owne House, then hee may doe in his Inne; and at parting, if he give some few pence to the Chamberlin and Ostler, they wish him a happy journey.

Source: The Journeys of Celia Fiennes, in 1697 and 1698.

The house thats call'd Buxton Hall which belongs to the Duke of Devonshire its where the warme Bathe is and Well, its the largest house in the place tho' not very good, they are all Enter-taining houses and its by way of an Ordinary, so much a piece for your dinners and suppers and so much for our Servants besides; all your ale and wine is to be paid besides, the beer they allow at the meales is so bad that very little can be dranke, you pay not for your bed room and truely the other is so unreason-able a price and the Lodgings so bad, 2 beds in a room some 3 beds and some 4 in one roome, so that if you have not Company enough of your own to fill a room they will be ready to put others into the same chamber, and sometymes they are so crowded that three must lye in a bed; few people stay above two or three nights its so inconvenient: we staid two nights by reason one of our Company was ill but it was sore against our wills, for there is no peace nor quiet with one Company and another going into the Bath or coming out;

... my Landlady brought me one of the West Country tarts, this was the first I met with, though I had asked for them in many places in Sommerset and Devonshire, its an apple pye with a custard all on the top, its the most acceptable entertainment that could be made me; they scald their creame and milk in most parts of those countrys and so its a sort of clouted creame as we call it, with a little sugar, and soe put on the top of the apple pye; I was much pleased with my supper tho' not with the custome of the country, which is a universall smoaking both men women and children have all their pipes of tobacco in their mouths and soe sit round the fire smoaking, which was not delightfull to me when I went down to talke with my Landlady for information of any matter and customs amongst them; ...

CHAPTER XXVII

THE POOR

In the late fifteenth century and throughout the sixteenth, society was changing rapidly and, while many people were becoming richer, the poor were becoming poorer. Unemployment was general and the roads were swarming with beggars, many of whom were a danger to life and property. Much private charity was given, as men's consciences were pricked by the conditions in which the more unfortunate of their fellow countrymen existed.

It was in the towns that the problem of the poor was most acute. Countrymen pushed off the land took refuge there, and mixed with soldiers returned from the wars, with beggars, thieves and rogues. Charity and Church collections were unable to cope with the need and poor relief became a question of prime importarce in England. Many authorities were very cruel in their treatment: persistent vagrants were whipped or burned through the ear and sent back to the parish of their birth. London, Ipswich and Norwich were the most progressive towns in dealing with the problem. A compulsory poor rate was levied and hospitals, houses of correction, asylums and training schools were established.

In the years 1594–1597 England suffered a series of bad harvests and there was much scarcity and distress, and as a result Parliament tackled the question of poor relief on a national basis and passed a bill establishing a compulsory poor rate, giving J.P.s power to appoint overseers of the poor in every parish, and to set the able-bodied to work, to provide for the infirm poor, and to bind poor children as apprentices.

AN ACTE AGAYNST VACABOUNDS AND BEGGARS (11 Henry VII, c. 2, 1496–7)

... that the shiref, maires, baillifs, high constables and pety constables and all other governors and officers of citees burghes townes townshipps villeges and other placis, within iij daies after this acte proclaimed, make due serch, and take or cause to be taken all suche vagaboundes idell and suspecte persones lyvyng suspeciously, and theym so taken to sette in stokkes, ther to remayne by the space of iij daies and iij nyghtes, and ther to have noon other sustenaunce but brede and water; and after the seid

iij daies and iij nyghtes to be had oute and set at large and then
to be commanded to avoide the towen; And if eftsomes he be
taken in suche defaute in the same town or township then he
to be sette in the like wise in stokkis by the space of vj daies with
like diete as is before reherced; and if eny persone or persones
geve eny other mete or drinke to the seid mysdoers being in
stokkes in fourme aforseid, or the same prisoners favour in their
mysdoyng, that then they forfeite for every tyme so doing xij d.

LEGACIES FOR THE RELIEF OF THE POOR

Source: Testamenta Eboracensia (Surtees Soc., 1868), Vol. IV.

(Dame Joan Chamberleyn of York, 1502.) To the exhibicion of
Marten Andrewson (at) schole x s. I wyll that Richard Diotson,
ydiott, be fonden of my goodes as longe as he levith. . . . To
every persone in the castell or in other prisons within the cetie
of Yorke j d., and to every leper house beyng in the subbarbes
of the said cetie, to every person, j d. I wit to my executores
my place in Hundgate, which place I wyll they sell; and the
money for the said to be disposid for the wele of my saule; that is
to say to the exhibicion of pure chylder apte to lerne at scoles,
pore maydens well disposyd to mariages, and to wayes or briges,
brokon or hurte to the neuance or nivertie of Cryston people,
amendynge and reparinge.

Source: John Stow, *A Survey of London,* ed. Kingsford (1908), Vol. I.

Henrie Keble, Grocer, Maior (of London), 1511, . . . gave to
high wayes, 200 pound, to poore maides marriages, 100 Markes,
to poore husband men in Oxford and Warwickshires, 140 Plough-
shares and 140 Cultars of iron, and in London to seven almes
men, sixpence the week for ever.

Sir Thomas Roe, Marchant Taylor, Mayor (of London), 1568,
gave to the Marchant Taylors lands or Tenements, out of them
to bee given to ten poore men Clothworkers, Carpentars, Tilars,
Plasterers, and Armorers, 40 pounds yearely, viz. 4 pounds to
each, also 100 pounds to bee lent to 8 poore men.

PUNISHMENT OF VAGABONDS

Source: Harrison, *A Description of England,* 1577.

... The roge being apprehended, committed to prison, and tried in the next assises, ... if he happen to be convicted for a vagabond, either by inquest of office, or the testimonie of two honest and credible witnesses upon their oths, he is then immediatlie adjudged to be greevouslie whipped and burned through the gristle of the right eare, with an hot iron of the compasse of an inch about, as a manifestation of his wicked life, and due punishment received for the same. And this judgement is to be executed upon him, except some honest person woorth five pounds in the queenes books in goods, or twentie shillings in lands, or some rich housholder to be allowed by the justices, will be bound in recognisance to reteine him in his service for one whole yeare. If he be taken the second time, and proved to have forsaken his said service, he shall then be whipped againe, bored likewise through the other eare, and set to service; from whence if he depart before a yeare be expired, and happen afterward to be attached againe, he is condemned to suffer paines of death as a fellon ... without benefit of clergie or sanctuarie, ...

ON ALMES HOUSES, 1550

Source: Select Works of Robert Crowley, ed. J. M. Cowper. (E.E.T.S., 1872).

A Marchaunte, that longe tyme hadde bene in straunge landis,
Returned to his contrey, whiche in Europe standes.
And in his returne, hys waye laye to passe
By a Spittlehouse, not farre from where his dwelling was.
He loked for this hospitall, but none coulde he se;
For a lordely house was builte where the hospitall should be.
Good Lorde (sayde this marchaunt) is my contrey so wealthy,
That the verye beggers houses be builte so gorgiouslye?
Than, by the waye syde, hym chaunced to se
A pore manne that craved of hym for charitie.
Whye (quod thys Marchaunt) what meaneth thys thynge?
Do ye begge by the waye, and have a house for a kyng?

Alas! syr (quod the pore man) we are all turned oute,
And lye and dye in corners, here and there aboute.
Men of greate riches have brought our dwellinge place,
And whan we crave of them, they turne awaye their face.
Lorde God! (quod this merchaunt) in Turkye have I bene,
Yet amonge those heathen none such crueltie have I sene.
The vengeaunce of God muste fall, no remedye,
Upon these wicked men, and that verye shortelye.

BEGGARS

Source: Select Works of Robert Crowley, ed. J. M. Cowper (E.E.T.S., 1872).

I heard two beggars that under an hedge sate,
Who did with long talk their matters debate.
They had both sore legs most loathsome to see,
All raw from the foot well most to the knee.
'My leg' quoth the one, 'I thank God is fair'.
'So is mine' quoth the other, 'in a cold air.
For then it looketh raw and as red as any blood,
I would not have it healed for any world's good.
No man would pity me but for my sore leg,
Wherefore if I were whole I might in vain beg.
I should be constrained to labour and sweat,
And perhaps sometime with scourges be beat'.

ORDERS FOR THE HOUSE OF CORRECTION AT BURY, SUFFOLK, Anno 1588

Source: Sir Frederic Eden, *The State of the Poor*, 1797.

Item, It is ordered, that every person committed to the said house, shall have for theire dietts, theis portions of meate and drinke followinge, and not above, (viz). At every dynner and supper on the fleshe daies, bread made of rye, viij ounces troye waight, with a pynte of porredge, a quarter of a pound of fleshe, and a pinte of beare, of the rate of iijs. a barrell, every barrell to conteyne xxxvj. gallands; and on every fysche daie at dynner and supper the like quantitie, made eyther of milk or pease or such lyke, and the thurd part of a pound of chese, or one good heringe, or twoe white or redd, accordinge as the keper of the house shall thinke meete.

Item, It is ordered, that such persons as will applie theire worke, shall have allowance of beare and a little bread between meales, as the keper of the house shall fynd that he doth deserve in his said work.

Item, It is ordered, that they which will not worke shall have noe allowance but bread and beare onley, untill they will conforme themselves to worke.

A POOR LANDOWNER

The poor family owning a piece of land has never been so badly off as those without. Thus in 1577 Harrison reported:

. . . a poore man peradventure dooth dwell in one of them (houses)—who, not being able to repare it, suffereth it to fall down,—and thereto thinketh himselfe verie friendlie dealt withall, if he may have an acre of ground assigned unto him, whereon to keepe a cow, or wherein to set cabbages, radishes, parsneps, carrets, melons, pompons, or such like stuffe, by which he and his poore household liveth as by their principall food, sith they can doo no better. And as for wheaten bread, they eat it when they can reach unto the price of it, contenting themselves in the meane time with bread made of otes or barleie: a poore estate God wot!

ERRING SERVANTS

Source: Pepys's Diary.

Dec. 1st, 1660. This morning, observing some things to be laid up not as they should be by the girl, I took a broom and basted her till she cried extremely, which made me vexed, but before I went out I left her appeased.

Feb. 19th, 1665. At supper, hearing by accident of my mayds letting in a rogueing Scotch woman to helpe them to washe and scoure in our house, I fell mightily out, and made my wife, to the disturbance of the house and neighbours, to beat our girle, and then we shut her down into the cellar, and there she lay all night.

CHAPTER XXVIII

CRIME AND PUNISHMENT

IN THE STOCKS.

Crime of all kinds was widespread and punishments seem, to our more tolerant eyes, wickedly severe. There was widespread belief that crime could be diminished by increased severity.

Londoners were accustomed to seeing traitors hung, drawn and quartered, heretics burned at the stake and thieves hanged, and these had become one of the main sights enjoyed by visitors to the capital. In other towns minor crimes were punished by whipping, branding, and by exhibiting the wrongdoer in the stocks or the pillory, for the mockery and ill-treatment of the citizens.

A PROCLAMATION ORDERING SOWERS OF FALSE RUMOURS TO BE SET IN THE PILLORY, 1486-7

Source: Letters and Papers of Henry VII.

Forasmuch as many of the king our sovereign lord's subjects been disposed daily to hear feigned, contrived and forged tidings and tales, and the same tidings and tales, neither dreading God nor his Highness, utter and tell again as though they were true, to the great hurt of divers of his subjects and to his grevous displeasure: Therefore in eschewing of such untrue and forged tidings and tales, the king our said sovereign lord straitly chargeth

276

PLATE 29

The top of a casket embroidered in stump-work. On white satin, in coloured silks, gold thread and seed-pearls. It illustrates a biblical story

PLATE 30

Mirror with embroidered shutters and surrounds

and commandeth that no manner person, whatsoever he be, utter nor tell any such tidings or tales but he bring forth the same person the which was author and teller of the said tidings or tales upon pain to be set in the pillory, there to stand as long as it shall be thought convenient to the mayor, bailiff, or other officer

of any city, borough, or town where it shall happen any such person to be taken and accused for any such telling or reporting of any such tidings or tales. Furthermore the same our sovereign lord straitly chargeth and commandeth that all mayors, bailiffs and other officers diligently search and inquire of all such persons tellers of such tidings and tales not bringing forth the author of the same, and them set on the pillory as it is above said.

PUNISHMENT OF THIEVES

Source: Sir Thomas More, *Utopia*, 1516.

It chanced on a certain day, when I sat at his table, there was also a certain layman cunning in the laws of your realm. Who . . . began diligently and earnestly to praise that strait and rigorous justice which at that time was there executed upon felons, who, as he said, were for the most part twenty hanged together upon one gallows. And, seeing so few escaped punishment, he said he could not choose but greatly wonder and marvel, how and by what evil luck it should so come to pass that thieves, nevertheless, were in every place so rife and rank.

Nay, sir, quoth I . . . marvel nothing hereat: for this punishment of thieves passeth the limits of justice, and is also very hurtful

T

to the weal-public. For it is too extreme and cruel a punishment
for theft, and yet not sufficient to refrain and withhold men from
theft. For simple theft is not so great an offence that it ought
to be punished with death. Neither there is any punishment
so horrible that it can keep them from stealing which have no
other craft whereby to get their living. Therefore in this point
not you only but also the most part of the world be like evil
schoolmasters, which be readier to beat than to teach their
scholars. For great and horrible punishments be appointed for
thieves, whereas much rather provision should have been made
that there were some means whereby they might get their living,
so that no man should be driven to this extreme necessity, first
to steal and then to die.

A HOKER, OR ANGGLEAR

The activities of rogues and swindlers were sharply specialized:
priggers or prancers worked exclusively as horse-thieves, lock-pickers
did not act as card-sharpers or pickpockets, and so on. Here a writer
describes the activities of a hoker, or angglear:

Source: Thomas Harman, *A Caveat or Warening for Commen Cursetors,
vulgarly called Vagabones,* 1567.

. . . when they practise there pylfringe, it is by night; for, as
they walke a day times from house to house, to damaund charitie,
they vigelantly marke where or in what place they maye attayne
to there praye, casting there eyes up to every wyndow, well
noting what they se their, whether apparall or linnen, hanginge
nere unto the sayde wyndowes, and that wyll they be sure to have
the next night folowing; for they customably carry with them a
staffe of v. or vi. foote long, in which, within one ynch of the tope
therof, ys a lytle hole bored through, in which hole they put an
yron hoke, and with the same they wyll pluck unto them quickly
any thing that they may reche ther with, which hoke in the day
tyme they covertly cary about them, and is never sene or taken
out till they come to the place where they worke there fete: . . .

FLEETWOOD TO BURGHLEY ON A SCHOOL FOR PICKPOCKETS IN LONDON, 7 July, 1585

Source: Lansdowne MSS., No. 44, Art. 38.

Right honourable and my verie good Lord, uppon Thursdaye laste, beinge the crastinn of Trinitie Terme, we kepte a Sessions of Inquyrie in London in the forenone, and in the afternoone we kepte the lyke att Fynsburie for Middlesex, in which two severall Sessionses all such as were to be arrayegned for felonye at the Goale deliverye were indyted. Uppon Frydaie last we sate at the Justice hall at Newgate from vij in the morninge untill vij at night, where were condempned certen horsestealers, cutpurses, and such lyke, to the number of x, whereof ix were executed, and the tenthe stayed by a meanes from the Courte. These were executed uppon Saterdaye in the morninge. There was a Showmaker also condempned for wyllfull murder commytted in the Blacke Fryers, who was executed uppon Mondaie in the morninge. The same daye my Lord Maior beinge absente abowte the goods of the Spannyards, and also all my Lords the Justices of the Benches beinge also awaye, we fewe that were there did spend the same daie abowte the searchinge out of sundrye that were receptors of Felons, where we fownd a greate manye as wel in London, Westminster, Sowthwarke, as in all other places abowte the same. Amongest our travells this one matter tumbled owte by the waye, that one Wotton, a gentilman borne, and sometyme a marchauntt man of good credyte, who fallinge by tyme into decaye kepte an Alehowse att Smarts keye neere Byllingesgate, and after, for some mysdemeanor beinge put downe, he reared upp a newe trade of lyffe, and in the same Howse he procured all the Cuttpurses abowt this Cittie to repaire to his said howse. There was a schole howse sett upp to learne younge boyes to cutt purses. There were hung up two devises, the one was a pockett, the other was a purse. The pocket had in yt certain cownters and was hunge abowte with hawkes bells, and over the toppe did hannge a litle sacring bell; and he that could take owt a cownter without any noyse, was allowed to be a publique Foyster; and he that could take a peece of sylver owt of the purse without the

noyse of any of the bells, he was adjudged a judiciall Nypper.
Nota that a Foister is a Pick-pockett, and a Nypper is termed a
Pickepurse, or a Cutpurse.

PUNISHMENTS

The Civil Law on the Continent condemned no man unless he confessed his guilt, and so was often driven to torture to extract a confession. English law relied upon the sense of the community as
expressed in the verdict of a jury of twelve men.

Source: Essex Record Office, Q/SR 148/10, Quarter Sessions Roll, 1599.

Agnes Osier alias Beggar of Brook Street in South Weald,
Spinster, for breaking into the house of William Reynolds of
the same in the night-time, and stealing two flaxen sheets worth
4s. 4d. and 6os. in money, belonging to the said William. Guilty,
to be hanged.

*Source: Essex Record Office, Court Rolls of Manor of Ging Joyberd
Laundry, Harvard Stock, 1558.*

Thomas Boteworth is fined 4d. because he is a common
brawler and disturber of his neighbours and to give him warning
to leave it or else he is to be carried in a dung cart about the town
in open assembly, and then to be put in the stocks and then to be
banished out of the lordship.

*Source: Essex Record Office, D/DL M6, Estreat Roll of Manor of Aveley,
1592.*

The wife of Walter Hycocks and the wife of Peter Philips do
be common scolds and therefore it is ordered that they shall
be admonished thereof in the church, to leave their scolding.
But upon complaint made by their neighbours the second time
they shall be punished by the ducking stool according to the
discretion of the constable.

TRIAL BY JURY

Source: Italian Relation (Camden Soc.), pp. 32–3.

. . . Nor are proceedings carried on in this country by the deposi-
tion of anyone, or by writing, but by the opinion of men, both in

criminal and civil causes. And if anyone should claim a certain sum from another, and the debtor denies it, the civil judge would order that each of them should make choice of six arbitrators, and when the twelve are elected, the case they are to judge is propounded to them: after they have heard both parties, they are shut up in a room, without food or fire, or means of sitting down, and there remain till the greater number have agreed upon their common verdict. But before it is pronounced each of them endeavours to defend the cause of him who named him, whether just or unjust; and those who cannot bear the discomfort, yield to the more determined, for the sake of getting out sooner. This practice extends also to criminal causes, and any one may be accused of great and glaring crimes, and be put to the torture, (if they 'stood mute', i.e. refused to plead) though he may openly deny the truth of the accusation. But when the chief magistrate of the place has received notice of any such malefactor, he causes him immediately to be thrown into prison, and then twelve men of that place are elected, who must decide according to their consciences, whether the prisoner has or has not committed the crime of which he is accused, and if the greater number vote that he has, he is considered to be guilty. He is not, however, punished at that time; but it is necessary that twelve other men should be chosen, who must hear the cause over again; and if their verdict should agree with the former one, the days of the delinquent are brought to a close. It is the easiest thing in the world to get a person thrown into prison in this country, for every officer of justice, both civil and criminal, has the power of arresting any one, at the request of a private individual, and the accused person cannot be liberated without giving security, unless he be acquitted by the judgment of the twelve men above named; nor is there any punishment awarded for making a slanderous accusation.

EVIL MAY DAY, 1517

Londoners had for centuries felt a strong resentment against foreign merchants, and Englishmen who 'coloured' the goods of foreigners (that is, imported and sold them under their name) were severely punished.

The most striking manifestation of the Londoner's dislike of foreigners occurred in Easter week, 1517, and had tragic consequences:

Source: Hall's Chronicle in Henry VIII, by Edward Hall, ed. Charles Whibley (1904), Vol. I.

. . . Then sodeynly was a commen secret rumour, and no man could tell how it began, that on May daye next the citie would rebell and slaye all Aliens, in so muche as diverse straungers fled out of the citie. This brute ranne so farre that it came to the kinges counsail, insomuch as the Cardinall, beyng lord Chauncelour, sent for Jhon Rest, Mayre of the citie, and other of the counsayl of the citie, and demaunded of the Mayre in what case the citie stode; to whom hee aunswered that it was wel and in good quyet. Nay, sayd the Cardinalle, it is informed us that your young and ryotous people wyll ryse and distresse the straungers; heare ye of no such thing? No surely, sayd the Mayre, and I trust so to governe them that the kynges peace shalbe observed, and that I dare undertake, yf I and my brethren the Aldermen may be suffered. Wel, said the Cardinal, go home and wisely forsee this matter, for and yf any suche thinge be, you may shortly prevent it. The Mayre came from the Cardinals at iiii of the clocke at after none on May even, and demaunded of the officers what they harde; diverse of them aunswered that the voyce of the people was so, and had been so ii or iii dayes before. This heryng, the Mayre sent for al his brethern to the Guylde hall in great hast, and almost vii of the clocke or the assemble was set. Then was declared to them by Master broke the recorder how the kynges counsail had reported to them that the comminaltie that night would ryse, and distresse al the Aliens and straungers that inhabited in the citie of London; the Aldermen aunswered they harde say so, but they mistrusted not the matter, but yet they sayd that it was wel done to forsee it. Then, sayd the recorder, it were best that a substancial watche were set of honest persons, housholders, whiche might withstand the evell doers. An Alderman sayde, that it was evell to rayse men in harneys, for if suche a thinge were entended, they coulde not tel who woulde take their parte. Another Alderman sayd that it were best to kepe the younge men asonder, and every man to shut in hys doores, and to kepe hys servauntes within. Then with these opinions was the recorder sent to the Cardinal before viii of the clocke, and then he, with suche as were of the kynges counsayll at his place, commaunded that in no wyse watche shoulde be kept, but that every man shoulde repayre to his awne house, and there to kepe hym and hys servauntes tyl vii of the clocke of the mornynge; with whiche commaundment the sayde Rycharde brooke, sergeaunt at the lawe and recorder, and syr Thomas Moore, late undershrife of London and then of the kynges counsaill, came to the Guylde hall halfe houre and before ix of the clocke, and there shewed the commaundement of the kynges counsayl. Then in all hast, every Aldermen sent to his warde that no man should styrre after ix of the clocke out of his house, but to kepe his doores shut and hys servauntes within tyll vii of the clocke in the mornynge.

After this commaundement syr Jhon Mondy, Alderman, came from his warde, and founde two young men in Chepe plaiynge at Buckerels, and a great company of young men lokynge on them, for the commaundement was then skace knowen, for then it was but ix of the clocke. Master Mondy, seyng that, bade them leave, and the one young man asked hym why? and then he sayd, thou shalt know, and toke hym by the arme to have had him to the counter. Then all the young men resisted the Alderman, and toke him from master Mondy, and cryed prentyses and clubbes. Then out of every doore came clubbes and weapons, and the Alderman fled, and was in great daungier. The more people arose out of every quarter, and oute came servynge men and water men and Courtiers, and by xi of the clocke there were in Chepe vi or vii hundreth. And oute of Paules churcheyard came iii hundreth, whiche wist not of the other and so out of all places they gathered, and brake up the counteryes, and tooke out the prisoners that the Mayre had thether committed for hurtynge of the straungers, and came to Newgate and tooke out Studley and Petyt, committed thether for that cause. The Mayre and Shrifes were there present, and made Proclamacion in the kynges name, but nothynge was obeyed. Thus they ranne a plump thorow sainct Nycholas Shambels, and at saynct Martyns gate there met with them syr Thomas Moore and other, desyrynge theym to go to their lodgynges. And as they were intreatyng and had almost brought them to a staye, The people of saynct Martynes threwe oute stones and battes, and hurte dyverse honest persones, that were perswadynge the ryotous people to ceasse, and they bade theim holde their handes, but still they threwe oute bryckes and hoate water. Then a sergeaunt of Armes called Nycholas dounes, whiche was there with master Moore, entreatynge them, beynge sore hurt, in a fury cryed doune with them. Then all the misruled persons ranne to the doores and wyndowes of saynct Martyn, and spoyled all that they founde, and caste it into the strete and lefte fewe houses unspoyled. And after that they ranne hedlynge into Cornehill by Leaden hal, to the house of one Mutuas, a Frencheman or Pycardy borne, whiche was a greate bearer of Frenchemen, were they pyckpurses, or howe evell disposicion soever they were of, and within hys gate, called Grenegate, dwelled dyverse Frenchmen that kalendred Worsted, contrary to the kynges lawes; and al thei were so borne out by the same Mutuas, that no man durst medle with them, wherfore he was sore hatet, and yf the people had found hym in their fury they would have striken of his head; but when they found hym not, the water men and certeyn young priestes that were there fell to riflynge; some ranne to Blanchechapelton and brake the straungers houses, and threwe shooes and bootes into the strete.

This from x or xi of the clocke continued these ryotous people, durynge whiche tyme a knight called syr Thomas parr in great hast went to the Cardinall and tolde him of thys ryot, which incontinent strengthened his house with men and ordinaunce. And after this knight roade to the king to Richemond, and made the report much more than it was. Wherfore the king hastely sent to London, and was truly advertised of the matter, and how that the ryot was ceassed and many of the doers apprehended. But while this ruffling continued syr Richard Cholmeleye, knight, Lieutenant of the Towre, no great frende to the citie, in a frantyke fury losed certayn peces of ordinaunce and shot into the citie, which did litle harme, howbeit his good wyl apered. About iii of the clocke, these ryotous persons severed and went to their places of resorte, and by the waye they were taken by the Mayre and the heddes of the citie, and some sent to the

Towre and some to Newgate, and some to the Counters, to the number of iii c.; some fled, and specially the watermen and priestes and servyng men, but the poore prentises were taken. About fyve of the clocke the erles of Shrewesbury and Surrey, whiche had harde of this ryot, came to London with suche strength as they had, so dyd the Innes of court, and diverse noble men; but or they came all the ryot was ceased and many taken, as you have heard.

Then were the prisoners examined, and the sermon of doctor Bele called to remembraunce, and he taken and sent to the Towre, and so was Jhon Lyncoln; but with this ryot the Cardinall was sore displeased. Then the iiii. day of may was an Oyer and determiner at London before the Mayre, the duke of Norffolke, the erle of Surrey and other . . . And upon examination it could never be proved of any metyng, gathering, talking, or conventicle at any daye or tyme before that day, but that the chaunce so happened without any matter prepensed of any creature saving Lyncoln, and never an honest person in maner was taken but onely he. Then Proclamacions were made that no women shoulde come together to bable and talke, but all men should kepe their wyves in their houses. All the stretes that were notable stode full of harnessed men, which spake many opprobrious wordes to the citezens, whiche greved them sore, and yf they woulde have been revenged the other had had the worsse, for the citezens were ii.c to one; but lyke true subjectes they suffered paciently.

When the lordes were set, the prisoners were brought in thorough the stretes tyed in ropes, some men, some laddes, some chyldren of xiii. yere. There was a great mournyng of fathers and frendes for their chyldren and kynsfolke. Emong the prisoners many were not of the citie, some were priestes, and some husbandmen, and laborers, the whole some of the prisoners were ii. c. lxxviii persones. The cause of the treason was because the kyng had amitie with all Christen princes, that they had broken the truce and league, contrary to the statute of kyng Henry the V. Of this treason diverse were endited, and so for that tyme the lordes departed. And the next day the duke came agayn, and the erle of Surrey with ii.M. armed men, which kept the stretes. When the Mayre, the duke, and the erle of Shrewsbury and Surrey were set, the prisoners were arreigned, and xiii. founde giltye of high treason and adjudged to be hanged, drawen and quartered, and for execucion wherof were set up xi. payre of galowes in diverse places where the offences were done, as at Algate, at Blanchechapelton, Gracious strete, Leaden hal, and before every counter one, and at Newgate, at S. Martens, at Aldrisgate, at Bishops gate. This sight sore greved the people to se galowes set in the kynges chamber. Then were the prysoners that were judged brought to the places of execucion, and executed in the most rigorous maner, for the lord Edmond haward, sonne to the duke of Northfolke, and knight Mershal, shewed no mercy but extreme cruelty to the poore yongelinges in their execucion, and likewise the dukes servauntes spake many opprobrious wordes, some bad hange, some bad drawe, some bad set the citie on fyer, but all was suffred.

On Thursday the vii. day of May was Lyncoln, Shrywyn, and two brethren called Bets and diverse other adjudged to dye. Then Lyncoln said: my lordes, I meant well, for and you knew the mischief that is ensued in this realme by straungers, you would remedy it, and many tymes have I complained, and then I was called a busy felow; now our lord have mercy on me. Then all the sayd persons were layd on hardels and drawen to the standarde in Chepe, and first was Jhon Lyncoln executed, and as the other had the rope about their neckes, there came a commaundment from the kyng to respite execution. Then the people cried, God save the king. Then was the Oyer and determiner deferred tyll another daye, and the prisoners sent agayn to warde, and the harnessed men departed oute of London, and all thynges quyet.

(The rest of the prisoners, 'poore younglinges and olde false knaves . . . to the number of iiii.c. men and xi. women,' were subsequently pardoned.)

PRISON CONDITIONS

Conditions in prisons were appalling. Ordinary prisoners lived on starvation diet in misery and filth, but those who could afford it lived comfortably by bribing their gaolers. Many citizens were sickened by the violence and cruelty meted out to those in prison:

Source: Stubbes, *Anatomie of Abuses,* 1585.

Beleve me, it greeveth me to heare (walking in the streetes)
the pittifull cryes and miserable complayntes of poore prisoners
in duraunce for debte, and like so to continue all their life, desti-
tute of libertie, meate, drink, (though of the meanest sorte), and
clothing to their backes, lying in filthie straw and lothsome dung,
worse than anie dogge, voyde of all charitable consolation and
brotherly comforte in this worlde, wishing and thirsting after
deathe, to set them at libertie and loose them from their shackles,
. . . and iron bandes.

MASS EXECUTIONS

Source: Thomas Platter, *Travels in England,* 1599.

This city of London is not only brimful of curiosities, but so
populous also that one simply cannot walk along the streets
for the crowd.

Especially every quarter when the law courts sit in London
and they throng from all parts of England for the terms, to litigate
in numerous matters which have occurred in the interim, for
everything is saved up till that time; then there is a slaughtering
and a hanging, and from all the prisons (of which there are several
scattered about the town where they ask alms of the passers by,
and sometimes they collect so much by their begging that thee
can purchase their freedom) people are taken and tried; when the
trial is over, those condemned to the rope are placed on a cart,
each one with a rope about his neck, and the hangman drives
with them out of the town to the gallows, called Tyburn, almost
an hour away from the city, there he fastens them up one after
another by the rope and drives the cart off under the gallows
which is not very high off the ground; then the criminals' friends
come and draw them down by their feet, that they may die all
the sooner. They are then taken down from the gallows and
buried in the neighbouring cemetery. . . .

CHAPTER XXIX

FOREIGN TRADE

In Tudor and Stuart times it was assumed that the Government should control the economic life of the nation. Foreign trade was almost entirely in the hands of the merchants who had bought a charter from the Crown and had the sole right to trade in a given area. Nevertheless

sectional interests, then as now, tried to suppress or foster particular trades. There were those who considered all trade to be an inferior occupation and who bemoaned the mercantile developments.

The volume of internal trade was far greater than the external. Imports were still mainly luxury goods, and the mass of English people were fed and clothed by English products. In the early sixteenth century trade still ran mainly along the coasts of Northern Europe and into the Mediterranean. By Elizabeth's reign many of these markets had closed and new markets further afield were being sought. Sir Francis Drake and other seamen had shown that English ships could successfully sail long distances, and trade with the Far East seemed likely to be profitable. New trading companies were formed by adventurous London merchants, and throughout the seventeenth century England became the centre of new and expanding trade routes. As merchants became more powerful in the community, they resented royal interference in trade, and Stuart misuse of the granting of monopolies was one of the factors which led to the Civil War.

INCONVENIENCEES OF ENLARGYNG ANY POWER TO BRYNG ANY MORE WYNE INTO THE REALME

Source: Notes by Burghley on Trade, 1581. (S.P.D. Eliz., Vol. XLI, No. 58).

It is manifest that nothyng robbeth the realm of England, but whan moore marchandisees is brought In to the realme than is carryed forth; as for example, if viij thowsand poundes worth of forrayn Commoditees be brought In, and but vj thousand poundes worth of the Commoditees of england carryed furth, the realme must spend uppon the stock yerly ij thousand poundes which must be payd with mony, and it is manifestly seene allredy by the Custommers accomptes in the exchequer that yerly the forrayn commoditees doo surmount the Commoditees of the land.

The remedy hereof is by all pollycyes to abridg the use of such forrayn commoditees as be not necessary for us; wherof the excess of silkes is one, of wyne and spyce is an other; and therfor wyttyngly to make a law to increase any of theis is to consent to the robbery of the realm.

Of all theis iij excesses none is more hurtfull to the realm than wyne:

first, it enrycheth fraunce, whose power england ought not increass.

secondly, for the more part the wynes of france, . . . ar bought with sendyng redy monny thyther. For in burdeaux they have an ordonnance forbyddyng barteryng with englishmen for wynes, so as what so ever excess groweth in bryngyng home of wynes, therby the gold which is or shuld be by merchantes brought out of spayne or the low Contreis for the Commodities of england is conveyed into france.

Thyrdly, the multiplyeng of Taverns, which must nedes insew by repealyng the statute of King Edward the vj, is an evident course of disorder of the vulgar people, who by hastyng therto wast ther small substance which they wekly gett by ther hand labor, and committ all evills that accompany dronkenes.

Fourthly, the excessyve drynkyng of wyne deminisheth the use of ale and beare, and consequently decayeth tillage for grayn, which of all labors in the realme wold be favored and cherished, and preferred before such an unnecessary forrayn commoditee as wyne is; addyng therto, that in tyme of peace wisdom wold thynk what maye chance in warrs, and not to laye downe the use of our natural foode for the entysement of a forrayn that by occasion of warrs may be kept from us, and than the tyme may prove to late to recover our owne so soone as our nede shall be; and whan so ever france shall fynd this oportunite to pynch us, as it is no dout but ther pollycy seeth farr in all practisees, we may percase smart when no remedy will be found to ease our payne.

A TREATISE CONCERNING THE STAPLE AND THE COMMODITIES OF THIS REALME, c. 1519–35

Source: Drei Volkswirtschaftliche Denkschriften aus der Zeit Heinrichs VIII von England, ed. R. Pauli (1878). The author of this treatise was probably Clement Armstrong.

. . . The bredyng of so many merchaunts in London, rison owt of pore mens sonnes, hath ben a mervelous distruction to the holl reame, wher first worshipfull men bownd ther yong children to be merchaunts in London, unto so many were bownd prentisses, that ther masters wold never giff theym no wages, after they cam owt of ther termes, and than, havyng no frends to giff theym nor lend theym a stokke of redy money to occupie their occupacion (that is ther instrument to occupie byeng and seelyng of merchaundise) nor havyng no handy crafte, wherby to gete ther levyng, with no instruments on hande, must nedes lose all ther tyme of prentishod and their yougth, than to seke theym some other lyvyng, to be a servytour by some other meane, or elles to seke to bye merchaundises for respite to gete a stokke to begyn with by such meanes. So wer all yong merchaunts, comyng owt of ther prentishod and cowd have no wages of ther masters, compellid to borow clothes of clothe makers for respite, and caried the same clothes to the marts beyende see to sell, and ther must nedes sell theym, and the money to bestow it on wares to bryng home to sell, to make money to pay ther creditors at ther dayes. So abowt a fifty years agoo such yong merchaunts begane to encrease in nomber, that bought so many clothes of cloth-makers for respit and sold theym in Flaunders at the martes of goode chepe to make retorn to pay ther creditours, that in short tyme they distroyed the price of wollen clothes, causyng all the old merchaunts to fall from byeing and sellyng clothes.

THE ... OTHE, MINISTRED TO THE CAPTAINE

The spice islands of the east and the fabulous wealth of China were a great attraction to English trading companies, but the Mediterranean route to this area was blocked by the Turks, and the Portuguese and Spaniards were a menace in the west. The only alternative was to find a route to the north, and in 1555 Willoughby and Chancellor set out to look for a north-east passage. These voyages led to the setting up of the Muscovy Company, to trade with the Tsar's dominions, and the Eastland Company, to trade with Scandinavia.

Some idea of the appalling conditions which had to be faced by these early traders is given in the following note found in one of the two ships which wintered in Lappia, where Sir Hugh Willoughby and all his companions were frozen to death.

You shall sweare to be a faithful, true, and loyal subject in all points, and duties, that to a subject appertaineth, to our soveraigne Lord the kings Majestie, his heires, and successors: and that you shall wel and truely to the uttermost of your capacitie, wit, & knowledge, serve this present voiage, committed to your charge, and not to give up, nor sooner intermit the same, until you shall have atchieved the same, so farre foorth, as you may without danger of your life, and losse of the fleete: you shall give good, true, and faithful counsell to the said societie, and to such as shal have the charge with or under you, and not to disclose the secrets, or privities of the same to any person by any maner of meane, to the prejudice, hurt, or damage of it. You shal minister justice to all men under your charge, without respect of person, or any affection, that might move you to decline from the true ministration of justice. And further, you shal observe, and cause to be observed, as much as in you lieth, all and singular rules, articles, provisions, hitherto made, or heerafter to be made for the preservation or safe conduct of the fleete and voyage, and benefit of the company. You shall not permit nor suffer the stocke or goods of the company to be wasted, imbezeled, or consumed, but shall conserve the same whole and entire, without diminishment, untill you shall have delivered, or cause to be delivered the same, to the use of the companie. And finally you shal use your selfe in all points, sorts, and conditions, as to a faithfull captaine, and brother of this companie shall belong and appertaine: So helpe you God, &c.

REGULATIONS AS TO CONDUCT

The regulations as to conduct on board ship were laid down in May 1553 by Sebastian Cabot, as governor of the Company of the Merchant Adventurers.

11. Item, if any Mariner or officer inferiour shalbe found by his labour not meete nor worthie the place that he is presently shipped for, such person may bee unshipped and put on lande at any place within the kings Majesties realme & dominion, and one other person more able and worthy to be put in his place, at the discretion of the captaine and masters, & order to be taken that the partie dismissed shalbe allowed proportionably the value of that he shall have deserved to the time of his dismission or discharge, & he to give order with sureties, pawn, or other assurance, to repay the overplus of that he shall have received, which he shall not have deserved, & such wages to be made with the partie newly placed as shalbe thought reasonable, and he to have the furniture of al such necessaries as were prepared for the partie dismissed, according to right and conscience.

12. Item, that no blaspheming of God, or detestable swearing

PLATE 31

A family group

PLATE 32

Paris Cher Mory i' Trotaria.

Sold by C.Dicey & Co Alldermary Church Yard.

A coffee house. Notice hats on pegs, news-sheets and smoking

be used in any ship, nor communication of ribaldrie, filthy tales, or ungodly talke to be suffred in the company of any ship, neither dicing, carding, tabling, nor other divelish games to be frequented, whereby ensueth not onely povertie to the players, but also strife, variance, brauling, fighting, and oftentimes murther to the utter destruction of the parties, and provoking of Gods most just wrath, and sworde of vengeance. These and all such like pestilences, and contagions of vices, and sinnes to bee eschewed, and the offenders once monished, and not reforming, to bee punished at the discretion of the captaine and master, as appertaineth.

31. Item, there are people that can swimme in the sea, havens, & rivers, naked, having bowes and shafts, coveting to draw nigh your ships, which if they shal finde not wel watched, or warded, they wil assault, desirous of the bodies of men, which they covet for meate; if you resist them, they dive, and so will flee, and therefore diligent watch is to be kept both day & night, in some Islands.

INSTRUCTIONS TO MERCHANTS

The following letter from the Muscovy Company to their Agents in Russia tells us which commodities were most in demand at the time. The 'remembrance' given to Anthonie Jenkinson reminds us of the extent to which these merchants' representatives fulfilled an almost diplomatic function.

5th May, 1560. The wares that we would have you provide against the comming of the shippes are, Waxe, Tallowe, trayne Oyles, Flaxe, Cables and Ropes, and Furres, such as we have written to you for in our last letters by the shippes: and from hencefoorth not to make any great provision of any rich Furres except principall Sables & Lettes: for now there is a Proclamation made that no furres shall be worne here, but such as the like is growing here within this our Realme. Also we perceive that there might be a great deale of tallowe more provided in a yeere then you send. Therefore our minde is, you should enlarge somewhat more in the price, and to send us if you can three thousand podes a yeere: for we doe most good in it.

U

Source: A remembrance given by us the Governours, Consuls, and Assistants of the company of Merchants, trading into Russia, the eight day of May 1561, to our trustie friend Anthonie Jenkinson, at his departure towards Russia, and so to Persia, in this our eight journey.

8th May 1561. First you shall understand that we have laden in our good ship, called the Swallow, one Chest, the keyes whereof we doe heere deliver you, and also a bill, wherein are written particularly the contents in the sayd Chest, and what every thing did cost: and because, as you know, the sayd Chest is of charge, we desire you to have a speciall regard unto it, and when God shall send you unto Mosco, our mindes and will is, that you, with the advise of our Agents there, doe appoint some such presents for the Emperour and his sonne, either wine, cloth of golde, scarlet, or plate, as to your good discretion shall be thought meet, and when you have delivered unto him the Queenes Majesties Letters, and our sayd present in the name of the Company, we thinke it good that you make your humble sute unto his Highnesse in our name, to get his licence or safe conduct for you and all other our servants or Agents at all times hereafter with such wares and merchandise as you at this time, or they hereafter at all other times shall thinke good to passe out of his dominions towards Tartaria, Persia, or other places, and also to returne unto Mosco with such wares and merchandises as you shall bring or send from any land or countrey that is not in his dominions, . . .

A ROYAL CHARTER

Each of the Merchant Companies had a royal charter assigning to it a geographical sphere of operations and laying down certain other trading rules:

Source: An Act for the corporation of Merchants adventurers for the discovering of new trades, made in the eight yeere of Queene Elizabeth. Anno 1566.

. . . And for the better maintenance of the Navie and Mariners of this Realme, be it provided and inacted, that it shall not be lawfull to the saide fellowship and company, nor to any of them to cary and transport, or cause to be caried and transported any commodie of this Realme to their newe trade, but onely in

English ships, and to be sailed for the most part with English Mariners, nor also to bring into this Realme nor into Flanders from their saide new trade, any merchandizes, or other commodities but in English ships, and sailed for the most part by the English Mariners, on paine to forfeit for every such offence two hundred pounds, whereof the one moitie shall be to the Queenes Majestie, her heires and successors, the other moitie to the head officers of any port towne, having any haven or harborough decayed, by what name soever they bee incorporate, to the reparation of such harborough, that will sue for the same in any Court of Record, by action, bill, plaint or information, wherein no essoine, protection, or wager of lawe for the defendant shall be admitted or allowed.

Provided also, and be it enacted, that no maner of person or persons shall from henceforth carrie or transport, or cause to bee carried or transported out of this Realme of England, any maner of clothes or karsies into any of the partes where the said fellowship and societie is priviledged to trade by this Act, before the same clothes and karsies shall be all dressed, and for the most part died within this Realme, upon paine of forfeiture for every such cloth and karsie, otherwise caried and transported, five pounds: the one halfe thereof to the Queenes Majestie, her heires and successors, the other halfe to the Master and Wardens of the Clothworkers in the Citie of London for the time being, by what name soever they be incorporate that wil sue for the same.

INSTRUCTIONS TO A MERCHANT DYER

As well as buying and selling, there was useful information to be acquired by the representatives of the Muscovy Company.

Source: Certaine directions given by M. Richard Hackluit of the Middle Temple, to M. Morgan Hubblethorne, Dier, sent into Persia, 1579.

1. For that England hath the best wool & cloth of the world, and for that the clothes of the realme have no good vent, if good dying be not added: therefore it is much to be wished, that the dying of forren countreyes were seene, to the end that the arte of dying may be brought into the Realme in greatest excellency:

for thereof will follow honour to the Realme, and great and ample vent of our clothes: and of the vent of clothes, will follow the setting of our poore on worke, in all degress of labour in clothing and dying: for which cause most principally you are sent over at the charge of the city: and therfore . . . it behooves you to have care to returne home with more knowledge then you caried out.

2. . . . . the price of a cloth . . . riseth by the colour and dying: and therefore to devise to die as good colours with the one halfe of the present price were to the great commodity of the Realme, by saving of great treasure in time to come. And therefore you must have great care to have knowledge of the materials of all the countreys that you shall passe thorow, that may be used in dying, be they hearbs, weeds, barks, gummes, earths, or what els soever.

3. In Persia you shall finde carpets of course thrummed wooll, the best of the world, and excellently coloured: those cities & townes you must repaire to, and you must use meanes to learne all the order of dying of those thrummes, which are so died as neither raine, wine, nor yet vineger can staine: and if you may attaine to that cunning, you shall not need to feare dying of cloth: For if the colour holde in yarne and thrumme, it will holde much better in cloth.

4. For that in Persia they have great colouring of silks, it behooves you to learne that also, for that cloth dying & silke dying have a certaine affinity, and your merchants mind to bring much raw silke into the Realme, and therefore it is more requisit you learne the same.

5. In Persia there are that staine linnen cloth: it is not amisse you learne it if you can: it hath bene an olde trade in England, whereof some excellent clothes yet remaine: but the arte is now lost, and not to be found in the Realme.

6. They have a cunning in Persia to make in buskins of Spanish leather flowers of many kindes, in most lively colours, and these the Courtiers do weare there: to learne which arte were no harme.

7. If any Dier of China, or of the East parts of the world, be to be found in Persia, acquaint yourselfe with him, and learne what you may of him.

8. You shall finde Anile there, if you can procure the herbe that it is made of, either by seed or by plant, to cary into England, you may do well to endevour to enrich your countrey with the same; but withall learne you the making of the Anile, and if you can get the herbe, you may send the same dry into England, for possibly it groweth here already.

9. Returne home with you all the materials and substances that they die withall in Russia, and also in Persia, that your company may see all.

10. In some little pot in your lodging, I wish you to make daily trials in your arte, as you shall from time to time learne ought among them.

11. Set downe in writing whatsoever you shall learne from day to day, lest you should forget, or lest God should call you to his mercy; and by ech returne I wish you to send in writing whatsoever you have learned, or at the least keepe the same safe in your coffer, that come death or life your countrey may enjoy the thing that you goe for, and not lose the charge, and travell bestowed in this case.

12. Learne you there to fixe and make sure the colour to be given by logge wood: so shall we not need to buy woad so deare, to the enriching of our enemies.

13. Enquire of the price of leckar, and all other things belonging to dying.

14. . . .

15. If before you returne you could procure a singular good workeman in the arte of Turkish carpet making, you should bring the arte into this Realme, and also thereby increase worke to your company.

'CERTAINE TRIFLES' TO BRING HOME

Source: Notes in writing, besides more privie by mouth, that were given by M. Richard Hakluyt of Eiton in the Countie of Herefore, Esquire, Anno 1580: to M. Arthur Pet, and to M. Charles Jackman, sent by the Merchants of the Moscovie companie for the discovery of the Northeast straight, not altogether unfit for some other enterprises of discovery, hereafter to be taken in hand.

Bring home with you (if you may) from Cambalu or other civil place, one or other yong man, although you leave one for him.

Also the fruites of the Countreys if they will not of themselves dure, drie them and so preserve them.

And bring with you the kernels of peares and apples, and the stones of such stonefruits as you shall find there.

Also the seeds of all strange herbs & flowers, for such seeds of fruits and herbs comming from another part of the world, and so far off, will delight the fansie of many for the strangenesse, and for that the same may grow, and continue the delight long time.

If you arrive at Cambalu or Quinsay, to bring thence the mappe of that countrey, for so shall you have the perfect description, which is to great purpose.

To bring thence some old printed booke, to see whether they have had print there before it was devised in Europe as some write.

. . . . . .

TRIFLES TO TAKE

Take with you the mappe of England set out in faire colours one of the biggest sort I meane, to make shew of your countrey from whence you come.

And also the large Mappe of London to make shew of your Citie. And let the river be drawn full of Ships of all sorts, to make the more shew of your great trade and traffike in trade of merchandize.

THE EAST INDIA COMPANY

The Merchants trading in the Levant (Middle East) were near enough to the east to know how profitable trade with that region would be. Money and enterprise were provided by a group of London merchants, but out of three ships sent to the east in 1591 one sank and the other two failed to reach the Indian Ocean.

In 1599 another group of merchants contributed £30,000 and founded the East India Company, which was given its charter by the Queen on the last day of 1600:

Source: H. Stevens, *The Dawn of British Trade to the East Indies as recorded in the Court Minutes of the India East Company* 1599–1603.

An assembly of the persons heerunder named holden the xxiiijth of September, 1599.

(Fifty-seven names)

Whereas the severall persons abovenamed together with divers others . . ., by the suffraunce of almightie god after Royall assent of our Soveraigne Lady the Queenes most excellent Maiestie first therunto had and obteyned, do entend for the honor of our native Cuntrey and for thadvauncement of trade of merchaundize within this Realme of England uppon ther severall adventures accordinge to the severall proportions of the sommes of money by them severally sett downe and inregistred under ther owne handes, To set forthe a vyage this present yere to the Est Indies and other the Ilandes and Cuntries theraboutes, and ther to make trade by the sale of suche commodities as uppon further deliberation shalbe resolved to be provided for these partes or otherwyse by buying or barteringe of suche goodes wares jewelles or merchaundize as those Ilandes or Cuntries may yeld or afforthe; And for the better ordering and disposinge of the said viage intended and for thencoragement of all suche as have already determined to adventure in the same or shall before the viage set forthe determine to adventure therein. They have thought it meete to direct them selfes by certen Rules and orders to be holden and observed, aswell in the preparinge of suche shippinge as shalbe thought fitt for this enterprice, as of all other provision of wares merchandize bullion and suche other thinges as are to be provided and adventured in the same.

A TRADE VENTURE TO AFRICA

Source: Pepys's Diary.

Oct. 3rd, 1660. . . . This day I heard the Duke speak of a great design that he and my Lord of Pembroke have, and a great many others, of sending a venture to some parts of Africa to dig for gold ore there. They intend to admit as many as will venture their money, and so make themselves a company. £250 is the lowest share for every man. . . .

CHAPTER XXX

COLONIZATION

One of the most influential writers of the sixteenth century was Hakluyt, author of *The Principall Navigations, Voiages and Discoveries of the English Nation*. This book described in three volumes the deeds of Hawkins, Drake, Frobisher, Raleigh and other seamen, and directed the thoughts of many people to the possibilities of adventure across the seas and of colonizing as a means of personal betterment.

SIR FRANCIS DRAKE

Source: Letter of Don Francisco da Zarate to Don Martin Enriquez, Viceroy of New Spain (*New Light on Drake*, ed. Z. Nuttall).

He is called Francisco Drac, and is a man of about 35 years of age, low of stature, with a fair beard, and is one of the greatest mariners that sail the seas, both as a navigator and as a commander. His vessel is a galleon of nearly four hundred tons, and is a perfect sailor. She is manned with a hundred men, all of service, and of an age for warfare, and all are as practised therein as old soldiers from Italy could be. Each one takes particular pains to keep his arquebus clean. He treats them with affection, and they treat him with respect. He carries with him nine or ten cavaliers, cadets of English noblemen. These form a part of his council, which he calls together for even the most trivial matter, although he takes advice from no one. But he enjoys hearing what they say and afterwards issues his orders. He has no favourite. . . . He is served on silver dishes with gold borders and gilded garlands, in which are his arms. He carries all possible dainties and perfumed waters. He said that many of these had been given to him by the Queen.

None of these gentlemen took a seat or covered his head before him, until he repeatedly urged him to do so. This galleon of his carries about thirty heavy pieces of artillery and a great quantity of firearms with the requisite ammunition and lead. He dines and sups to the music of viols. He carries trained carpenters and artisans, so as to be able to careen the ship at any time. Besides being new, the ship has a double lining. I understood that all the men he carries with him receive wages, because, when our ship was sacked, no man dared take anything without his orders. He shows them great favour, but punishes the least fault. He also carries painters who paint for him pictures of the coast in its exact colours. . . .

I managed to ascertain whether the General was well liked, and all said that they adored him.

VIRGINIA, 1576

The first English expedition to America sailed in 1497 under John Cabot, the first attempt at colonizing was led by Sir Humphrey Gilbert in 1583, but failed.

Source: Captain John Smith, *The Generall Historie of Virginia,* 1624.

The most famous, renowned and ever worthy of all memory for her courage, learning, judgment and virtue, Queen Elizabeth granted her letters patent to Sir Walter Ralegh for the discovering and planting new lands and countries, not actually possessed by any Christians. This patentee got to be his assistants Sir Richard Grenville the valiant, Master William Sanderson, a great friend to all such noble and worthy actions, and divers other gentlemen and merchants, who with all speed provided two small barks, full furnished with all necessaries, under the command of Captain Philip Amidas and Captain Barlow. The twenty-seventh of April they set sail from the Thames, the tenth of May passed the Canaries, and the tenth of June the West Indies: which unneedful southerly course (but then no better was known) occasioned them in that season much sickness.

The second of July they fell with the coast of Florida in shoal water, where they felt a most delicate sweet smell, though they saw no land, which ere long they espied, thinking it the continent: an hundred and twenty miles they sailed not finding any harbour. The first that appeared with much difficulty they entered, and anchored; and after thanks to God they went to view the next land adjoining, to take possession of it for the Queen's most excellent Majesty: which done, they found their first landing place very sandy and low, but so full of grapes that the very surge of the sea sometimes overflowed them; of which they found such plenty in all places, both on the sand, the green soil and hills, as in the plains as well on every little shrub, as also climbing towards the tops of high cedars, that they did think in the world were not the like abundance.

We passed by the sea-side towards the tops of the next hills being not high: from whence we might see the sea on both sides, and found it an isle of twenty miles in length and six in breadth, the valleys replenished with goodly tall cedars. Discharging our muskets, such a flock of cranes, the most white, arose by us, with such a cry as if an army of men had shouted all together. This isle hath many goodly woods and deer, conies, and fowl in incredible abundance, and using the author's own phrase, the woods are not such as you find in Bohemia, Muscovy, or Hercynia, barren and fruitless, but the highest and reddest cedars of the world, bettering those of the Azores, Indies, or Libanus; pines, cypress, sassafras, the lentisk that beareth mastic, and many other of excellent smell and quality. Till the third day we saw not any of the people, then in a little boat three of them appeared. One of them went on shore, to whom we rowed, and he attended us without any sign of fear; after he had spoke much though we understood not a word, of his own accord he came boldly aboard us. We gave him a shirt, a hat, wine and meat, which he liked well; and after he had well viewed the barks and us, he went away in his own boat; and within a quarter of a mile of us in half an hour, had laden his boat with fish, with which he came again to the point of land, and there divided it in two parts, pointing one part to the ship, the other to the pinnace, and so departed.

The next day came divers boats, and in one of them the king's brother, with forty or fifty men, proper people, and in their behaviour very civil; his name was Granganameo, the king is called Wingina, the country Wingandacoa. Leaving his boats a little from our ships, he came with his train to the point, where spreading a mat he sat down. Though we came to him well armed, he made signs to us to sit down without any show of fear, stroking his head and breast, and also ours, to express his love.

After he had made a long speech unto us, we presented him with divers toys, which he kindly accepted. He was greatly regarded by his people, for none of them did sit nor speak a word, but four, on whom we bestowed presents also, but he took all from them, making signs all things did belong to him.

The king himself, in a conflict with a king, his next neighbour and mortal enemy, was shot in two places through the body and the thigh, yet recovered: whereby he lay at his chief town six days' journey from thence.

A day or two after showing them what we had, Granganameo taking most liking to a pewter dish, made a hole in it, hung it about his neck for a breastplate: for which he gave us twenty deer skins, worth twenty crowns: and for a copper kettle, fifty skins, worth fifty crowns. Much other truck we had, and after two days he came aboard, and did eat and drink with us very merrily. Not long after he brought his wife and children; they were of mean stature, but well favoured and very bashful. She had a long coat of leather, and about her forehead a band of white coral, and so had her husband; in her ears were brecelets of pearl, hanging down to her middle, of the bigness of great peas. The rest of the women had pendants of copper, and the noblemen five or six in an ear; his apparel as his wives', only the women wear their hair long on both sides, and the men but on one; they are of colour yellow, but their hair is black, yet we saw children that had very fair chestnut coloured hair.

After that these women had been here with us, there came down from all parts great store of people, with leather, coral, and divers kinds of dyes, but when Granganameo was present, none durst trade but himself and them that wore red copper on their heads, as he did. Whenever he came, he would signify by so many fires he came with so many boats, that we might know his strength. Their boats are but one great tree, which is but burnt in the form of a trough with gins and fire, till it be as they would have it. For an armour he would have engaged us a bag of pearl, but we refused, as not regarding it, that we might the better learn where it grew. He was very just of his promise, for oft we trusted him, and he would come within his day to keep his word. He sent us commonly every day a brace of bucks, conies, hares and fish, sometimes melons, walnuts, cucumbers, peas and divers roots. This author saith, their corn groweth three times in five months; in May they sow, in July reap; in June they sow, in August reap; in July sow, in August reap. We put some of our peas in the ground, which in ten days were fourteen inches high.

The soil is most plentiful, sweet, wholesome, and fruitful of all other; there are about fourteen several sorts of sweet smelling timber trees; the most parts of the underwood, bays and such like, such oaks as we, but far greater and better . . .

This discovery was so welcome into England that it pleased her Majesty to call this country of Wingandacoa, Virginia.

VIRGINIA, 1649

Source: A Perfect Description of Virginia, . . . sent from Virginia, at the request of a Gentleman of worthy note, who desires to know the true state of Virginia as it now stands. 1649.

Worthy Captaine Matthews, an old Planter of above thirty yeers standing, one of the Counsell, and a most deserving Common-wealthsman, I may not omit to let you know this Gentlemans industry.

He hath a fine house, and all things answerable to it; he sowes yeerly store of Hempe and Flax, and causes it to be spun; he keeps Weavers, and hath a Tan-house, causes Leather to be dressed, hath eight Shoemakers employed in their trade, hath forty Negroe servants, brings them up to Trades in his house: He yeerly sowes abundance of Wheat, Barley, &c. The Wheat he selleth at four shillings the bushell; kills store of Beeves, and sells them to victuall the ships when they come thither: hath abundance of Kine, a brave Dairy, Swine great store, and Poltery; he married the daughter of Sir Tho. Hinton, and in a word, keeps a good house, lives bravely, and a true lover of Virginia; he is worthy of much honour.

RULES FOR SUCCESSFUL COLONIZATION

No colony was successfully established during the lifetime of Queen Elizabeth, but much experience was gained which greatly helped those who left England to settle in the New World during the seventeenth century.

In his essay *Of Plantations*, Francis Bacon wrote:

. . . I like a plantation in a pure soil; that is, where peoples are not displanted, to the end to plant in others; for else it is rather an extirpation than a plantation. Planting of countries is like planting of woods; for you must make account to lose almost twenty years' profit, and expect your recompense in the end: for the principal thing that hath been the destruction of most plantations hath been the base and hasty drawing of profit in the first years. It is true, speedy profit is not to be neglected as far as may stand with the good of the plantation, but no further. It is a shameful and unblessed thing to take the scum of people and wicked condemned men to be the people with whom you plant; and not only so, but it spoileth the plantation; for they will ever live like rogues, and not fall to work, but be lazy, and do mischief, and spend victuals, and be quickly weary, and then certify over to their country to the discredit of the plantation. The people wherewith you plant ought to be gardeners, plough-men, labourers, smiths, carpenters, joiners, fishermen, fowlers, with some few apothecaries, surgeons, cooks, and bakers. In a country of plantation, first look about what kind of victual the country yields of itself to hand: as chestnuts, walnuts, pine-apples, olives, dates, plums, cherries, wild honey, and the like; and make use of them. Then consider what victual or esculent things there are which grow speedily and within the year; as parsnips, carrots, turnips, onions, radish, artichokes of Jerusalem, maize, and the like; for wheat, barley, and oats, they ask too much labour; but with pease and beans you may begin, both because they ask less labour, and because they serve for meat as well as bread; . . . Above all, there ought to be brought store of biscuit, oatmeal, flour, meal, and the like in the beginning till bread may he had. For beasts and birds take chiefly such as are least subject to diseases and multiply fastest; as swine, goats, cocks, hens, turkeys, geese, house-doves, and the like. The victual in a plantation ought to be expended almost as in a besieged town; that is, with certain allowance; and let the main part of the ground employed to gardens or corn, be to a common stock; and to be laid in and stored up and then delivered out in proportion; besides some spots of ground that any particular person will manure[1] for his own private. Consider likewise what commodities the soil where the plantation is doth naturally yield, that they may some way help to defray the charge of the plantation: so it be not, as was said, to the untimely prejudice of the main business, as it hath fared with tobacco in Virginia. Wood commonly aboundeth but too much; and therefore timber is fit to be one. If there be iron ore, and streams whereupon to set the mills, iron is a brave commodity where wood aboundeth. Making of bay-salt, . . . growing silk . . . pitch and tar, . . . drugs and sweet woods, . . . soap-ashes . . . but moil not too much underground, for the hope of mines is very uncertain, and useth to make planters lazy in other things. For government, let it be in the hands of one, assisted with some council; and let them have commission to exercise martial laws, with some limitation. . . . Let there be freedom from custom till the plantation be of strength; and not only freedom from custom, but freedom to carry their commodities where they may make their best of them, except there be some special cause of caution. . . . If you plant where savages are, do not only entertain them with trifles and gingles, but use them justly and graciously, with sufficient guard nevertheless; and do not win their favour by helping them to invade their enemies, but for their defence it is not amiss; and send oft of them over to the country that plants, that they may see a better condition than their own, and commend it when they return. When the plantation grows to strength, then it is time to plant with women as well as men; that the plantation may spread into generations, . . .

WELCOME IN THE NEW LANDS

The motives of those who emigrated from England in the early seventeenth century were very mixed. A great many went for political and religious reasons and hoped to establish a new society based upon toleration. Others went to better themselves economically and were attracted by the promise of free land and opportunity. The government sent out convicts and, later, prisoners of the Civil Wars.

All these suffered great hardships on the voyage, and a large proportion of the first colonists died before arrival or in the difficult conditions in which they settled. A number of contemporary records give a happier picture.

[1] manure = cultivate.

Source: The Third Voyage of Master Henry Hudson, written by Robert Juet, of Lime-house. 1609.

. . . This day the people of the countrey came aboord of us, seeming very glad of our comming, and brought greene tobacco, and gave us of it for knives and beads. They goe in deere skins loose, well dressed. They have yellow copper. They desire cloathes, and are very civill. They have great store of maize or Indian wheate, whereof they make good bread. The countrey is full of great and tall oakes. . . . Our men went on land there, and saw great store of men, women, and children, who gave them tabacco at their comming on land. So they went up into the woods, and saw great store of very goodly oakes and some currants. For one of them came aboord and brought some dryed, and gave me some, which were sweet and good. This day many of the people came aboard, some in mantles of feathers, and some in skinnes of divers sorts of good furres. Some women also came to us with hempe. They had red copper tobacco pipes, and other things of copper they did weare about their neckes.

PROBLEMS OF SETTLEMENT

It was realized that some form of control and government would be needed from the very start. This was best decided upon just before arrival, when it was known how many had survived the voyage:

Source: G. Mourt (Ed.), *A Relation or Journall of the Beginnings and Proceedings of the English Plantation settled at Plimouth in New England by certain English Adventurers.* 1622.

This day before we came to harbour, observing some not well affected to unitie and concord, but gave some appearance of faction, it was thought good there should be an association and agreement, that we should combine together in one body, and to submit to such government and governours, as we should by common consent agree to make and choose, and set our hands to this that followes word for word.

In the name of God, Amen. We whose names are under-written, the loyall Subjects of our dread soveraigne Lord King James, by the grace of God of Great Britaine, France, and Ireland, King, Defender of the Faith, &c.

Having under-taken for the glory of God, and advancement of the Christian Faith and honour of our King and Countrey, a Voyage to plant the first Colony in the Northerne parts of VIRGINIA, doe by these presents solemnly & mutually in the presence of God and one of another, covenant, and combine ourselves together into a civill body politike, for our better ordering and preservation, and furtherance of the ends aforesaid; and by vertue hereof to enact, constitute, and frame such just and equall Lawes, Ordinances, acts, constitutions, offices from time to time, as shall be thought most meet and convenient for the generall good of the Colony; unto which we promise all due submission and obedience. In witnesse whereof we have here-under subscribed our names, Cape Cod 11th of November, in the yeare of the reigne of our soveraigne Lord King James, of England, France, and Ireland 18. and of Scotland 54. Anno Domini 1620.

ADVICE TO NEW SETTLERS

The following is part of a letter from Edward Winslow who had recently arrived in Plymouth, New England. After giving optimistic news of the planting undertaken and of the relations with the Indians, he wrote 'certain useful directions for such as intend a voyage into those parts':

Source: G. Mourt (Ed.), *A Relation . . . of the English Plantation . . . at Plimouth in New England . . . 1622.*

... Now because I expect your comming unto us with other of our friends, whose companie we much desire, I thought good to advertise you of a few things needfull; be carefull to have a very good bread-roome to put your Biskets in, let your Cask for Beere and Water be Iron-bound for the first tyre if not more; let not your meat be drie salted, none can better doe it then the Saylers; let your meale be so hard trodd in your Cask that you shall need an Ads or Hatchet to work it out with: Trust not too much on us for Corne at this time, for by reason of this last company that came, depending wholy on us, we shall have little enough till harvest; be carefull to come by some of your meale to spend

by the way, it will much refresh you. Build your Cabbins as open
as you can, and bring good store of clothes, and bedding with
you; bring every man a Musket or fowling Peece, let your Peece
be long in the barrell, and feare not the waight of it, for most
of our shooting is from Stands; bring juyce of Lemons, and take
it fasting, it is of good use; for hot waters, Anni-seed water is
the best, but use it sparingly; if you bring any thing for comfort
in the Country, Butter or Sallet oyle, or both is very good; our
Indian Corne even the coursest, maketh as pleasant meat as Rice,
therefore spare that unlesse to spend by the way; bring Paper,
and Linced oyle for your Windowes, with Cotton yarne for your
Lamps; let your shott be most for bigge Fowles, and bring store
of Powder and shot: I forbeare further to write for the present,
hoping to see you by the next returne, so I take my leave, com-
mending you to the LORD for a safe conduct unto us. Resting in
him

    Plimmouth in New-England
    this 11. of December.

      1621.   Your loving Friend.
                                       E. W.

ENCOURAGEMENT TO NEW SETTLERS

There was much discussion, both in England and in New England,
as to the wisdom and lawfulness of settling in the new lands. The
following is a part of a document written by a Mr. Cushman, in the
hope of persuading good persons who were hesitant to join the colony.
Mr. Cushman had just spent a month with the Pilgrims at Plymouth
and had returned to London in February 1622.

Source: G. Mourt (Ed.), *A Relation . . . of the English Plantation . . .
at Plimouth in New England . . . 1622.*

. . . I am perswaded, that howsoever the frailties of men are
principall in all contentions, yet the straitnes of the place is such,
as each man is faine to plucke his meanes as it were out of his
neighbours throat, there is such pressing and oppressing in
towne and countrie, about Farmes, trades, traffique, &c., so as a
man can hardly any where set up a trade but he shall pull downe
two of his neighbours.

x

The Townes abound with young trades-men, and the Hospitals are full of the Auncient, the country is replenished with new Farmers, and the Almes-houses are filled with old Labourers, many there are who get their living with bearing burdens, but more are faine to burden the land with their whole bodies: multitudes get their meanes of life by prating, and so doe numbers more by begging. Neither come these straits upon men alwaies through intemperancy, ill husbandry, indiscretion, &c. as some thinke, but even the most wise, sober, and discreet men, goe often to the wall, when they have done their best, . . .

A TREATY WITH THE INDIANS

Encounters with the Indians were sometimes difficult and dangerous, sometimes friendly. The following account is of a peace treaty with King Massasoyt.

Source: G. Mourt (Ed.), *A Relation . . . of the English Plantation . . . at Plimouth in New England . . .* 1622.

. . . They could not well expresse in English what they would, but after an houre the King came to the top of an hill over against us, and had in his trayne sixtie men, that we could well behold them, and they us: we were not willing to send our governour to them, and they unwilling to come to us, so Squanto went againe unto him, who brought word that wee should send one to parley with him, which we did, which was Edward Winsloe, to know his mind, and to signifie the mind and will of our governour, which was to have trading and peace with him. We sent to the King a payre of Knives, and a Copper Chayne, with a Jewell at it. . . . our Messenger made a speech unto him, that King James saluted him with words of love and Peace, and did accept him as his Friend and Alie, and that our Governour desired to see him and to trucke with him, and to confirme a Peace with him, as his next neighbour: he liked well of the speech and heard it attentively, though the Interpreters did not well expresse it; . . . Captaine Standish and master Williamson met the King at the brooke, with halfe a dozen Musketiers, they saluted him and he them, so one going over, the one on the one side, and the other on the other, conducted him to an house

then in building, where we placed a greene Rugge, and three or
foure Cushions, then instantly came our Governour with
Drumme and Trumpet after him, and some few Musketiers.
After salutations, our Governour kissing his hand, the King
kissed him, and so they sat downe. The Governour called for
some strong water, and drunke to him, and he drunke a great
draughte . . .; he called for a little fresh meate, which the King
did eate willingly. . . . Then they treated of Peace, which was:

1. That neyther he nor any of his should injure or doe hurt to
any of our people.

2. And if any of his did hurt to any of ours, he should send
the offender, that we might punish him.

3. That if any of our Tooles were taken away when our people
were at worke, he should cause them to be restored, and if ours
did any harme to any of his, wee would doe the like to them.

4. If any did unjustly warre against him, we would ayde him;
If any did warre against us, he should ayde us.

5. He should send to his neighbour Confederates, to certifie
them of this, that they might not wrong us, but might be likewise
comprised in the conditions of Peace.

6. That when their men came to us, they should leave their
Bowes and Arrowes behind them, as wee should doe our Peeces
when we came to them.

Lastly, that doing thus, King JAMES would esteeme of him
as his friend and Alie: all which the King seemed to like well,
and it was applauded of his followers; . . .

COLONIZATION SATIRIZED

Jonathan Swift commented satirically in *Gulliver's Travels* on the
English system of colonizing.

A crew of pirates are driven by a storm they know not whither;
at length a boy discovers land from the topmast; they go on
shore to rob and plunder; they see a harmless people, are enter-
tained with kindness; they give the country a new name; they
take formal possession of it for their king; they set up a rotten

plank or a stone for a memorial; they murder two or three dozen of the natives; bring away a couple more by force for a sample; return home and get their pardon. Here commences a new dominion acquired with a title by divine right. Ships are sent with the first opportunity; the natives driven out or destroyed; their princes tortured to discover gold; a free licence given to all acts of inhumanity and lust, the earth reeking with the blood of its inhabitants; and this execrable crew of butchers, employed in so pious an expedition, is a modern colony, sent to convert and civilise an idolatrous and barbarous people.

FURTHER READING

GENERAL: 1485–1700

H. Ellis, *Original Letters illustrative of English History* (3 vols.). London, 1825.

F. J. Fisher (ed.), *Essays in the Economic and Social History of Tudor and Stuart England.* In Honour of R. H. Tawney. Cambridge.

F. J. C. Hearnshaw (ed.), *Social and Political Ideas of the 16th & 17th centuries.*

Christina Hole, *English Home-life, 1500–1800.* Batsford, 1947.

Mitchell & Leys, *A History of the English People.* 1950.

M. & C. H. B. Quennell, *A History of Everyday Things in England, 1500–1799.* Batsford.

G. M. Trevelyan, *English Social History (Illustrated).* Vol. 1: 'Chaucer's England and the Early Tudors'; Vol. 2: 'The Age of Shakespeare and the Stuart Period.'

Thomas Tusser, *Five Hundred Points of Good Husbandry* (Ed. Payne & Heritage, 1878).

GENERAL: *Tudor Period*

S. T. Bindoff, *Tudor England.*
Rawdon Brown, *Four Years at the Court of Henry VIII.* 1854.
Cavendish, *Life of Cardinal Wolsey.*
Connoisseur Period Guides: *The Tudor Period, 1500–1603.* 1956.
L. Einstein, *Tudor Ideals.* 1921.
G. R. Elton, *England under the Tudors.* Methuen, 1955.
F. G. Emmison, *Tudor Secretary.* 1961.
James Gairdner, *The Reign of Henry VIII.* 1884.
D. Harrison, *Tudor England.* Cassell, 1953.
Hartley & Elliott, *Life and Work of the People of England, 15th c.* 1925.
A. F. Pollard, *The Reign of Henry VII from Contemporary Sources.* 3 vols.
A. F. Pollard, *Henry VIII.*
A. F. Pollard, *Wolsey.* 1929.
A. L. Rowse, *Tudor Cornwall.* Cape, 1941.
E. Gurney Salter. *Tudor England through Venetian Eyes.* 1930.
L. F. Salzman, *England in Tudor Times.* 1926.
Tawney & Power, *Tudor Economic Documents* (3 vols.). 1924.
G. M. Trevelyan, *English Social History (Illustrated),* Vol. 1. 1949.
J. A. Williamson, *The Tudor Age.* Longman's 2nd ed., 1958.

GENERAL: *Elizabethan Period*

Bindoff, Hurstfield & Williams (eds.), *Elizabethan Government and Society*. 1961.
J. W. Burgon, *Life and Times of Sir Thomas Gresham*. 1839.
Burton & Kelly, *The Elizabethans at Home*. 1958.
M. St. C. Byrne, *The Elizabethan Home*. 1949.
M. St. C. Byrne, *Elizabethan Life in Town and Country*. Methuen, 7th edit., 1954.
Caroll Camden, *The Elizabethan Woman*, 1540–1640. 1952.
Connoisseur Period Guides: *The Tudor Period*, 1500–1603. 1956.
A. H. Dodd, *Life in Elizabethan England*. 1961.
G. B. Harrison, *Elizabethan Journal* (3 vols.).
Hartley & Elliott, *Life and Work of the People of England*, 16th c. 1925.
J. E. Neale, *Queen Elizabeth*. 1947.
Allardyce Nicol, *The Elizabethans*. C.U.P., 1957.
C. T. Onions (ed.), *Shakespeare's England*. 1916.
L. E. Pearson, *Elizabethans at Home*. Stanford U.P., 1957.
A. L. Rowse, *The England of Elizabeth—the Structure of Society*. 1961.
G. M. Trevelyan, *English Social History (Illustrated)*, Vol. 2. 1950.
Victoria & Albert Museum, *Elizabethan Art*. 1953.
Wernham & Walker, *England under Elizabeth*. 1932.
Dover Wilson, *Life in Shakespeare's England*.
L. W. Wright, *Middle Class Culture in Elizabethan England*. 1958.

GENERAL: *Stuart Period*

Maurice Ashley, *England in the* 17th *Century*.
William Bray (ed.), *The Diary & Correspondence of John Evelyn*.
Richard, Lord Braybrooke (ed.), *The Diary & Correspondence of Samuel Pepys*. 1858.
S. Reed Brett, *The Stuart Century*, 1603–1714. Harrap.
A. Browning (ed.), *English Historical Documents*, 1660–1714. Eyre & Spottiswoode, 1953.
Arthur Bryant (ed.), *Letters, Speeches and Declarations of Charles II*. 1935.
Burnet, *History of My Own Times* (ed. Osmund Airy).
Burton & Kelly, *The Jacobeans at Home*. 1962.
Sir George Clark, *Three Aspects of Stuart England*. (The Whiddon Lectures, 1960) O.U.P.
Alice Clark, *The Working Life of Women in the* 17th. *c*. Routledge, 1919.
Mary Coate, *Social Life in Stuart England*. Methuen, 1924.
Mary Coate (ed.), *English Historical Documents*, 1603–1660. 1962.
Connoisseur Period Guides: *The Stuart Period*, 1603–1714. 1957.
G. B. Harrison, *Jacobean Journal*, 1603–6.
Hartley & Elliott, *Life and Work of the People of England*. 17th c.

Christopher Hill, *The Century of Revolution*. Nelson, 1961.
W. Notestein, *English Folk*. Cape, 1938.
Hesketh Pearson, *Charles II. His Life and Likeness*. 1960.
Charles Petrie, *The Stuarts*. 1937.
G. Scott Thompson, *Life in a Noble Household*, 1641–1700. Cape, 1950.
G. M. Trevelyan, *England under the Stuarts*.
F. P. Verney, *Memoirs of the Verney Family*.
B. Willey, *The 17th-century Background*.

GENERAL: *Cromwell and the Commonwealth*

Connoisseur Period Guides: *The Stuart Period*, 1603–1714. 1957.
Sir Charles H. Firth, *Cromwell*. 1950.
John Morley, *Oliver Cromwell*. 1900.
Lord Nugent, *Memorials of John Hampden*.

2. TOWNS

Sir Walter Besant, *London in the Time of the Stuarts*.
Thomas Burke, *The English Townsman*. 1946.
Byrne, *Elizabethan Life in Town and Country*. 1934.
Mitchell & Leys, *A History of London Life*.
T. F. Ordish, *Shakespeare's London*. 1904.
Riley, *Memorials of London*.
Stow, *Survey of the Cities of London and Westminster*.
George Unwin, *The Gilds and Companies of London*. 1908.
Norman Wymer, *English Town Crafts*. 1949.

3. DRESS

Barfoot, *Discovering Costume*. 1961.
C. W. & C. Cunnington, *English Costume in the 17th century*. 1955.
C. W. & C. Cunnington, *A Picture History of English Costume*. 1960.
Kelly & Schwabe, *Historic Costume*. 1929.
James Laver (Costume of the Western World) *Early Tudor*, 1485–1558. 1951.
Graham Reynolds (Costume of the Western World), *Elizabethan & Jacobean*, 1558–1625. 1951.
London Museum, *The Cheapside Hoard of Elizabethan & Jacobean Jewellery*. 1928.

4 and 5. HOMES

M. W. Barley, *The English Farmhouse and Cottage*. Routledge, 1961.
C. J. Charles, *Elizabethan Interiors*.
Ralph Dutton, *The English Interior*, 1500–1900. Batsford. 1948.
F. G. Emmison, *Jacobean Household Inventories*. 1938.

R. Fastnedge, *English Furniture Styles from 1500 to 1830*. Pelican, 1955.
G. E. Fussell, *The English Rural Labourer*. 1949.
Elizabeth Godfrey, *Home Life under the Stuarts*. 1903.
Molly Harrison, 'Homes,' *E. S.A. Information Book*, 1960.
Hilary Jenkinson, *English Wallpapers of the 16th and 17th centuries*. 1925.
Margaret Jourdain, *English Decoration and Furniture of the Early Renaissance*, 1500–1650. 1924.
Margaret Jourdain, *English Interior Decoration*, 1500–1830. Batsford, 1950.
J. S. Lindsay, *Iron and Brass Implements of the English House*. 1927.
McQuoid & Edwards, *Dictionary of English Furniture* (3 vols.). 1954.
W. B. Rye, *England as seen by Foreigners*. 1865.
F. W. Steer (ed.), *Farm and Cottage Inventories of Mid-Essex*, 1635–1749.

6 and 7. FOOD, HEALTH AND MEDICINE

Drummond & Wilbraham, *The Englishman's Food*. 1958.
G. E. Fussell, *The English Rural Labourer*. 1949.
Molly Harrison. 'Food,' *E.S.A. Information Book*, 1955.
Mitchell & Leys, *History of London Life*.
Joan Parkes, *Travel in England in the 17th century*. O.U.P., 1925.
William Vaughan, *Naturall and Artificial Directions for Health*, 1602.

8. LEISURE

Tom Brown. *London Amusements*. 1700.
Charles Cotton, *The Complete Gamester*. 1674.
Firth (ed.), *Memoirs of Colonel Hutchinson*. 1885.
Izaak Walton, *The Compleat Angler*. 1640.
Norman Wymer, *Sport in England*. 1949.

9. DRAMA

Marchette Chute, *Shakespeare of London*. 1951.
Allardyce Nicol, *A History of Restoration Drama*, 1660–1700. C.U.P., 1928.
Allardyce Nicol, *Stuart Masques and the Renaissance Stage*. 1938.

10. MUSIC

O. Anderton, 'Early English Music' (15th and 16th Centuries), *Musical Opinion*. 1920.
Sir Frederick Bridge, *Shakespearean Music*.
Campion & Rosseter, *Book of Ayres*. 1601.
Fellowes, *The English Madrigal*. 1925.
F. W. Galpin, *Old English Instruments of Music*.

Karl Geiringer, *Musical Instruments (Stone Age to Present Day).* 1943.
Hipkins & Gibbs, *Musical Instruments.* 1945.
John Playford, *An Introduction to the Skill of Music.* 1654.
John Playford, *The English Dancing Master.*
Raymond Russell, *Early Keyboard Instruments.* Victoria & Albert Museum. 1959.
Percy Scholes, *The Puritans and Music.*
Christopher Simpson, *Compendium of Practical Music.* 1667.
John Stevens, *Music and Poetry in the Early Tudor Court.* 1961.

11. PAINTING

Dr. E. Auerbach, *Tudor Artists.* 1954.
Graham Reynolds, *English Portrait Miniatures.* 1952.
Ellis Waterhouse, *Painting in Britain,* 1530–1790. Pelican, 1953.
Margaret Whinney & Oliver Millar, *English Art,* 1625–1714. 1957.
C. Winter, *Elizabethan Miniatures.* King Penguin, 1943.

12, 13, 14. RELIGION

Robert Barclay (of Tottenham), *Religious Societies of the Commonwealth.* 1876.
Robert Barclay (the Elder), *Apology—an Explanation and Vindication of the Principles and Doctrines of Quakers.* 1676.
W. C. Braithwaite, *The Beginnings of Quakerism.* C.U.P., 1955.
W. H. Frere, *The English Church in the Reigns of Elizabeth and James I.* Macmillan, 1904.
Thomas Fuller, *The Church History of Britain* (3 vols.). 1655
James Gairdner, *History of the English Church . . . from the Accession of Henry VIII to the Death of Mary.* 1902.
James Gairdner, 'The Reformation' (pamphlet). 1899.
Christina Hole, *Witchcraft in England.*
W. K. Jordan, *The Development of Religious Toleration in England,* 1558–1660 (4 vols.). Allen & Unwin, 1932–1940.
T. M. Parker, *The English Reformation to* 1558. O.U.P., 1950.
R. H. Tawney, *Religion and the Rise of Capitalism.* Murray, 1926.
W. B. Whitaker, *Sunday in Tudor and Stuart Times.* Houghton, 1933.
W. T. Whitley, *A History of British Baptists.* Griffin, 1932.

15–18. EDUCATION

J. Howard Brown, *Schools.* 1961.
E. Cocker, *England's Perfect Schoolmaster,* 1699.
M. H. Curtis, *Oxford and Cambridge in Transition,* 1558–1642. O.U.P., 1959.
Erasmus, *On the Liberal Education of Boys.*
Firth (ed.), *Memoirs of Colonel Hutchinson.* 1885.

Elizabeth Godfrey, *Home Life under the Stuarts*. Richards, 1903.
Magdalen King-Hall, *The Story of the Nursery*. Routledge, 1958.
John Locke, *Some Thoughts concerning Education*.
John Milton, *Tractate of Education*. 1644.
William Nelson (ed.), *A 15th-century School Book*. Oxford, 1956.
G. Scott Thompson, *Life in a Noble Household*. 1936.
Andrew Tuer, *History of the Horn-book*.
J. Foster Watson, *The English Grammar School to* 1660. C.U.P., 1908.
J. Foster Watson, *Return from Parnassus*. Clarendon Press, 1886.

19. SCIENCE

Marie Boas, *The Scientific Renaissance*, 1450–1630. Collins, 1962.
H. Butterfield, *Origins of Modern Science*. Bell, 1949.
A. C. Crombie, *Augustine to Galileo*, Vol. 2, 'Science in the later Middle Ages, 13c. to 17th c.' Heinemann, 1952.
A. R. Hall, *The Scientific Revolution*, 1500–1800. Longman's, 1954.
Thomas Sprat, *History of the Royal Society*. 1667.
A. Wolf, *A History of Science, Technology and Philosophy in 16c. and 17c.* 1935.

20. AGRICULTURE

M. W. Beresford, *The Lost Villages of England*. Lutterworth, 1954.
M. Campbell, *The English Yeoman under Elizabeth and the Early Stuarts*. Yale U.P. 1942.
Drummond & Wilbraham, *The Englishman's Food*. 1958.
Lord Ernle, *English Farming, Past and Present*. Longman's, 5th ed., 1936.
R. H. Tawney, *The Agrarian Problem in the 16th century*. Longman's, 1912.
J. Thirsk, 'Tudor Enclosures' (Historical Association Pamphlet G.41). Routledge, 1959.

21–24. TRADE AND INDUSTRY

J. H. Clapham, *Concise Economic History of Britain to* 1730. C.U.P., 1949.
M. G. Davies, *The Enforcement of English Apprenticeship*, 1563–1642. Harvard U.P., 1956.
H. Hamilton, *The English Brass and Copper Industries to* 1800. Longman's, 1926.
H. Heaton, *The Yorkshire Woollen and Worsted Industries*. O.U.P., 1920.
R. K. Kelsall, *Wage Regulation under the Statute of Artificers*. Methuen, 1938.
S. Kramer, *English Craft Gilds*. Columbia U.P., 1927.
E. Lipson, *Economic History of England*, Vols. 2 and 3. Black, 7th ed., 1961.

J. U. Nef, *The Rise of the British Coal Industry*. Routledge, 1932.
W. B. Rye, *England as seen by Foreigners*, 1865.
G. Unwin, *Industrial Organization in the 16th & 17th centuries*. O.U.P., 1904.
G. Unwin, *Gilds and Companies of London*. Allen & Unwin, 3rd. ed., 1938.
W. B. Whitaker, *Sunday in Tudor and Stuart Times*. Houghton, 1933.

25, 26. TRAVEL

R. & R. C. Anderson, *The Sailing Ship*. Harrap, 1926.
Thomas Burke, *Travel in England*. 1942.
G. S. Laird Clowes, *Sailing Ships* (Part I. H.M.S.O., 1959).
W. T. Jackman, *A History of Transportation in England* (2 vols.). C.U.P., 1916.
Joan Parkes, *Travel in England in the 17th Century*. O.U.P., 1925.
W. B. Rye, *England as seen by Foreigners*, 1865.

27. THE POOR

Drummond & Wilbraham, *The Englishman's Food*. 1958.
D. M. Stuart, *The English Abigail*.

28. CRIME AND PUNISHMENT

A. V. Judges, *The Elizabethan Underworld*. Routledge, 1930.

29, 30. FOREIGN TRADE AND COLONIZATION

G. M. Asher (ed.), *Henry Hudson, the Navigator*. 1860.
Black, *The Age of Drake* 3rd ed., 1952.
N. Boteler, *Six Dialogues about Sea Services*. 1685.
William Bradford, *History of Plimouth Plantation*, 1606–1646. Printed 1856.
Francis Drake, *World Encompassed*. 1628.
John Evelyn, *Mundus Muliebris, or Voyage to Marryland*. 1690.
Peter Force, *Tracts and other Papers* (collected by). Washington, 1938.
Sir W. Foster, *England's Quest of Eastern Trade*. Black, 1933.
Hakluyt, *Voyages*. 12 vols.
Thomas Hariot, *A Briefe and True Report of the New Found Land of Virginia*. 1588.
B. Krishna, *Commercial Relations between England and India*, 1601–1757. Routledge, 1924.
G. D. Ramsay, *English Trade in the Centuries of Emergence*. Macmillan, 1957.
E. G. R. Taylor, *Tudor Geography*, 1485–1583. 1930.

E. G. R. Taylor, *Late Tudor and Stuart Geography*. 1934. (With very full bibliography.)

T. S. Willan, *The Early History of the Russia Company*, 1553–1603. Manchester U.P., 1956.

T. S. Willan, *Studies in Elizabethan Foreign Trade*. Manchester U.P., 1959.

J. A. Williamson, *A Short History of British Expansion*. Macmillan. 2nd. ed., 1930.

A. C. Wood, *A History of the Levant Company*. O.U.P., 1935.

INDEX